D1435785

INTRODUCING
THE OLD TESTAMENT

Introducing the Old Testament

Based upon
John R. Sampey's *Syllabus*

By

Clyde T. Francisco

Assistant Professor
of Old Testament Interpretation
Southern Baptist Theological Seminary

BROADMAN PRESS
Nashville, Tennessee

PRINTED IN THE UNITED STATES OF AMERICA
2.5 AT 51 CL

To my father
L. T. FRANCISCO
Whose love for the Bible
inspired his son

Preface

This is the first book to come from the pen of this author, but it will not be the last. He is a scholar of great promise as his academic record both at the University of Richmond and at the Southern Baptist Theological Seminary indicates. He has a passion to master the field of Old Testament interpretation, but greater still is his passion to experience for himself and to teach others the truths of the Old Testament.

The nature and purpose of this book are clearly indicated by the title, INTRODUCING THE OLD TESTAMENT. It is not intended to be an exhaustive presentation or interpretation of the Old Testament. Rather, it is an introduction to this vast field of study. The book will have great value for those who desire to secure an elemental knowledge of the Old Testament, but it will be equally valuable to those who will use it as the foundation of a comprehensive study of the Old Testament.

The author, who is professor of Old Testament interpretation in the Southern Baptist Theological Seminary, wrote the book primarily to meet the needs of his own students but also to put into the hands of other teachers of the Old Testament a book which will serve their purpose and aid their students.

Since there is so much "written in the law of Moses, and the prophets, and the psalms" concerning the Christ, things which Christ himself said "must needs be fulfilled," a knowledge of the Old Testament is indispensable to all students who would understand the message and the ministry of our Lord and Saviour. Hence, the tremendous value and importance of this book.

ELLIS A. FULLER
President

Southern Baptist Theological Seminary
Louisville, Kentucky

Foreword

It was with great hesitation that I undertook the writing of this book. But the great need of our classes at the Southern Baptist Theological Seminary for a text of this type has necessitated such an effort. Without the assistance of material from John R. Sampey's *Syllabus for Old Testament Study* the book might have been permanently delayed. The wise counsel of Dr. J. B. Weatherspoon and Dr. Ellis A. Fuller has proved invaluable. Dr. D. W. Deere has labored tirelessly over many details of the manuscript. Dr. Kyle M. Yates and Dr. J. Leo Green, my former teachers, and Dr. J. J. Owens, my colleague, will certainly recognize my indebtedness to them in much of what I have written. To Dr. R. T. Daniel, professor of Old Testament at Southwestern Baptist Theological Seminary, goes my sincerest appreciation for his helpful advice.

It is not the purpose of this book to deal in the technicalities of scholarly research. Such a study, it is hoped, will appear later. The inclusion of technical material in this work would defeat the primary purpose of its writing, which is to acquaint the average reader with the essential history and teachings of the Old Testament. Any intense study would dampen his interest and cloud his understanding.

As far as possible I have tried to make the material of such a sort as to be helpful to the Sunday school teacher, interested layman, college student, or seminary beginner. Such a purpose may be impossible of achievement, but one cannot be blamed for the attempt. There is an important need today for a position which emphasizes the positive teachings of the Old Testament, regardless of opinions about critical problems. Before this can be achieved, however, these problems must be carefully studied and thoughtfully weighed, for we cannot bury our heads in sand. But after such a procedure, surely there remains some positive truth. INTRODUCING THE OLD TESTAMENT seeks to present the abiding truths that survive this battle of the scholars.

The scriptural quotations contained herein, unless otherwise designated, are from the American Standard Version. Where there is disagreement with that version, the author is giving his own translation. Each book quoted is used by permission of the publisher listed in the footnote below the quotation.

Contents

INTRODUCTION

THE NATURE OF THE OLD TESTAMENT

Although the Bible is by far the best seller among the world's publications, it is not being read by the average person. It is kept in the parlor and referred to by the preacher but is generally regarded as dull reading or as a sealed Book to be interpreted only by experts. This apathy is especially pronounced in regard to the Old Testament. To some extent naive expositors are to blame for this deplorable condition, when they ignore historical settings in trying to locate in the Old Testament a complete New Testament. If the Old Testament is only the New Testament in hieroglyphics, it is much more simple for one to read the New Testament. If it is studied in complete disregard of historical setting, the breath of life departs from it.

Many higher critics have also made their contribution to this tragic disregard of the Old Testament by tearing its contents into meaningless fragments or relegating its revealed truth to the realm of the ordinary. As one scholar has put it, what was "begun with a pen-knife, continued with a hatchet."[1] Perhaps, as another has said, they have been enticed "by the fascinating devices of the naughty man."[2] Although it has made a valuable contribution to the study of the Old Testament in its insistence upon the fact that a passage cannot be understood apart from its historical setting, the critical method has been pursued with such minute analysis that weightier spiritual truths have been neglected. Its evolutionary emphasis has led to the conviction that the only portions of the Old Testament worth studying

[1] C. C. Torrey, *The Second Isaiah* (New York: Charles Scribner's Sons, 1928), p. 13.

[2] N. H. Snaith, *The Distinctive Ideas of the Old Testament* (Philadelphia: The Westminster Press, 1946), p. 13.

I

are the eighth century prophets, in which Old Testament religion reaches its peak. To the New Testament writers, however, the Old Testament was of a quite different nature. They did not confine their attention to those portions of the Old Testament that most nearly approximated the teachings of Jesus but viewed the whole history of the Hebrews as culminating in God's dealing with spiritual Israel through his incarnate Son. In Jesus one finds the same attitude. He always regarded the Scriptures as a unity rather than a compilation.

Still another group has encouraged the neglect of the Old Testament—those who minimize its importance as compared with the New Testament. It is their claim that since the New Testament is the fulfilment of the Old, the study of the Jewish Scriptures is of little value. Such an opinion is as unreasonable as that of the student who imagines he should start his study of the language of the Old Testament in a class of advanced Hebrew, since only in the advanced group can the complete revelation be secured. Yet, in order to understand such Hebrew, one must necessarily pass through the preliminary valley of the shadow. Just so, those who try to master the New Testament apart from the Old are glaringly guilty of tragic errors of misinterpretation. Such an attempt at study has led many scholars to interpret New Testament conceptions according to Greek thought exclusively, ignoring the Hebrew concepts that gave them root. This has been a characteristic feature of the history of Christian thought. In recent years, however, perhaps the most important emphasis of New Testament scholarship has been upon the essential unity of the Bible. As one writer has ably stated, "No further progress in the understanding of primitive Christianity is possible, unless the ark of New Testament exegesis be recovered from its wanderings in the land of the Philistines and be led back to its home in the midst of the classical Old Testament Scriptures, to the Law and the Prophets."[3] Conversely, of course, the Old Testament must never be studied independently of the New, for it is the New Testament that unlocks many of the mysteries of the Old, revealing the purpose behind its revelation.

[3]Cf. R. V. G. Tasker, *The Old Testament in the New Testament* (Philadelphia: The Westminster Press, 1945), p. 9.

Perhaps the greatest hindrance confronting the person wishing to understand the Old Testament is an improper understanding of the nature of its literature. The medium through which the writers wished to convey their thoughts was language. The art of speech is the chief means by which the ideas of one person may be passed on to others. Language has definite forms which carry with them their own definite laws of use and interpretation. If a biblical writer used a particular type of literature, one must interpret that passage in accordance with the universal laws of that mode of expression. Until one is able to determine whether a passage is daring poetical imagery or a prosaic statement of scientific fact, his interpretation must necessarily be precarious. If this cannot be adequately determined, the meaning of the passage must remain in doubt.

One glance at the English Bible will suffice to show that little help is given the average reader in discovering the type of literature a particular section may be. If one opens it at random, he will discover that it is arbitrarily divided into books, chapters, and verses. Unmindful of the fact that the chapter and verse divisions were inserted for facility in ready reference, the average reader comes to believe that those divisions have always been there, although the originals had neither chapter nor verse distinctions. Surely these are invaluable in a study of the Scriptures, but the literature has suffered considerably because of such a pragmatic dismemberment. One can imagine what would happen if Tennyson's poems were edited in chapter and verse sections that pay no regard to his original arrangement. Yet such a fate has befallen the Scriptures.

There are some who regard the literary study disapprovingly, as if admiring the exquisite beauty of a flower would hinder one from realizing its sweet fragrance. Before something can be appreciated, it must first of all attract. Theological handling of the Scriptures has destroyed much of their attractiveness to the world. We need to renew an appreciation of the beauty of the biblical accounts, for it is the open door to the realization of the fundamental revelation. It is a tragedy of modern civilization that through schools and colleges students are taught to appreciate the beauty and sublimity of the works of Byron, Shakespeare, and Browning but are left completely uninformed on the greatest literature the world has ever known, just because it is in the Bible. If it were anywhere else, the literary world would bow before it.

It has not always been thus in our English-speaking world. An American professor of English has written that the most important event in English history was not the defeat of the Spanish Armada, nor the Battle of Waterloo, but the translation of a Book. "It was in the sixteenth century that the translation of the Bible into the vernacular by Tyndale and Coverdale made the English people the people of a book—and that book, the Bible. . . . The mental habits of the English people became Hebraic."[4]

Saintsbury speaks of the Authorized Version of 1611 as having been the training ground of every man and woman of English speech in the noblest uses of their language. Its phrasing is evident in the speeches of Patrick Henry and in the great addresses of Lincoln. James Russell Lowell and Nathaniel Hawthorne were noticeably affected by its contents. Pfeiffer[5] has listed many concrete expressions which our speech today has borrowed from the Hebrew: "to lick the dust"; "the sweat of thy face"; "gall and wormwood"; "to heap coals of fire"; "a land flowing with milk and honey"; "the stars in their courses"; "a broken reed"; "bone of my bone and flesh of my flesh"; "an eye for an eye"; "the flesh pots"; "the skin of my teeth"; "a little cloud . . . like a man's hand"; "hewers of wood and drawers of water"; "the wife of thy bosom." An appreciation of the sublime beauty of Old Testament literature will never destroy its religious interest; it will both encourage and enhance it.

It is hoped that the studies contained in this book will contribute toward a better understanding of the nature of the Old Testament. The importance of the Hebrew Scriptures in the gracious plan of salvation can never be overestimated. Their personalities, when once they are known, are timeless in the

---

[4]E. C. Baldwin, *Types of Literature in the Old Testament* (New York: The Ronald Press Co., 1929), p. 15.

[5]R. H. Pfeiffer, *Introduction to the Old Testament* (third edition, New York: Harper and Brothers, 1941), p. 15.

lessons of their experiences with God. Heaven and earth may pass away, but this Word will live on forever.

PRINCIPLES OF INTERPRETATION

The preceding discussion has emphasized certain methods that the student should follow in interpreting any Old Testament passage. It may be profitable to observe them more closely. Upon attempting to discover the significance of a section of the Hebrew Scriptures, one should determine the following data, which are arranged in the correct order of procedure:

1. The historical position of the writer. This includes the history of the times and the social and religious conditions. Something must be known of the author's personal life, if possible, and his background.

2. The original language in which he wrote. It is impossible to translate one language into another, for every translation is actually an interpretation. A knowledge of Hebrew is essential to sound Old Testament exposition. If it is not possessed, the student must take the second best course of studying good commentaries that are based on the Hebrew text.

3. The context of the passage. Scripture writers did not write each verse in a vacuum but reasoned logically from one thought to another. Each verse must be properly related to those around it. Each passage must be studied in the light of the book that contains it, and each book must be examined as it is related to the over-all progress of Old Testament revelation.

4. The nature of the literature. As has been suggested in the preceding section, the type of literature is of major significance in the understanding of a passage of the Old Testament.

5. The relationship to its later fulfilment. Old Testament critical study, with its emphasis upon the historical approach, has led many to stop with the fourth procedure. Neither Jesus nor the New Testament authors followed such a method. Just as the life of a man makes explicit the hidden tendencies of his infancy, the New Testament reveals the concealed truths of the Old. Truths that neither the authors themselves nor later

Jewish expositors saw lie dormant in many Old Testament utterances, made evident only in Jesus Christ. One should be cautious lest he read into Old Testament passages the teachings of the New Testament; yet he must never forget that Jesus is the key to the only true understanding of the dream of the prophets. One must therefore determine first what the passage meant to the writer and his own generation. Then he must perceive its relationship to the eternal plan of God, which relationship even the inspired writer may not have seen, but is plainly evident to those who live in the fulness of the light.

ORIGINAL LANGUAGES

All the New Testament is in Greek, whatever may have been the original in which Matthew, James, and others wrote. The Old Testament was composed by men who spoke and wrote Hebrew; and Hebrew is the original language of all the Old Testament Scriptures, except about six chapters in Daniel (2:4 to 7:28), about three in Ezra (4:8 to 6:18; 7:12–26), and one verse in Jeremiah (10:11). These chapters are in the Aramaic tongue, a sister to Hebrew. If one wishes to read in the original the entire Bible, he must learn Hebrew, Aramaic, and Greek.

STATE OF THE HEBREW TEXT

The Jews have for two thousand years been extremely careful about preserving their sacred books in primitive purity. They have spared no pains to preserve a pure text. At the same time one must not forget that the Hebrew Scriptures were often in great danger. Antiochus Epiphanes (c. 167 B.C.) burned all the copies he could find. Many rolls were destroyed during the terrible Roman wars (c. A.D. 70). Moreover, scribal errors may have crept into the text long before the days of Ezra and his school of scribes. In addition to unintentional errors of copyists, the original text was perhaps subjected to more or less of editorial revision.

The earliest complete manuscripts of the Hebrew Bible now extant are dated about A.D. 1000. At least two manuscript editions of the Old Testament in Greek are as old as the middle of the fourth century A.D. There are small fragments of both Hebrew and Greek that are dated in the second century B.C. Quite recently a complete Hebrew manuscript of Isaiah was discovered that is dated tentatively in the first century B.C.

The modern Massoretic text, with its accompanying citations of variant readings, is a witness to the need for textual criticism in the Old Testament. S. Baer and Franz Delitzsch from time to time during more than twenty years published in parts an edition of the Massoretic Hebrew text. C. D. Ginsburg is the author of a carefully compiled Massoretic text. Kittel has published a good edition of the Hebrew Bible. The footnotes make much use of the ancient versions and the conjectures of modern scholars. This is the best edition of the Hebrew Bible for critical study.

The ancient Hebrews wrote without indicating the vowels. The consonantal text is still used in the synagogue rolls. Somewhere from the sixth to the eighth century A.D. the present system of vowel points was devised by the Massoretic scholars, and copies of the Scriptures have since that time indicated the vowels that accompany the consonantal text. Modern Hebrew Bibles follow the Palestinian system, which employs pointing above, below, and in the middle of the consonantal letters. The Babylonian system was supralinear. Of course, the absence of the vowels left a larger margin for ambiguity, and the ancient versions, especially the Septuagint, give evidence that the same consonantal text was variously read and understood.

THE ANCIENT VERSIONS

1. Greek

(1) The *Septuagint* was probably the first version of the Hebrew Scriptures. The Pentateuch was translated in Egypt about 250 B.C. Josephus records the marvelous story of the work of the seventy translators. Scholars

are agreed that the story has been "dressed up"; but the fact that the Septuagint version of the Law was made in Egypt long before the Christian Era is well established. The Prophets and the Hagiographa were translated later. The Greek of the Septuagint is far removed from the classical idiom. Different books of the Bible evidently fell into different hands; and while some of the translators knew Hebrew quite well, and Greek tolerably well, others were not at home in either language. Most of the translators were quite faithful to the original Hebrew, while others leaned toward a paraphrase. The Pentateuch is best rendered. The book of Daniel is the worst. The apostles quote quite frequently from the Septuagint, and the idiom of New Testament Greek (Koine) is anticipated, for the most part, in this early Greek translation.

(2) Three other Greek versions of the Old Testament were made from A.D. 100 to A.D. 200 by Jews. Exact dates are not known, and only fragments of these translations have been preserved. (1) The version of Aquila probably dates from the second quarter of the second century A.D. It was slavishly literal. The Jews quoted it in opposition to the Christian use of the Septuagint. (2) Theodotion, in the latter half of the second century, made a version more closely resembling the LXX (Septuagint). (3) Symmachus, near the end of the second century, made a version that aimed to be smooth. He is sometimes paraphrastic.

Origen's Hexapla (c. A.D. 230) contained, in addition to the Hebrew text and a Greek transliteration of the Hebrew, the four Greek versions named above. Only fragments of Origen's great work remain. Perhaps no complete copy of this *magnum opus* was ever made.

2. The Syriac

A Syriac version was probably made between 150 and A.D. 200 for the benefit of Christians who spoke Syriac. The *Peshitta,* made somewhat later, is the standard version.

3. The Targums

Long before Christ, the Hebrew Scriptures were probably translated orally by public interpreters in the synagogues. Written Aramaic versions may have been made as early as the first century of our era.

(1) The *Targum of Onkelos* is a fairly literal translation of the Pentateuch into Aramaic. The date is unknown but is assigned to periods as far apart as the first and third centuries A.D.

(2) The *Targum of Jonathan* on the Prophets was probably made in the third century A.D.

4. Latin Versions

(1) The *Old Latin* belongs to the second century A.D. It is a literal translation of the Septuagint and not of the Hebrew.

(2) *Jerome's Version*, afterwards known as the *Latin Vulgate*, was completed in A.D. 405. It is a good piece of work, though not an infallibly accurate translation of the true text of the Bible, as the Council of Trent affirmed. The *Douay Version*, an accredited English translation of the Latin Vulgate, is the authorized Roman Catholic Bible for English readers.

The value of the ancient versions is twofold: (1) For purposes of textual criticism. They occasionally bear witness to the true reading in places which have been corrupted in the Hebrew text. (2) As aids to interpretation. Every translation partakes of the nature of a commentary, and these early versions are helps to the understanding of the Bible. They are the most ancient commentaries.

THE DIVISIONS OF THE OLD TESTAMENT

The Jewish classification of the Old Testament books is threefold:

1. The *Law*, or the five books of Moses. This was most highly esteemed as the foundation of the Hebrew Bible.

2. The *Prophets*. (1) The Former Prophets: Joshua, Judges, Samuel, and Kings. (2) The Latter Prophets: Jeremiah, Ezekiel, Isaiah, and the twelve minor prophets.

3. The *Writings*. (1) Poetical books: Psalms, Proverbs, Job. (2) Five rolls: Canticles, Ruth, Lamentations, Ecclesiastes, Esther. (3) Daniel, Ezra-Nehemiah, Chronicles.

By counting Ezra and Nehemiah as one book, and the twelve smaller prophets as one roll, the Jews made their canon to contain twenty-four books. By combining Ruth with Judges, and Lamentations with Jeremiah, they sometimes reckon their sacred books as twenty-two, the exact number of letters in the Hebrew alphabet. The book of Daniel, made up of both history and apocalypse, was classed with the Hagiographa, or Writings.

A SUMMARY OF THE HISTORY OF THE OLD TESTAMENT CANON[6]

Any examination of the evidence in dating the inclusion of a book among those regarded by the Jews as of divine authority must take into account the three divisions into which the Hebrew Scriptures were divided. The *Law* was by its very history and nature first so regarded. When the Law in the present form was first recognized as of divine institution it is impossible to tell. We are told that Moses received most of the legislative material and that it was immediately regarded as authoritative. Amos and Hosea of the eighth century are acquainted with much of the historical material in the Pentateuch. Deuteronomy was regarded as divinely inspired when it was found in 621 B.C.

By the time of Ezra and Nehemiah (c. 400) we can be sure the Law as we now have it was accepted by the Jews. It may have been so regarded before that time, but of that date we can be certain for the following reasons:

(1) The Samaritan schism occurred about 400 B.C. Since the Samaritans have the Pentateuch as their Scriptures, they must have received it before the schism. They claim that their Penta-

---

[6]Although the term "canon" was not applied to the books of the Old Testament until the fourth century A.D., the concept of canonicity was much older.

teuch dates from 722 B.C., but scholars universally deny this, from the nature of the manuscripts.

(2) The Law in Ezra's day consumed a long period of time when read, from dawn until midday (Neh. 8:3).

(3) The post-Exilic writers, during and after the period of Ezra, refer to the Law with special reverence (cf. Mal. 4:4).

The *Prophets* were the next group to be accepted as divinely inspired. In the prologue to Ecclesiasticus, Jesus ben Sirach (c. 132 B.C.) writes that there were already three divisions in the Hebrew Scriptures: the Law, Prophets, and other books. In Ecclesiasticus itself, Jesus ben Sirach the elder (c. 180 B.C.) names Isaiah, Jeremiah, Ezekiel, and the twelve minor prophets, showing that the Hebrew prophetic canon was closed by then. Of course, individual prophets had been accepted long before, but we know only that the present grouping had been settled before 180 B.C. How long before is unknown.

The *Writings* were the last group to be approved as a whole. The indefinite reference of Jesus ben Sirach to this section as "other books" indicates this. An inclusion of a book in this group does not necessarily mean that it originated late. It may rather be present because later sections have been added, as in the case of Psalms and Proverbs, or because of the character of its literature, or due to the fact that its inclusion in the canon was disputed for some time.

When were the *Writings* closed? References from the books of Maccabees, Josephus, and the New Testament indicate that Jesus and the apostles possessed the Old Testament substantially as we have it today.[7] The date of the completion of the Septuagint translation would certainly clarify this matter, but that is not at all certain, for that translation was not finished before 100 B.C. and probably later.

There is no evidence that the Apocryphal books (which appear in the Latin Vulgate) were ever included in the Hebrew Scriptures by the Jews themselves. Jerome himself denied their validity.

---

[7]Cf. Matt. 23:35. Zechariah was not the last martyr in the Old Testament from the point of time. The account of his murder occurs in Chronicles. In the present Hebrew canon, Chronicles is the last book. This reference indicates that Jesus possessed the present canon. Compare our expression, "from Genesis to Malachi."

The student will note that until the first century A.D. there was no organized body, so far as is definitely known, meeting to determine what books should be included in or excluded from the Scriptures. The Councils of Jamnia (A.D. 90, 118) composed of Jewish scholars, did not settle on the canon; rather they discussed the problem of leaving certain books in the canon that were already there. Public opinion had determined the books in the Old Testament before the scholars met to discuss them. Book after book found acceptance by the people as they sifted them out from the mass of material available, on the basis of how the books agreed with God's past revelation and met the needs of the human soul. Thus God guided the formation of the canon as surely as he inspired the writers of its books.

PART I

The Pentateuch

The five books of Moses early came to be known as the Law, or the Law of Moses. They contain the commandments and ordinances that lay at the basis of the Hebrew commonwealth. The Jews esteemed these books above all others. The Pentateuch might properly be classed with the historical books, for the legislative codes are vitally connected with the history of the Mosaic period. It is common now to speak of the Hexateuch, the book of Joshua being regarded by many scholars as the necessary conclusion of the historical narratives found in the five books commonly ascribed to Moses.

Authorship of the Pentateuch

Biblical criticism has two departments: (1) *Lower Criticism*, consisting of (a) textual criticism, the search for a text closest to the original; (b) linguistic criticism, examinaton of root meanings of words and significance of idioms; (2) *Higher Criticism*, consisting of (a) literary criticism, which seeks to solve the problems of date and authorship of books; (b) historical criticism, which investigates their reliability.

The term "Higher Criticism" is often used carelessly by controversialists as synonymous with radicalism. A higher critic, however, may be either conservative or liberal, depending upon his conception of the nature of the Old Testament. It is in the field of historical criticism that the actual controversy has raged. Denial of the reliability of Old Testament statements concerning authorship and divine inspiration have inevitably aroused the opposition of those who believe in the authority of the Scriptures.

Criticism of the Pentateuch is the most important critical task confronting students of the Old Testament. Fundamental and difficult, it calls for patience, industry, and the ability to sift evidence and estimate its value. It requires logical discipline and a well-balanced mind. There is much poor reasoning on the part of learned men. Some specialists collect a multitude of facts without being able to arrange them or to show their bearing on debated questions.

The opinion of Jews and Christians for over two thousand years was almost unanimous in favor of the Mosaic authorship. A few assailants of this view appeared between 1650 and 1750 (a century of beginnings of modern criticism), such as Hobbes, Peyrerius, Spinoza, Richard Simon, and Le Clerc.

1. The Early Documentary Hypothesis

Francis Astruc, a French physician (1753), published a work which started modern criticism on its way. He thought he had found in Genesis two main documents, one employing *Elohim*, the other *Jehovah* for God (thus called "Elohistic" and "Jehovistic"), and ten smaller documents. His book was entitled *Conjectures concerning the Original Memoranda which Moses is supposed to have used in composing the Book of Genesis*. Eichhorn's *Introduction to the Old Testament* (1782) fortified Astruc's partition by adducing arguments drawn from differences in style. Astruc and Eichhorn, while separating Genesis into documents, held that Moses was the author of the Pentateuch. All this was seemingly harmless speculation. But this small beginning was to lead to greater things.

2. The Fragmentary Hypothesis

Alexander Geddes, in 1800, resolved the Pentateuch into a number of fragments without logical or chronological connection. Vater (1802–5) and Hartmann (1831) taught that the Penrateuch consisted of a number of brief post-Mosaic fragments, which grew until combined into our present Pentateuch. However, the order and unity of the narratives were too apparent to allow such an hypothesis to win the field.

3. The Supplementary Hypothesis

The way for this hypothesis was cleared by De Wette, who wrote in 1805 an epoch-making book on the date of Deuteronomy, placing this important book just prior to the reformation under Josiah in 621 B.C. Bleek (1830), Tuch (1838), Staehelin (1843), and Knobel (1852) belonged to this school. According to this hypothesis, the *Elohim* document formed the basis of the Pentateuch, and the *Jehovah* writer worked this up, making additions and other modifications. This school also denied Mosaic authorship.

But the supposed original document, when separated from the so-called Jehovistic additions, was incomplete, lacking those sections assigned to the Jehovist. Moreover, in the Elohistic sections there were references to events recorded in the sections assigned to the Jehovist. Keil, Hengstenberg, and others defended the unity and authenticity of the Pentateuch. The term "Hexateuch" now came into use, *Joshua* being regarded as a necessary part of the early history, since evidences of these documents were found therein.

4. The Later Documentary Hypothesis

Hupfeld (1853) contended that, apart from Deuteronomy, there are three historical compositions at the basis of the Pentateuch, two Elohistic and one Jehovistic. Hupfeld thus divided the main Elohistic document into two. From 1853 to the present, scholars have contended for four main documents (J, E, D, P). This theory was supported at once by Schrader, Noeldeke, Dillmann, and others. These documents were distributed from the time of David on down to the time of Josiah.

Graf (1865) transferred all the legislation, as now found in Exodus, Leviticus, and Numbers, to a time subsequent to the Babylonian Exile (586 B.C.). He at first held that the historical sections scattered throughout these middle books were more ancient, but later on brought them in like manner into the period after the Captivity. Wellhausen adopted this theory, placing the important priestly document about

500 B.C. Thus there are, according to modern scholars, four main component parts of the Hexateuch:

(1) *J.* Narrative of the ninth century B.C. (c. 850), written by a prophet of Judah, in which Jehovah is the name of the deity. He is called the Jahvist or Yahwist. The author is regarded as patriotic and is the master of the narrative style. It is he who includes the details of human interest that make the stories of the Pentateuch so unforgettable. His conception of God is definitely anthropomorphic. (Cf. Genesis chapters 2–4.)

(2) *E.* Narrative of the eighth century B.C. (c. 750), by a prophet of Ephraim, using Elohim as the name of deity until Exodus, chapter 3, when the name Jehovah (Yahweh) was declared to Moses. After this both names are used for God. The author is called the Elohist (formerly called the Second Elohist). This document is not discovered until Genesis, chapter 15, for it begins with Abraham. The Elohist has more antiquarian interest than the author of the J document. To him God is sublime and majestic and is conceived in less anthropomorphic terms than in J. Yet he seems more remote from men. More emphasis, therefore, is put upon the supernatural. The Elohist also seems to be more aware of moral issues than the earlier author of J.

These two documents are observed to be closely akin in style and spirit, however, and are often difficult to disentangle. It is claimed that they were fused into one narrative by a writer using Jehovah (Yahweh) for God, whom Wellhausen calls the Jehovist. The combined prophetic narrative is represented by the symbol JE.

It is not claimed that these writers invented history, but rather that they wrote down what was the tradition of the Hebrew people in that day, narratives that had been handed down for centuries.

(3) *D.* Author of Deuteronomy, whose hand is detected also in sections of Joshua; date before 621 B.C., during the reign of Manasseh. There is a recent tendency to

date the basic sections of Deuteronomy earlier than Manasseh, however.

(4) P. Priestly writer (or school of writers) who composed the legal sections and the history bound up with laws; date about 500 B.C. The style of the P document is unmistakable. (Cf. Gen. chapter 1, and the book of Leviticus.) It is formal, repetitious, precise, abstract in the description of God. Yet it is minutely concrete in the description of objects of priestly interest, such as the tabernacle or methods of sacrifice. The author (or authors) had a legal mind, being especially interested in genealogies and statistical details. His characters are more remote from life than those of J and E. He differs from J and E as much as the author of Chronicles varies from the attitude of the writers of the books of Samuel and Kings.

Many subdivisions are made within these documents, and editors are introduced at various points by different critics. The history is considered untrustworthy in many places and most of the laws post-Mosaic. Recent criticism has greatly multiplied the number of authors and editors. It is now customary to parcel out the materials of J, E, D, and P among schools of writers. Critics speak of J^1, J^2, E^1, E^2, S (Pfeiffer). We might almost consider the latest theories as a return to the Fragmentary Hypothesis.

Any tenable view concerning the authorship of the Pentateuch must at once question the views of modern criticism on certain issues:

1. The incredibility of the history narrated in the Pentateuch. It is "manufactured history." It is claimed that Deuteronomy was invented by the prophetic party in order to enforce centralization. The name of Moses was used to give it authority, although he had nothing to do with its distinctive teaching. The priestly document, which includes the book of Leviticus and the legislative material in Exodus and Numbers, was composed to assure the acceptance of a priestly system which had little relationship to Moses. Such a view contradicts the biblical concept that the

religion of Israel is a result of the revelation of God. Such motives of writing are unworthy of the inspired writers of Scripture. Accounts may be based upon ancient tradition but certainly not deliberately falsified. Minor discrepancies may occur, but the general trustworthiness of the history cannot be denied.

2. The impossibility of the supernatural in the Old Testament. Many modern scholars have an aversion to the supernatural. All narratives recounting miracles are thereby discredited. It is not difficult to accept the doctrine of miracles in the Old Testament when one believes in the incarnation and the resurrection.

3. Denial of special revelation to the authors of the Old Testament. The Hebrew Scriptures are not only on a par with other ancient literature but must be viewed also as their superior and of an entirely different nature, written under the inspiration and direction of God.

Not only must erroneous views be denied, but also the student must reach a view consistent with the following claims of the Bible:

1. The internal claims of the Pentateuch as to Mosaic contributions (Ex. 17:14; 24:4; 34:27; Num. 33:1–2; Deut. 31:9,24. "Jehovah spake unto Moses" occurs again and again in Leviticus).

2. The external evidence that Moses is the substantial author of the Pentateuch (Josh. 1:7f.; Judg. 3:4; 2 Chron. 25:4; Ezra 6:18; 7:6; Mal. 4:4; Matt. 8:4; Mark 7:10; 10:5; Luke 20:37; John 5:45–47; 7:19).

The essential issue in the study of the Pentateuch is, not the existence of sources for its writing, but its inspiration and reliability in its present form. If this is viewed as inspired and trustworthy, all other considerations are only of academic interest.

THE BOOK OF GENESIS

The Jews divide their sacred books into three sections—the Law, the Prophets, and the Writings. The Law corresponds to our Pentateuch, the first five books of the Bible. The rabbis call the first of these books *Bereshith* ("In beginning"), which is the first Hebrew word in the book. Our English term comes from the Greek through the Latin and carries the idea of "origin" or "beginnings." Genesis is a book of beginnings, the first eleven chapters forming an admirable introduction to the Scriptures. In the absence of these opening chapters, many fundamental questions in theology would go without a satisfactory answer. The doctrines of creation, the fall of man, election, and providence are set forth here most clearly. If the interpreter could unfold in its entirety the theology of Genesis, he would bring into view most of the great doctrines of the Bible. It is also interesting to note that this single book covers much more time than all the remainder of the Bible.

In arrangement, the book shows every evidence of careful planning. The key to the structure is the Hebrew word *toledhoth* ("generations"), a term used to introduce each section of history. The ten *toledhoth* are preceded by a magnificent introductory passage (1:1 to 2:3). The ten divisions are the *toledhoth* of the heavens and the earth (2:4 to 4:26), of Adam (5:1 to 6:8), of Noah (6:9 to 9:29), of the sons of Noah (10:1 to 11:9), of Shem (11:10–26), of Terah (11:27 to 25:11), of Ishmael (25:12–18), of Isaac (25:19 to 35:29), of Esau (36:1 to 37:1), of Jacob (37:2 to 50:26).

The book of Genesis is not a textbook on the history of mankind but is concerned only with events that bear directly upon the selective plan of God in his redemptive work. Its treatment narrows from a survey of the whole human race in the early chapters to a detailed portrayal of a small Hebrew family in the closing passages. Neither is the book intended to be the latest treatise on science. It is completely silent on the *method* of creating, leaving science free to pursue its investigation of that mystery; but rather it is insistent upon the *source* of creation, God, and its *purpose*, a human race that would walk with and serve him.

Genesis is a book of religious fundamentals. Written at a period long before modern scientific research, and not designed to take the place of such research, it uses the language of appearance and everyday life. Respect for the book of Genesis has led men to pore over its pages; and every age has tried to find in the Genesis story confirmation of its hypotheses in the realm of science as well as in theology. Had not the story been so well told, surely the book had been torn to pieces by rival interpreters. And if it conformed in every detail to today's scientific theory, tomorrow it would be out of date. Only the wisdom of God could guide the writing of such passages so permanent in their truth that they can be understood in light of the scientific theory of any age.

The physical sciences have done much to enlarge our view of the immensity of space. Stellar photography reveals innumerable worlds. Time also has expanded. Estimates of scientists differ widely—from ten million years to six billion years—for the life of the universe. With such discoveries the greatness of the Creator increases in man's mind. The value of the book of Genesis loses nothing when such considerations are kept in mind. In fact, it is enhanced. One of the most remarkable aspects of the biblical account is its agreement with modern science on the principle of progress from lower to higher in creation, thus anticipating modern theory by thousands of years. There can never be any essential conflict between religion and true science. The attempts of little men on both sides to make it so will always end in ultimate failure.

In archaeology there has also been development. Scholars speak of civilizations as far back as 5000 B.C., or even earlier. The wonderful similarity between the Hebrew, or biblical, account of the beginnings of the human race and the Babylonian-Assyrian view can now be traced. How can we account for this similarity?

1. Some have suggested accidental coincidence, or spontaneous development. No sober student can now take this view.

2. The Babylonian account might have drawn from the Hebrew, but the Babylonian account is too old for such an origin.

3. The Hebrew account might have been derived from the Babylonian. Many critics entertain this view, and it may have elements of truth. Abram must have learned much from the civilization about him in Babylonia.

4. The Hebrew and Babylonian accounts may have been derived from the same original, whether written or merely oral tradition. This would account for the differences as well as the similarities. Divine revelation, however, has freed the Hebrew account of all the polytheism of the Babylonian account and has fitted the story into the eternal plan of God.

Both Jewish and Christian traditions hold that Moses was the author of the book. However, the majority of Old Testament scholars believe that the book is composed of three main documents, all dating after the time of Moses—J (Jehovah) and E (Elohim) in the ninth and eighth centuries B.C., and P (Priestly) about 500 B.C. This view is based upon (1) the variation of the names for God; (2) a difference in style, theology, and viewpoint; (3) double accounts of the same event.

NOTES ON GENESIS 1–12

1:1. "In beginning" has no article in the Hebrew. "God" (Hebrew, *Elohim*) is a plural word. This does not imply polytheism but is an example of the Hebrew custom of pluralizing a noun to indicate excellence or transcendence. Note how this name recurs throughout chapter 1. "Created" is a word that is used only of God's activity, never that of man. It may bear the significance, therefore, of "making without the use of pre-existing materials."

1:2. There is not a catastrophe and a new creation between verses 1 and 2, as some contend. Verse 1 is the introductory statement for the whole account of the creation; verses 2ff. show how it was done. The earth on which we now live is the first God created. (Cf. Rev. 21:1.)

1:5. The word for "day" (Hebrew, *yom*) is not necessarily limited to a twenty-four-hour period. It is often used of longer expanses of time. (Cf. the prophetic phrase, "in that day.") The sun, which determines our twenty-four-hour day, was not created until the fourth day (1:16).

1:6. "Expanse" rather than "firmament."

1:26. "Let us make man" may be a reference to the Trinity, but it is probably an allusion to the heavenly council. (Cf. 3:22.)

1:27. The "image of God" means spiritual nature, that in man which is different from the animals.

1:28. "Be fruitful, and multiply." The sexual relationship was not the sin in the garden of Eden. The growth of the race by the birth of children was a part of God's plan prior to the Fall.

1:29. God intended that men and animals be vegetarians.

2:4. Note the use of "Jehovah" in the following passages. The name "Jehovah" is a strange product of scholars' imagination. The original Hebrew had no vowels but only four consonants, YHWH, or by another scheme of transliteration, JHVH. In later Jewish history the name became too holy for the reader to pronounce, since it is the covenant name of the God of Israel. When the reader came to the name, he would say Adonai (Lord), instead. The Massoretic scholars, when they added vowels to the consonantal text, inserted the vowels of Adonai with the four sacred consonants, since Adonai was the name to be read. Pronounced together, a strange term results, foreign to every Hebrew, "Jehovah." The actual vowels belonging with the name are unknown, but apparently the original form of the word was Yahweh or Jahveh. This term will be used in the remaining sections of our study.

2:8ff. No such arrangement of rivers can be found today. Some scholars contend that the flood changed the course of the streams. The mention of the Tigris and the Euphrates indicates that the garden was somewhere in the fertile Mesopotamian Valley.

2:15. Labor antedates the Fall. After the Fall labor becomes toil.

2:17. The test of man's obedience.

2:18. The purpose of the creation of woman. Man's companion and helper. She is not to be his servant but his inspiration.

2:24. God's intention in marriage. No allowance made for divorce. (Cf. Deut. 24; Mark 10:11ff.)

3:6. "Her husband with her." Was Adam present during the temptation?

3:15. The foundation promise in redemption. Some contend that the verse describes only the eternal conflict between man and the serpent, without an assurance of victory on either side, since it is the heel of the man the serpent always strikes and the head of the serpent that is most vulnerable. Although the verse may not in itself assure victory over evil for man, the context of the passage does. God will not be defeated in the most important of his ventures. He will provide a way for his purpose to be accomplished. The wiles of the serpent can never match the wisdom of God.

3:22. Eternal life was not bestowed upon man at creation. It had to be achieved. Now man has shown his unworthiness and can never taste of it until a way is found to atone for his sin.

4:3ff. Why was Cain's offering rejected and Abel's accepted? Abel had faith, while Cain was unbelieving (Heb. 11:4). Also note that Abel offered the best he possessed. The content of the offering was not involved. Provision was made in the sacrificial system for offering the products of the soil as well as animals to God. Only animals were used for the sin offering, but no word is mentioned here that theirs was for such a purpose. Furthermore, the Mosaic legislation had not yet been pronounced.

4:15. The sign was for protection, not a condemnation. There is no indication of what it was.

4:17. Who was Cain's wife? This is a proverbial question. Adam and Eve had begotten other sons and daughters (5:4).

23

In order for the human race to expand, these first brothers necessarily married sisters. Then cousins married, and men began to scatter over the face of the earth. Incest is a terrible sin because of the evils attendant upon a family's inbreeding. These dangers were avoided in these early marriages because of the youth of the race and the constantly widening intervals of relationships.

4:19. Lamech, of the line of Cain, is the first known polygamist.

Chapter 5. The longevity of the patriarchs has been an outstanding objection to the accuracy and trustworthiness of Genesis. Many explanations have been given of their length of life: (1) Differences in reckoning of time. (2) The years given are not references to the length of individual lives, but of existence of families. (3) The race was young, and sin had not shortened the life-span.

5:24. The fate of Enoch must have set men thinking about the possibility of a blessed life after death.

5:27. Methuselah lived the longest life of the patriarchs; yet all that could be said of him was that he died. Enoch lived only one third as long. It is not *how long* a man lives but *how* that matters. There is a possibility that Methuselah died in the flood.

6:2. Two interpretations: (1) Angels entered into marital relations with women, a nation of giants resulting. This is a doubtful explanation since such angels would not be apt to bother with the formal ceremonies of marriage. The expression used is that of legal marriage. (2) The sons of Seth chose wives from the beautiful but sinful daughters of Cain. The Hebrew idiom "sons of God" means godly sons, or the sons of Seth. "Daughters of men" are fleshly daughters, or daughters of Cain. Hebrew has few adjectives and frequently uses the idiom "son of" for this purpose. (Cf. Isaiah 5:1, "a very fruitful hill" —Hebrew, "a hill, the son of fatness.")

6:3. The conflict between Spirit and flesh can result only in the destruction of the flesh. Its doom would come in 120 years. The 120 years could not refer to individual life-spans, for the patriarchs after the flood lived several hundred years.

6:4. Nephilim (Hebrew, "fallen ones"). Mighty men, many of whom were giants, who were descended from the marriages in 6:2. (Cf. Num. 13:33.)

6:9. Noah was completely on God's side. The word for perfection carries the idea of completion rather than moral perfection.

6:15ff. The ark was 525 feet long, 87½ feet wide, 52½ feet high. A cubit varies from 18 to 21 inches, since it is the length between the tip of the fingers and the elbow.

9:3. Man now permitted to eat flesh because the animals owe their very existence to Noah's provision for them in the ark.

9:13. Probably not the first time a rainbow had appeared. But from now on it would have a new significance.

9:20ff. The Bible portrays men as they are. Righteous Noah found strong drink too much even for him to handle.

Chapter 10. The location of Noah's family. Japheth settled in the territory of Asia Minor and southern Europe. Ham migrated to Africa and Palestine. Some of his descendants stayed in Babylonia. Shem remained in the Mesopotamian Valley. From him the Semites were descended, of which the Hebrews were a branch.

Chapter 11. The Tower of Babel was an expression of human pride and possibly a grim determination to resist any effort of the Almighty to destroy the human race a second time by a flood.

11:7. Not only did this confusion of language prevent man's co-operating in evil projects, but it has also hindered his efforts toward peace. (Cf. Zeph. 3:9.)

12:1–3. A study of the remainder of Genesis reveals that the instructions and promises contained in Genesis 12: 1–3 are the several elements of the later specified covenant with Abraham, which covenant was confirmed by the strange sacrifice described in chapter 15 and which carried the mark of circumcision. The possession of Canaan, a distinguished name, a numerous posterity, a great nation, divine favor for himself and friends, and divine judgment upon his enemies are subordinate or contributory matters. They are means to a greater end stated in: "and in thee shall all the families of the earth be blessed"

(12:3, Hebrew, "bless themselves"). This is the primary element and the ultimate purpose of the promise. It appears five times, with slight variations, in the book of Genesis, three times to Abraham (12:3; 18:18; 22:18), once to Isaac (26:4), and once to Jacob (28:14). A fuller statement, including all the elements of the variants, is: "In thee and in thy seed shall all the nations of the earth be blessed." This seems to be the promise to which the New Testament writers referred many times, and Paul (Gal. 3:16) saw its complete fulfilment in Christ. (Cf. Psalm 72:17.)

THE LIFE OF ABRAHAM

1. From His Birth Until His Departure for Canaan. 11:27 to 12:4

   (1) Early life in Ur, a city of culture, and especially devoted to idolatrous worship.
   (2) Journey to Haran in northern Mesopotamia. Death of his father.

2. From His Departure for Canaan Until the Birth of Ishmael. 12:5 to 16:16

   (1) First sojourn in Canaan.
      a. His first stop at Shechem. Yahweh appears to him, and Abram builds an altar.
      b. Second resting place near Bethel; builds an altar and worships.
      c. Passes through the South country (Negeb).
   (2) Abram's sojourn in Egypt. Note his deception and the disgrace which follows, also that he builds no altar there.
   (3) Abram returns to Canaan.
      a. Passes through the South country to Bethel. Renews his communion with God. Separation from Lot followed by renewal of the promise that this land should belong to his posterity.

    b. Removes to Hebron, where he builds an altar.

        (a) Rescues Lot from the eastern invaders; pays tithes to Melchizedek.

        (b) Yahweh renews his covenant with Abram, revealing to him the fate of his posterity during the four hundred years that would follow.

        (c) Sarai gives Hagar to Abram. Flight of Hagar, and birth of Ishmael.

3. From the Birth of Ishmael to the Birth of Isaac. 17:1 to 20:18

    (1) Renewal of the covenant between Yahweh and Abram. Abram's name changed to Abraham.

    (2) The covenant again renewed, with promise of the birth of Isaac.

    (3) The destruction of Sodom and Gomorrah, Lot being saved from the overthrow.

    (4) Abraham sojourns in Gerar; repeats his misrepresentation as to Sarah. He remains in the country of the Philistines many days, either at Gerar or in the neighborhood of Beer-sheba, thirty miles away.

    (5) Birth of Isaac.

4. From the Birth of Isaac to the Death of Sarah. 21:1 to 23:20

    (1) Hagar and Ishmael sent away.

    (2) Covenant with Abimelech at Beer-sheba.

    (3) Sacrifice of Isaac. Note Abraham's sublime faith and self-sacrifice.

    (4) Death of Sarah, who is buried at Hebron, in the cave of Machpelah.

5. From the Death of Sarah to the Death of Abraham. 24:1 to 25:18

    (1) Abraham seeks a wife for his son Isaac.

    (2) Abraham's marriage with Keturah. He makes Isaac his heir, but gives presents to the sons of Keturah.

    (3) Death of Abraham.

The Life of Jacob

1. His Life in Canaan. 25:19 to 28:9

    (1) The younger of twins. Esau his brother.
    (2) Jacob, a quiet, home-loving boy, secures his more athletic brother's birthright with a mess of pottage.
    (3) Rebekah and Jacob successfully scheme to secure Isaac's blessing also.
    (4) Jacob is forced to flee from the wrath of Esau.

2. Jacob's Flight and Sojourn in Haran. 28:10 to 31:21

    (1) The dream at Bethel. Jacob bargains with God.
    (2) He falls in love with Rachel his cousin, agrees to work seven years for her hand in marriage. Laban, her father, and brother of Rebekah, deceives Jacob in giving him Leah as his wife. Jacob works seven additional years to secure his right to Rachel.
    (3) The birth of eleven of Jacob's children and his prosperity.

3. His Return to Canaan. 31:22 to 35:29

    (1) The flight from Haran.
    (2) The stormy encounter between Laban and Jacob.
    (3) Jacob wrestles with an angel. His name changed to Israel.
    (4) The meeting with Esau.
    (5) The sojourn near Shechem. Dinah disgraced.
    (6) Back to Bethel. Profound effect on Jacob's spirit.
    (7) Birth of Benjamin and death of Rachel.
    (8) Jacob dwells with Isaac. He and Esau bury their father. Their last meeting. The Jacob story blends with that of Joseph.

THE LIFE OF JOSEPH

1. His Youth in Canaan. 37:1–36

   (1) A dreamer. Tells the truth about his brothers, despised by them.

   (2) Given a coat by his father that symbolizes that he is not to be a laboring man like his brothers. "A long coat" rather than "a coat of many colors." (Cf. Hebrew, "a coat of extremities.")

   (3) His visit to Dothan to spy on his brothers. He is sold to a passing band of merchants and taken to Egypt. The brothers convince Jacob of his death.

2. The Period of Servitude and Distress. 39:1 to 40:23

   (1) Sold to Potiphar, the captain of the guard of Pharaoh (of the Hyksos dynasty, composed of Semitic conquerors of Egypt). Grows in favor from day to day. Soon the chief lieutenant of the captain.

   (2) Great temptation, and how he withstands it.

   (3) Into the dungeon. Born to rule. Soon master of the prison.

   (4) Two noted prisoners committed to Joseph's hands. Their dreams interpreted.

   (5) Two years of weary waiting. Severe discipline reveals Joseph's nature. Faith in God keeps him sane and hopeful.

3. The Years of Plenty and the Years of Famine. 41:1 to 47:26

   Pharaoh's alarming dreams. Joseph, the interpreter, suddenly raised to the office of prime minister.

   (1) The seven years of plenty. Joseph's industry, good management, faith in the voice of God.

   (2) The seven years of famine.

      a. Treatment of the Egyptians not so harsh if compared

with the spirit and policy of other prime ministers of ancient times.

b. Treatment of his brethren.

   (a) He puts their love for one another to the test. Simeon bound. Will they return to redeem him? Later on, Benjamin taken for a slave. Will the brothers forsake him? Speech of Judah before Joseph one of the most pathetic in history. Affliction had done much for the brothers of Joseph.

   (b) He acknowledges them before the court of Egypt as his own brothers.

   (c) He gives them wise and affectionate counsel.

c. Transfer of Jacob and his family into Egypt. Joseph's thought for his father in providing wagons. Goes to meet him. Goshen becomes the home of Jacob, and he enjoys peace and prosperity even in years of famine.

4. Quiet Years of Power and Usefulness. 47:27 to 50:26

  (1) Jacob's closing days.

    a. Makes Joseph promise to bury him in Palestine.

    b. Blesses the two sons of Joseph.

    c. Blesses his twelve sons. Joseph and Judah the favored ones.

    d. Burial of Jacob.

  (2) Joseph quiets the fears of his brethren after the death of their father.

  (3) At the end, Joseph makes the children of Israel swear that they will take his body with them at the Exodus.

THE BOOK OF EXODUS

The name of the book is a Latinized form of the Greek word *exodos,* which means outgoing or departure. It comes down to us through the LXX and Vulgate. On the other hand, the Jews simply called it by the first words in the book, "And these are the names." The fact that no descriptive name was given to Genesis or Exodus by the Hebrews emphasizes the fact that they considered the whole Pentateuch or Torah as a unit. The five divisions were only for convenience in handling. The book of Exodus continues the story of Genesis. The fact that it begins with "And" shows its close connection with the first book of the Law. The date of the Exodus described in this book is a much disputed question. There are two principal views:

1. During the 18th dynasty in Egypt. This view is derived from biblical and Assyrian chronology and is favored by more conservative scholars. First Kings 6:1 says that there were 480 years from the Exodus to the building of the Temple of Solomon. The Temple was founded about 965 (computing from the known date of the Battle of Karkar in 853 B.C.). The Battle of Karkar must have occurred during the three years of peace between Israel and Syria (1 Kings 22:1), since Ahab and Benhadad were allied at the time of the battle, according to Assyrian records. This would be during the twentieth year of Ahab and the seventeenth of Jehoshaphat. Computing the reign of the kings before these two, the approximate date of the building of the Temple can be determined. If 480 is added to 965, the date 1445 B.C. results. There is some archaeological evidence to recommend this view.

2. During the 19th dynasty (c. 1300 B.C.), Seti I being the

Pharaoh of the oppression, and Rameses II the Pharaoh of the Exodus. Recent archaeological discoveries have increased the weight of the argument for this date. This view, however, is open to the objection that there is not a sufficient interval between Moses and David. The archaeological evidence in hand at the present is too contradictory to warrant a safe conclusion in either direction.

The change in attitude toward the Hebrews after the death of Joseph was probably due to the expulsion of the Semitic Hyksos kings from Egypt. These Hyksos rulers were friendly toward the Semitic Israelites, but when the native Egyptians assumed the rule (c. 1550 B.C.), the oppression of the Hebrews began.

Exodus differs from Genesis both in purpose and in contents. Genesis pictures God as the covenant God of a patriarchal family; Exodus reveals him as the covenant God of the Hebrew nation. A great deal happened during the sojourn. By the time the Hebrews reached Sinai, we can see a number of results of the Egyptian experience:

1. A family had become a nation determined to found a country of its own.

2. The Hebrews became tainted with idolatry. After the Exodus the spiritual leaders could see the impotence of the idols of Egypt, but the common people clung to their superstitions.

3. The Hebrews went into Egypt as nomads but came out as an agricultural and urban people.

4. Henceforth they had a marvelous experience to tide them over difficult times.

OUTLINE OF THE BOOK

Introduction—Death of Joseph, and subsequent increase of the Israelites. 1:1–7

1. The Oppression. 1:8 to 12:36

    (1) The children of Israel put under bondage. 1:8–14
    (2) Their male children put to death. 1:15–22

(3) Birth, education, and flight of Moses. 2:1–22

(4) Call of Moses to be the deliverer of Israel. 2:23 to 4:31

(5) First interview with Pharaoh and its discouraging outcome. 5:1 to 7:7

(6) Pharaoh having hardened his heart, the ten plagues come upon the land. 7:8 to 12:36

2. The Exodus and the March to Sinai. 12:37 to 19:1

(1) The Exodus, and directions as to the Passover. 12:37 to 13:16

(2) The march from Succoth through the Red Sea. 13:17 to 15:21

(3) From the Red Sea to Sinai. 15:22 to 19:1

3. Giving of the Law. 19:2 to 40:38

(1) Preparation of the people. 19

(2) The moral law. 20

(3) The civil law. 21:1 to 23:19

(4) A covenant between Yahweh and Israel. 23:20 to 24:18

(5) Pattern of the tabernacle. 25–31

(6) Breach and renewal of the covenant. 32–34

(7) Tabernacle made and set up. 35–40

The Book of Leviticus

This book is named after the tribe of Levi, which took over the ceremonial functions of Hebrew religion. However, it is more concerned with the priests than with the Levites as such. All Levites were not priests, although it was necessary that each priest be a Levite.

The Hebrew ritual and ceremonial laws were object lessons for a people in their religious kindergarten days. In Leviticus we have objective requirements that are unforgettable symbols of deeper spiritual truths. The pictures were given first to prepare the way for the spiritual discernment needed in later revelation. Underlying the whole system was the *holiness* of God. Sinful man must find a way to approach and commune with this Holy One. The best commentary on the book of Leviticus is the book of Hebrews in the New Testament.

Animal sacrifices were of four kinds: (1) The sin offering, with emphasis on blood, pictured the giving of life to secure forgiveness of sin. (2) The burnt offering, when the flesh was completely burnt, symbolized a full consecration to God. (3) The trespass offering, with its restitution, emphasized that there are certain divine and human boundaries that one cannot cross with impunity. (4) The peace offering, with its meal at the conclusion, pictured communion between God and man. These offerings were religious festivals in which portions of the offering were consumed on the altar, portions were eaten by the priests, and the remainder by the offerers and their families. These festivals enabled the offerer to give a more complete expression to some of the religious urges which did not find complete expression in the other sacrifices. They were needed

34

to give the offerer a more complete religious satisfaction, hence the *peace offering*.

One of these urges was to express in a satisfactory way one's gratitude for unmerited favors and blessings, the *thank offering*.

Another urge was to express one's feeling of obligation, or indebtedness, as well as one's joy upon the fulfilment or payment of a vow, *votive offering*.

A third urge was to express, voluntarily and in a special way, one's love and devotion to God, *freewill offering*.

Other than animal sacrifices there were two other types. The *meal offering* symbolized the dedication of the fruits of labor to God.

The *drink offering* is more difficult to analyze. The patriarchs offered drink offerings in Canaan centuries before the Mosaic period. This offering was not made alone but was always a part of, or along with, a burnt offering or one of the peace offerings. Its significance was the same as the offering with which it was made. It merely expanded the offering to include a portion from another source of food.

The laws of cleanness and uncleanness ever kept before Israel the distinction between holy and tainted, evil and good. God's people must be separate. The holy days of the Hebrews were likewise symbolical: (1) the sabbath—God as Creator; (2) the Passover—God as Redeemer; (3) Pentecost (spring) and Tabernacles (fall)—God as Provider; (4) Day of Atonement—God as holy and gracious.

OUTLINE OF THE BOOK

1. Laws as to Sacrifice, Purification, and Atonement. Chapters 1–16

    (1) The principal kinds of offerings, with supplemental directions to the priests. 1–7
    (2) Consecration of the priests, followed by the sin of Nadab and Abihu. 8–10

2. The Law of Holiness. Chapters 17–26

A miscellaneous collection of precepts dealing with moral and ceremonial requirements, much emphasis being laid on holiness.

THE BOOK OF NUMBERS

This book takes its title from a translation of the name that was given to the Septuagint version, so designated because of the two numberings of the children of Israel contained in it (chapters 1 and 26), and also since there is so much of numerical nature contained therein. The Jewish name for the book is probably the more correct, at least the more proper (*bemidh-bar,* "in the wilderness"), since this book records the fortunes of Israel in the Desert of Sinai. It forms a natural sequence to the book of Leviticus because the first part is of a statistical and Levitical character.

The writer of Numbers was not a mere recorder of the events which happened during the forty years of wandering in the wilderness. He was rather an interpreter of that history. He saw in each event God's hand, directing his Chosen People, tending to their needs, enduring their sins and weaknesses, keeping his covenant with them, and disciplining them. Kadesh-barnea will always be a condemnation of God's people of any age who refuse to go forward by faith.

OUTLINE OF THE BOOK

1. At Sinai. Numbering of the people, dedication of the altar, together with many precepts and regulations. 1:1 to 10:10

2. From Sinai to the Southern Border of Palestine. 10:11 to 14:45

3. From the First Sojourn at Kadesh-barnea Until the Return to the Same Place After the Period of Aimless Wandering. 15:1 to 20:21

4. From Kadesh-barnea to the Camp Opposite Jericho. 20:22 to 22:1

5. Events and Laws Connected with the Sojourn in the Plains of Moab. 22:2 to 36:13

The Book of Deuteronomy

The fifth book of the Law is a majestic, fascinating, and practical book. The Jews call it *'ellah haddevarim* ("these are the words," which compose the first two words in the Hebrew original). The English title "Deuteronomy," meaning second law or repetition of the law, is based on an erroneous Greek translation of three Hebrew words in 17:18, which should be rendered "a copy of this law." Though based on an inaccurate translation, the title is fairly appropriate; for Deuteronomy is in a real sense a repetition of the law found in the preceding books, although here the legislation is further interpreted, expanded, and applied.

Deuteronomy is primarily a book of oratory. It contains a series of discourses delivered by Moses to the Israelites in the plains of Moab during the brief interval (about forty days at the most) between the close of the wilderness wanderings and the entrance into the Land of Canaan. In these discourses the speaker constantly reminds the people of Yahweh's gracious dealings with them and appeals to them to respond to God's goodness by giving him their undivided love and loyalty.

There are three main discourses, with three short appendices. The first discourse (1:1 to 4:43) is mainly historical and hortatory. Moses rehearses in broad outline the experiences from Horeb to Moab and exhorts the Israelites to cleave to Yahweh and steer clear of idolatry. The second discourse (4:44 to 26:19) is principally hortatory and legislative. This is the longest discourse and constitutes the nucleus of the book. It gives a summary of the civil, moral, and religious laws and statutes of Israel. The tone is that of a father. The ideal is holiness. The

39

third discourse (27:1 to 31:30) is predictive and threatening. It deals primarily with the blessings of obedience and the curses of disobedience. Following these three discourses are three appendices: Moses' song (chapter 32), Moses' blessing (chapter 33), and the account of Moses' death and burial (chapter 34).

By whom and when was the book written? Tradition ascribes it to Moses. Many modern scholars claim that the book originated shortly before the Josianic reformation (621 B.C.). It was formulated by the prophetic party in the interest of centralization of worship and was then concealed in the Temple. After it was found, there soon followed the sort of revival they desired. The book itself does not claim to have been written by Moses but only that it contains his addresses (31:9; 31:24ff.; 1:1). There is strong evidence that the book took its final form considerably before the seventh century B.C. Thus it would not be a "pious fraud" but simply the final form of the addresses of Moses as edited by the prophetic party under the inspiration of God. This book, already recognized as authoritative, was lost during the reign of Manasseh and found in 621 B.C.

Deuteronomy is a book which has great religious value for today. Love is the key to the divine life. God is due all the loyalty of the human heart because of his grace. Deuteronomy was a favorite of our Lord. (Cf. Matt. 4:4,7,10; 22:37.)

The Life of Moses

1. From Birth Until Flight from Egypt. Ex. 1:1 to 2:15

   (1) Born in troublous times. Faith preserves him (Heb. 11:23).
   (2) Adopted into the family of Pharaoh. God overrules Pharaoh's plans so that he becomes the nourisher of Israel's deliverer. Though nominally the son of Pharaoh's daughter, Moses is nursed by his own mother. The nursing period was an important part of the education of Moses.

(3) Educated in all the wisdom of Egypt (Acts 7:22), trained in the midst of the highest civilization of the times.

(4) Chooses to ally himself with the people of God (Heb. 11:24–26). In a fit of indignation, he kills a cruel Egyptian.

(5) Flees from Egypt into the wilderness to Midian.

2. Period of Sojourn in the Desert. Ex. 2:16 to 4:28

(1) By chivalrous conduct secures a home and a wife.
(2) The discipline in the desert.
  a. He is content with a subordinate position, that of a shepherd.
  b. The solitude of the desert encourages reflection.
  c. He gains knowledge of the country through which he would lead Israel. These forty years were a preparation for his great work. They were not lost. They gave him time to think, time to become humble and meek, time to commune with God.
(3) The call of Moses to be the deliverer of Israel.
  a. In the marvelous symbol of the burning bush, God calls to him and lays upon him the task of rescuing Israel from Egypt.
  b. The objections of Moses and how God disposes of them:
    (a) "I am not equal to the task." God replies, "I will be with thee."
    (b) "By whose authority am I to go?" "I AM sends you—the one who is, the self-existing one, the ever-present one." A play on the name of YHWH.
    (c) "The elders of Israel will not believe me." The signs of the rod, the hand, and the water are given as proofs of his divine commission.
    (d) "I am not an eloquent speaker." "I will be with thy mouth."
  c. Now Moses tries to beg off without any excuse. "Send anyone except me!" He is afraid of the

wrath of Pharaoh. God becomes angry at Moses' stubbornness. He sends Aaron as his helper and spokesman and informs him that the Pharaoh is dead who sought his life.

(4) The departure for Egypt.

    a. Moses is accompanied by his family. A strange event happens at the lodging place. Neglect of circumcision in the family of Moses. Family sent back home.

    b. Moses meets with Aaron at the mount of God. They talk over their plans.

3. Moses the Deliverer, Leader, and Lawgiver of Israel

(1) The duel with Pharaoh. Ex. 4:29 to 15:21

    a. The elders convinced by the words and the signs. They give their consent to make the trial.

    b. Pharaoh, by way of reply, only increases their burdens.

    c. A sign given to Pharaoh. The rod of Moses swallows up the other rods.

    d. The contest in ten battles (plagues). These were actually contests between Yahweh and the gods of Egypt. The Egyptians worshiped the Nile, the sun, the sacred Apis bull, insects (scarab beetle).

    These plagues are suggested by phenomena in Egypt today; but two considerations prove that the plagues brought by Moses were miracles: (1) severity (2) coming and departure announced.

    God makes Pharaoh's heart strong; but only after Pharaoh willingly hardens his own heart. Pharaoh's freedom is not destroyed; but God's plan takes account of his wicked character.

    e. The Passover and the Exodus. Night of great excitement. The Israelites ask for rich presents and receive them. Mixed multitude goes out with them. Yahweh leads his people in the pillar of cloud and of fire.

    f. Deliverance at the Red Sea. Miraculous, though God uses means. Pharaoh must be more severely punished.

(2) The Journey to Sinai. Ex. 15:22 to 18:27

a. To Marah ("bitter"). Revelation at Marah: "I am thy healer."
b. To Elim (twelve springs of water).
c. To Wilderness of Sin. Here they receive manna and quails. (Cf. Deut. 8:2–6 for purpose.) The manna cannot be explained. It was miraculous bread from heaven.
d. Rephidim and its trials. Several events:
    (a) Water for their thirst. Water from the rock.
    (b) Battle with Amalekites. (Cf. Deut. 25:17–19.)
    (c) Visit of Jethro. He is wise enough to advise Moses to appoint judges.

(3) At Sinai
(See Numbers 33 for stages in Israel's journey. These stations in the desert are very hard to determine.)
a. Days of preparation for the giving of the Law. Ex. 19: 1–15
b. The great day in which the Ten Words were given. Ex. 19:16 to 20:21
c. The Book of the Covenant, and solemn ratification. Ex. 20:22 to 24:8
d. The first forty days on the Mount, during which Moses receives the pattern of the tabernacle and certain rules of worship. Ex. 24:12 to 31:18
e. The golden calf. Ex. 32:1 to 34:35
    (a) Conduct of Aaron blameworthy.
    (b) God announces the fall to Moses, and Moses intercedes for his people.
    (c) Moses, at the foot of the Mount, in anger breaks the tables.
    (d) There is war now in camp. Tribe of Levi destroys the chief offenders.
    (e) The second intercession of Moses. Forty days.
    (f) The growing promises and the vision of God.
    (g) The renewal of the covenant and the shining face. (Cf. 2 Cor. 3:12–18.)
f. The tabernacle built. The people offer willingly and freely. Ex. 35:1 to 40:38
g. Solemn anointing of Aaron and his sons. Lev. 8:1–36

h. The death of Nadab and Abihu. (A natural infer-
ence is that Nadab and Abihu were drunk.) Lev.
10:1–11

4. Journey from Sinai to Kadesh-barnea. Num. 10:11 to 14:45

An invitation extended to Hobab, Moses' brother-in-law, to
accompany them. Though declining at first, he seems to have
gone with them. (Cf. Judg. 1:16; 4:11.)
(1) The murmuring at Taberah.
(2) Kibroth-hattaavah, or the graves of lust. The seventy
elders prophesy. Observe the self-forgetful spirit of
Moses with respect to Eldad and Medad.
(3) At Hazeroth, Miriam and Aaron oppose Moses. Yahweh
defends Moses.
(4) The spies sent out from Kadesh. Moses and Aaron
have a terrible experience in connection with the great
rebellion at Kadesh.

5. The Period of Wandering (nearly thirty-eight years). Num.
16:1 to 17:13; 20:1. Deut. 1:19–46

The most important event of this period is the insurrection
of Korah, which is not only a revolt against the authority
of Moses but especially against the priesthood of Aaron.
Moses has great responsibilities during this period. He receives some new laws for Israel. The people have no hope.
At the beginning of the fortieth year they are at Kadesh-
barnea a second time.

6. From Kadesh-barnea to the Plains of Moab. Num. 20:1 to
21:35

(1) The death of Miriam.
(2) The sin of Moses and Aaron.
(3) Edom refuses to let Israel pass through his land.
(4) Aaron's death at Mount Hor.
(5) The Canaanites beaten off.
(6) Fiery serpents and the brazen serpent.

(7) The overthrow of Sihon and Og, and capture of eastern Palestine.

7. The Closing Days of Moses

    (1) Balaam and Balak cannot curse Israel, but lead the people into the worship of Baal-peor. Num. 22:1 to 25:5

    (2) After a second numbering of the people, Moses is warned of approaching death. Joshua appointed to be his successor. Num. 26:1 to 27:23

    (3) The war with Midian a war of extermination. Num. 31:1–54

    (4) The allotment of eastern Palestine to Reuben, Gad, and the half tribe of Manasseh. Many directions as to the western Palestine inheritance. Num. 32:1–42

    (5) Closing addresses of Moses in the last month of his life. Deuteronomy

PART II

STUDIES IN THE HISTORICAL BOOKS

INTRODUCTION

Herodotus is usually called the "Father of History," but the aging child can no longer acknowledge his parentage. Centuries before the honored Greek began his research, the Hebrews were writing history. The fact that this has not been recognized is due in part to prejudice of historians toward the Bible and the lack of acquaintance of secular scholars with pre-Greek civilization.[1] The historical portions of the Old Testament occupy more than half the entire volume. Not only do we have the exclusively historical books such as Samuel and Kings but also much historical writing included in the Law and the Prophets. The historical books are as different as their position in the canon, varying from the simple, popular stories embodied in Genesis to the ecclesiastical view of history which the late priestly writer of Chronicles presents. They contain the earliest and the latest teaching in the Old Testament. Yet there is throughout an underlying unity. This good order is derived from the Hebrew conception of the nature of history.

It is significant that the Hebrews were the first people in the ancient world to have a sense of history. Egypt and Babylonia, with older civilizations, offer no parallel. Although their records were abundant from ancient times, these raw materials were not utilized in forming a unified historical writing. The difference seems to be that Israel had a secret—"they discovered that human affairs were developing under a divine purpose. World events to their prophetic minds were not like the rise and fall of waves, but were a current moving toward a

---

[1] Cf. J. Philip Hyatt, *Prophetic Religion* (Nashville: Abingdon-Cokesbury Press, 1947), p. 76.

definite goal. Believing in the future they were interested in the past, not only in its facts, but in their meaning."[2] They were the first to assert that God manifests himself on the stage of time, controlling the destiny of men and nations. "The Hebrews affirmed the reality and importance of time. To them it was not an illusion, something from which man must escape, but something which must be redeemed."[3]

The Hebrews had a genius for storytelling, their historical imagination making ancient events vividly real. A thousand years seem but as a day as we read the stirring narratives which embellish Jewish historical writings. They possess a simple clearness that appeals to every type and class of man, and an undercurrent of earnest, strong feeling that stirs the heart of stone.

It is imperative that the modern reader understand at once that biblical history differs radically from modern historical writing. As Philip Hyatt has observed, historical writing is principally of two kinds, objective and subjective. Objective history gives account of events as they have occurred, avoiding as much as possible the personal prejudice of the investigator. Subjective history seeks to discover facts and to interpret their meaning for man. It consists of "events bound together by a thread of interpretation." Objective history seeks to be impersonal, while subjective history is personal to the core. The chief aim of the subjective type is to arouse interest so as to inspire action; the chief aim of its opposite is to supply information. The subjective historian has his eye on his readers, the objective on the facts he reports.

Modern historians are objective, having as their chief purpose the reporting of facts, whereas the Old Testament writers were subjective, interested primarily in the effect of the facts on the reader. It was not that they did not seek to report events as true to fact as possible but that their chief interest concerned the significance of these facts to the individual and the race. Present historians report; Old Testament historians exhorted.

---

[2]C. A. Dinsmore, *The English Bible as Literature* (Boston: Houghton Mifflin Company, 1931), p. 117.

[3]J. Philip Hyatt, *loc. cit.*

THE BOOK OF JOSHUA

As the book of Genesis begins the first division of the Hebrew Old Testament, known as the Pentateuch, the book of Joshua is the first of the second division, known as the Prophets. It also marks the beginning of that section of the Prophets known as the Former Prophets, which includes Joshua, Judges, First and Second Samuel, and the books of Kings. The name of the book is derived from its hero, although it is nowhere claimed that he is the author. The date of the writing appears to be during the time of the kings of Israel, even though the source material must have come directly from Joshua or an eyewitness of his conquests.

The man Joshua was born during the Egyptian bondage. He went out of the land during the Exodus, and soon was commander of the Hebrew armies under Moses. As a faithful attendant of the great lawgiver, he witnessed the historic events of the Wilderness. When the twelve spies were sent out to Canaan, he was probably their leader, and it was he and Caleb who brought back the challenge to take the land. After the death of Moses, Joshua led in the conquest of Canaan and in the allotment of tribal territory, coming to his death honored and revered by all, bequeathing to his people a great tradition and an unconquerable spirit. The name Joshua is equivalent to the name *Jesus,* and means "Yahweh is Saviour" or "salvation of Yahweh." Just as the first Joshua conquered the enemy country of Canaan, even so the second Joshua was victorious in his conquest of sin.

The moral problem of why God ordered Joshua to exterminate the inhabitants of Canaan may be met by the following considerations: (1) One cannot expect these early warriors to have attained the Christian concept of universal brotherly love, that so few have achieved today. (2) The destruction was an act of judgment upon the nations because of their sinfulness. The Hebrews were considered God's executioners.

THE CONQUEST OF PALESTINE

1. The Conquest of Eastern Palestine. Accomplished by Moses in the last year of his life.

   (1) The conquest of Gilead, country of Sihon.
   (2) The conquest of Bashan, country of Og.
   (3) The conquest of Midian. (A holy war, but land not occupied.)

2. The Conquest of Western Palestine. The whole country was overrun by Joshua; but many heathen were left in cities and villages. His strategy was to divide and conquer.

   (1) The conquest of Central Palestine.
      a. Jericho.
      b. Ai.
      c. Gideon.
      d. Beth-horon.
   (2) The conquest of Southern Palestine. Battle of Beth-horon was followed by the siege of Hebron and other cities in the south (Libnah, Lachish, Eglon, Hebron, Debir).
   (3) The conquest of Northern Palestine. The powerful league of Jabin was crushed at Lake Merom. This was followed by the capture of several cities and villages. These, with the exception of Hazor, were left standing, in order that the Israelites might occupy them.

OUTLINE OF THE BOOK

1. The Conquest of Canaan. Chapters 1–12
   (1) Preparation for invading Western Palestine. 1–2
   (2) The miraculous crossing of the Jordan. 3–4
   (3) The Conquest in three campaigns. 5–12
       a. Central Canaan. 5:1 to 10:15
       b. Southern Canaan. 10:16–43
       c. Northern Canaan. 11
       Summary. 12

2. The Division of Canaan Among the Tribes of Israel. 13–22
   (Study location of the twelve tribes.)
Conclusion—Two closing addresses by Joshua. 23–24

THE BOOK OF JUDGES

The Hebrew word translated "judges" is better rendered "deliverers" or "saviors," since the character of the men discussed in this book is best described by the latter terms. We have in this interesting book some of the most dramatic stories in the Old Testament, and one of the oldest folk songs—the song of Deborah. The first two chapters are introductory, forming a connecting link between the book and the preceding book of Joshua. Herein is found the writer's philosophy of history. Over and over again we have his theme recurring throughout the book. The people sin and fall away from God (apostasy); as a result they get into trouble (oppression); in trouble they repent and call upon God for help (penitence); God hears and delivers them (deliverance). Then the same cycle begins again.

The main body of the book begins with chapter 3 and continues through chapter 16. Here we meet with thirteen deliverers, the most outstanding of whom are *Ehud*, who slew the fat king of Moab, Eglon; *Deborah*, who defeated Sisera; *Gideon* the conqueror of the Midianites; *Jephthah* of the rash vow; and the muscular *Samson*. The remaining chapters (17–21) do not follow chapter 16 in time. Chapters 17–18 tell of the Danite migration and of Micah and his graven image, while chapters 19–21 tell of the almost total destruction of the tribe of Benjamin by fellow Israelites and of the attempt to find wives for the 600 Benjamites who were spared.

It is hardly likely that the various judges ruled consecutively. If we add their various terms of office, a total of 410 years is reached. However, 1 Kings 6:1 says that there were only 480 years from the Exodus to the fourth year of Solomon's reign (c. 965 B.C.). That would leave only seventy years for the forty years of wandering in the Wilderness, Joshua's conquest of Canaan, and the period of Eli, Samuel, Saul, and David. Evidently some adjustment is necessary in the chronology. Apparently several of the judges were in authority over only a part of Israel and ruled simultaneously with others. If this is true, the period can easily be shortened to 300 years, which is much more likely. If the Exodus occurred about 1300 B.C., the period must be shortened even more.

The author of the book of Judges is not known. From 18:30 it has been argued that the book was composed after the Babylonian Captivity (after 586 B.C.), or at least after 722 B.C.; but 18:31 would seem to show that the reference was rather to the captivity of the sacred ark in the days of Eli. The author lived either in the days of the united kingdom or just after.

OUTLINE OF THE BOOK

1. From the Conquest to the Period of the Judges. 1:1 to 3:6 (Part of this section overlaps with the book of Joshua.)

2. Sketch of Thirteen Judges, Six Major and Seven Minor. 3:7 to 16:31

   (1) Othniel overthrows the king of Mesopotamia
   (2) Ehud slays the king of Moab, and Shamgar beats down the Philistines
   (3) Deborah and Barak destroy the power of Jabin and Sisera
   (4) Gideon destroys the Midianites. Abimelech, Tola, and Jair act as judges over a more limited area
   (5) Jephthah drives out the Ammonites. He is followed by three minor judges—Ibzan, Elon, and Abdon
   (6) Samson defeats the Philistines in many encounters

3. Two Incidents Illustrating the Period Just Prior to the Judges. 17–21

The Book of Ruth

This little book is one of the master short stories of all time, and is so recognized among eminent students of this type of literature. We have in the story human interest, tragedy, humor, love, and an unexpectedly happy ending. The scene is laid during the period of the judges. As to the time of writing there is some disagreement. Many scholars claim that the viewpoint is that of a post-Exilic author. As evidence they present the arguments:

1. In the Hebrew canon the book of Ruth is not among the Former Prophets, where we find Judges, but is included among the Writings, which were the last material to be canonized.

2. Aramaic appears in the style of the author.

3. In 4:7 the author mentions a custom in Ruth's day long forgotten among the people he was addressing.

4. The idyllic life of the book, marked by simplicity and pastoral beauty, suggests that we have here a later idealization of the period of judges, since in the former book life is pictured as anything but idyllic.

If the book is written late, it is for the purpose of meeting a current post-Exilic problem. Naomi is the returning exile, Ruth represents the foreigners who came along at the same time, and Boaz represents the people of the land who were left behind when the others were taken into captivity. As in Obed the three were united to bring David, just so these three groups, united, will produce a great and permanent kingdom.

As attractive as this theory is, it is open to criticism. Ruth may be among the Writings because its sanction of foreign marriages might have delayed its canonization for some time. It may be observed that the style of Ruth is more similar to that of 1 and 2 Samuel than to that of Ezra and Nehemiah of the post-Exilic era. The allusion in 4:7 is possibly a later scribal note, and it is quite possible that idyllic communities existed during the age of judges. Unrest in the chief cities would not mean that life could not go quietly on in Bethlehem.

OUTLINE OF THE BOOK

1. Sojourn in Moab for Ten Years, During Which Time Naomi's Husband and Two Sons Die. 1:1-5

2. Return of Naomi with Ruth to Bethlehem. 1:6-22

3. Struggle with Poverty, Relieved by the Kindness of Boaz. Chapter 2

4. Bold Act of Ruth. Chapter 3

5. Redemption of Naomi's Property, and Marriage of Ruth. Chapter 4

The Books of Samuel

The two books of Samuel, like the two books of Kings, originally formed an undivided whole. They are now in the divided form only for the sake of convenience. Although the books deal with events sometime after the death of Samuel, these events are but the lengthening shadow of the great man; so the material rightly bears his name. First Samuel opens with the birth of Samuel, and 2 Samuel closes with the last days of David.

The author of the books could not be Samuel, for there is a unity of style and purpose throughout, even after the death of Samuel. When were these histories written? The pure Hebrew used indicates an early period. However, some time has elapsed since the events of the book occurred. The explanation of archaic terms (1 Sam. 9:9) and reference to obsolete customs (2 Sam. 13:18) as well as the use of the formula "unto this day" (1 Sam. 5:5; 6:18; 27:6; 30:25; 2 Sam. 4:3; 6:8; 18:18) indicate this. The writer is certainly in a period after David since the whole length of his reign is mentioned in 2 Samuel 5:5. The mention of the "kings of Judah" in 1 Samuel 27:6 shows that the kingdom is already divided, as do several allusions to a distinction between Judah and Israel. Therefore, the position of the writer appears to be that of one immediately following the division of the kingdom after the death of Solomon.

The writer, however, must have used sources for his material. These probably included: (1) Contemporary prophetical histories. First Chronicles 29:29 states that Samuel, Nathan, and Gad had accounts of their period. (2) The chronicles of King David (1 Chron. 27:24), which were probably statistical state records. (3) The character of the kingdom, written by

Samuel (1 Sam. 10:25). (4) The national poetical literature, among which was the book of Jashar (2 Sam. 1:18). (5) Oral tradition.

The books of Samuel give an interesting picture of the times. There are a number of statements that show the religious shortcomings of the period. Enemies were tortured, polygamy was common in the upper classes. Many considered David's departure from the land of Israel as excluding him from the presence and service of Yahweh (1 Sam. 26:19). However, there were many encouraging signs. The centralization of government exerted a strong unifying influence on religious thought and practice. The poor had a right to justice, adultery was recognized as a great crime, and more emphasis was placed on the rights of the individual.

OUTLINE OF BOOK I

1. Close of the Period of the Judges. Chapters 1–7

   (1) Early life of Samuel. 1:1 to 4:1a
   (2) Judgments on Eli and loss of the ark. 4:1b–7:1
   (3) Judicial life of Samuel. 7:2–17

2. Foundation of the Monarchy. 8–31

   (1) Appointment of the first king. 8–10
   (2) Saul's reign until his rejection. 11–15
   (3) The decline of Saul and the rise of David. 16–31

OUTLINE OF BOOK II

1. David's Reign at Hebron over Judah. Chapters 1–4

2. David's Prosperous Reign over All Israel Until His Great Sin. 5–11

3. Chastisement of David for His Terrible Sin. 12–20

    (1) Death of Bath-sheba's child. 12
    (2) Sin and death of Amnon. 13
    (3) Absalom's rebellion. 14–19
    (4) Rebellion of Sheba. 20

4. Group of Events and Sayings of Various Dates. 21–24

LIFE OF SAMUEL

Under the guiding hand of Samuel, the dissevered tribes of Israel became a united nation.

1. From His Birth Until the Capture of the Ark. 1 Sam. 1:1 to 4:22

    (1) He is given to his mother in answer to prayer. Samuel is dedicated to God as a Nazirite (Nazarite).
    (2) His early home training with a pious mother.
    (3) He becomes the assistant of the aged high priest as long as Eli lives. What influences are thrown around Samuel in the Tabernacle?
        a. The awful sins of Hophni and Phinehas. The picture of the three-pronged fleshhook reveals their character. Worse than gluttons, they are also guilty of adultery. Young Samuel may either follow after Eli or else imitate his wicked sons.
        b. The company of pious old Eli. Samuel is faithful to Eli and Eli becomes exceedingly fond of him, comes to lean upon him. He bestows blessings on Samuel's father and mother.
        c. The yearly visit of his parents.
    (4) There comes a warning to Eli from a man of God.
    (5) The boy Samuel receives a revelation from Yahweh, followed by yet other messages from God. He keeps growing in favor with God and man.

(6) The disastrous battle of Aphek and capture of the ark. Eli and both his sons perish in one day. The Philistines pitch near Aphek and slay four thousand men. The Israelites take counsel and decide to secure the ark and the two priests, Hophni and Phinehas. The Philistines become frightened and desperate. Next day the Philistines win and capture the ark. (Good example of superstitious religion. Israel put faith in the ark and not in God. Men today expect to be saved by the church or baptism.) Samuel is not mentioned in the day's incidents.

2. From the Capture of the Ark Until the Battle of Ebenezer. 1 Sam. 5:1 to 7:17

There is silence for twenty years, so far as Samuel is concerned. The ark is taken to Ashdod and presented to Dagon. Plagues come upon the possessors of the ark. They send it to Gath, then to Ekron. At length the lords of the Philistines send it to Beth-shemesh, where it is received by the Israelites. Seventy men are slain for irreverent curiosity. (The number in the text of 1 Sam. 6:19 is probably a scribal error.) What is Samuel doing during this twenty-year period?

(1) He probably begins to collect young men into schools and to teach them the law of God, and sacred music, with a view to promoting a revival throughout the land.

(2) He is teaching the people and weaning them from idolatry (1 Sam. 7:2–4). At the close of twenty years, Samuel holds a great assembly at Mizpah. Here they pour out water before God. While they are worshiping Yahweh, the Philistines come up to battle, and the Lord smites them. So the Philistines are subdued for a long period. The cities which the Philistines had captured are restored to Israel.

3. Samuel's Relations with Saul and David.

(1) His kind reception of Saul, and the secret anointing, followed by the kiss of homage. Saul is a changed man

after the anointing. The blessing of the Lord is upon him. "God gave him another heart." Saul also now seized with prophetic enthusiasm. 1 Sam. 8:1 to 10:16

(2) The formal choice of Saul by lot at the great assembly at Mizpah. Note the enthusiasm of Samuel over Saul's fine appearance. Samuel writes down the law governing the kingdom. (Cf. Deut. 17–14:20.) 1 Sam. 10:17–27

(3) After Saul's great victory at Jabesh-gilead, Samuel goes to Gilgal to renew the kingdom. Saul has won his crown by courage and good generalship. The eleventh chapter of 1 Samuel gives us a favorable opinion of Saul. Saul has gone back to the plow at Gibeah, until aroused by the news from Jabesh-gilead. He collects over three hundred thousand men and sweeps away the Ammonites like chaff.

Note the farewell address of Samuel as judge of Israel. He promises to pray for the people and instruct them, thus retaining his prophetic and priestly office. He challenges the world to find fault with his judicial life. 1 Sam. 11:1 to 12:25

(4) The Philistines having invaded the land, Saul becomes impatient and usurps the priestly office at Gilgal (30,-000 chariots almost certainly a mistake. The Septuagint, in Lucian's recension, and the Peshitta have 3,000.) Samuel rebukes Saul. 1 Sam. 13:1–15

(5) Samuel directs Saul to exterminate the Amalekites and their cattle. Saul spares Agag and the best of the cattle and sheep. Samuel says, "Obedience is better than sacrifice." Final separation between Samuel and Saul here takes place. 1 Sam. 15:1–35

(6) Samuel anoints David at Bethlehem. Samuel, having become afraid of Saul, does not tell the world of his purpose. 1 Sam. 16:1–13

(7) Several years after this first anointing, when chased from his home at the court of Saul, David takes refuge with Samuel at Ramah. Here Samuel is at the head of a company of prophets. Saul, upon his visit to arrest David, is again seized with the prophetic spirit. 1 Sam. 19:18–24

(8) During the period of David's wandering, Samuel dies, and is buried in the presence of a great multitude. I Sam. 25:1

(9) The incident with the witch of Endor. I Sam. 28. A good example of ancient spiritualism, which differs little from the modern form. Saul in his desperation is easily deceived. Note that he never sees Samuel.

LIFE OF DAVID

1. From His Birth to His Anointing

His ancestry was honorable (Ruth and Boaz, etc.). David was the youngest of eight sons, attractive, musical, and poetic. Serving as a shepherd in his youth, he was courageous in the face of danger. He was probably from sixteen to eighteen years of age at his anointing. I Sam. 16

2. From His Anointing to His Flight from the Court of Saul

(1) He is brought to Saul's court to soothe him with music. I Sam. 16:14–23. If David has been anointed, Saul knows nothing about it now. (Cf. Browning's "Saul.")

(2) He slays the giant Goliath. I Sam. 17. Saul probably did not recognize David. Still, Abner should have recognized him. Saul may have been frenzied when David played before him; moreover, David was now older and probably changed in dress and appearance. The Septuagint omits 17:12–31, 41, 48 (partly), 50, 55–58; 18:1–5, and greater part of 6, 9–11, 17–19, 29b, 30, etc. The Greek text here perhaps is to be preferred.

(3) David wins the love of Jonathan and is promoted by Saul to high command in the army; but his growing reputation makes Saul jealous. I Sam. 18:1–9

(4) Saul's jealousy manifests itself in various ways. I Sam. 18:10–30
   a. He tries to smite David to the wall with a javelin.
   b. Reduces him to the command of a thousand men.

      c. Having promised David the hand of Merab, Saul insults him by giving her to Adriel.

      d. Tries to entrap David by the strange dowry he requires for the hand of Michal.

      e. He even urges Jonathan and others to kill David.

(5) Jonathan persuades Saul to become reconciled to David. I Sam. 19:1–7

(6) David's new success in war revives Saul's jealousy. I Sam. 19:8 to 20:23

      a. He again tries to smite him to the wall.

      b. He tries to capture him in his house, but David is delivered by Michal.

      c. He tries in vain to arrest David in Ramah. David returns to seek Jonathan.

(7) Jonathan, having tried in vain to bring about a second reconciliation, renews his covenant with David and sends him away. I Sam. 20:24–42

3. David's Wanderings

(1) From his flight until Saul takes the field against him. I Sam. 21:1 to 23:13

      a. David flees by way of Nob to Achish, king of Gath.

      b. Having by a successful stratagem escaped from Gath, he retires to the cave of Adullam, where he receives his family and collects a band of men. These men were debtors and vagabonds. David is strong enough in will to control 400 such men.

      c. After a brief trip to land of Moab, he returns to his fortress. The prophet Gad directs David to return to the land of Judah, and he enters the forest of Hereth.

      d. He welcomes the fugitive Abiathar.

      e. He relieves Keilah from a Philistine invasion. Saul plans his capture.

(2) The period of Saul's pursuit of David. I Sam. 23:14 to 26:25

      a. Saul pursues David in the wilderness of Ziph. Jonathan has his last interview with David.

b. Invited by Ziphites, Saul returns to the chase in the wilderness of Maon, southeast of Ziph, and almost overtakes David.

c. While Saul is called away to meet a Philistine raid, David escapes to En-gedi. Here he spares Saul in the cave. David has a brief breathing space, during which he wins a new wife, Abigail. Polygamy commences in David's life.

d. The Ziphites try to betray David at the hill of Hachilah, but again it is Saul who is caught in the trap. (The Ziphites seem to hate David, and are spies of Saul.) Final interview between Saul and David. Saul goes home, never again to pursue David. Yet David at this time loses heart and hope.

(3) The period of exile in Philistia. 1 Sam. 27 to 2 Sam. 1

a. In despair, David flees to Achish, king of Gath, for refuge. He receives Ziklag as his city, and resides there sixteen months, making forays on his heathen neighbors. (Cf. 1 Chron. 12:1–7 for a reinforcement from the tribe of Benjamin.)

b. David is commanded to go forth with the Philistines against Saul. He obeys, but is sent home before the battle. Picture effect of David's conduct on the hearts of the men of Israel. David had to wait seven years for his throne over Israel. (Cf. 1 Chron. 12:19–22 for a reinforcement to David from the tribe of Manasseh.)

c. Meantime Ziklag had been plundered but was soon recovered.

d. David's beautiful elegy over Saul and Jonathan.

4. David's Reign at Hebron. 2 Sam. 2–4

(1) By divine direction, David goes up to Hebron, where the men of Judah anoint him as king. (Cf. 1 Sam. 30:26–31.) Abner sets Ish-bosheth (Esh-baal, 1 Chron. 8:33) on the throne of Israel, at Mahanaim, east of Jordan. Why did not all Israel turn as one man to David? His presence with the Philistine invaders became

known. Saul's partisans seized on this fact to wean the northern tribes from David.

(2) The contest at Gibeon between the soldiers of Ish-bosheth, under Abner, and the men of David, under three of David's nephews. The civil war, thus inaugurated, continues a long time.

(3) Abner, being angered, seeks to divert the whole kingdom from Ish-bosheth to David. Joab treacherously slays Abner at Hebron.

(4) David puts to death the two murderers of Ish-bosheth. David is gradually gaining favor with all Israel.

(5) David is anointed as king of all Israel, and decides to establish his new capital in Jerusalem. (Cf. 1 Chron. 12:23–40.)

5. David's Reign over All Israel at Jerusalem up to the Period of His Great Sin. 2 Sam. 5–10

It is impossible to locate all the events of David's reign in chronological order, for the treatment is topical.

(1) The capture of Jebus, and the transfer to the capital.

(2) Repulse of two Philistine invasions. (Brave deed of the three mighty men, while David was in the stronghold of Adullam.) 2 Sam. 23:13–17

(3) Removal of the ark to Jerusalem. Death of Uzzah followed by three months' delay in removing the ark. Preparation of Levites, David's joy, Michal's pride. Ark placed in tent.

(4) David, being now thoroughly established on his throne, desires to build a temple for the ark. He receives the promise of an everlasting kingdom.

(5) David shows kindness to Mephibosheth, the son of Jonathan. (Possibly after many of his campaigns against the surrounding nations. Cf. 2 Sam. 4:4; 9:12.)

(6) The famine probably occurred in the first half of David's reign. 2 Sam. 21:1–14. During this period of prosperity, he commences his preparations for the Temple.

(7) The Wars of David against:
   a. Philistines. Besides the two defensive campaigns at the beginning of David's reign, 2 Sam. 21:15–22 tells of four offensive campaigns.
   b. Moab. Two thirds of the captives put to death.
   c. Zobah and Damascus.
   d. Amalek.
   e. Edom. Almost exterminates the Edomites. 1 Kings 11:14–17
   f. Ammon. (Cf. 2 Sam. 8 for David's wars. The chronology cannot be made out.) The war against Ammon breaks out shortly before David's great sin. The turning point in David's career is about the fiftieth year of his life. The folly of Hanun brings on the war with David. The Ammonites secure help from the Syrians; but Joab and Abishai defeat the allies. David takes the field in person against a fresh army of Syrians and overthrows them. Joab undertakes the siege of Rabbah, while David enjoys the comforts of his palace.

6. The Period of David's Great Sin and Its Punishment

   (1) His sin with Bath-sheba. The Bible does not spare David. 2 Sam. 11
      a. Covetousness.
      b. Adultery.
      c. Murder. David's skill cannot hide his sin, and, in order to be free, he seeks to slay Uriah (Joab thus knew all about David's private life and secured a yet greater hold upon him.)
      d. Bath-sheba is taken by David to wife. Cruelty at the capture of Rabbah.
         Note the steps in David's sins. He did not pile up his sins in one day. His condition deplorable, as he lay entangled in the meshes of his own lust.
   (2) David's repentance. 2 Sam. 12
      a. The visit of Nathan.
      b. David repents. This was genuine, heartfelt sorrow for sin and a deliberate turning away from it.

    c. Bath-sheba's child dies. David's conduct startles his servants.
(3) Amnon's sin. 2 Sam. 13:1–19
(4) Absalom's revenge. 2 Sam. 13:20–39. Absalom flees for three years to Geshur, the home of his mother. (David sees at length the fruit of his own sin.)
(5) Joab secures permission for Absalom's return. For two years Absalom lives in Jerusalem, but he does not see the face of David. 2 Sam. 14:1–27
(6) Absalom forces Joab to bring him before the king. 2 Sam. 14:28–33
(7) Absalom's rebellion.
    a. Preparatory steps. 2 Sam. 15:1–12
      (a) He steals the hearts of the people, a shrewd politician.
      (b) He organizes a revolt at Hebron, under pretense of keeping a vow.
    b. Events up to death of Absalom. 2 Sam. 15:13 to 19:8
      (a) The flight of David from Jerusalem. He sends back the ark and the priests. Hushai also returns to do him service.
      (b) David is met by Ziba with supplies.
      (c) He is cursed by Shimei.
      (d) Absalom shows his firm determination to supplant David by publicly entering his harem.
      (e) Ahithophel's wise counsel to pursue David speedily is put aside by Hushai's skill, but David is warned by messengers to remove farther.
      (f) The suicide of Ahithophel.
      (g) David comes to Mahanaim. He is refreshed by Shobi (Ammon), Machir and Barzillai (Gileadites).
      (h) The great battle ends with death of Absalom and complete defeat of his army. David's excessive grief rebuked by Joab.
    c. Events connected with David's return to Jerusalem. 2 Sam. 19:9 to 20:2

(a) David is brought back by men of Judah. He promises to give Joab's office to Amasa.

(b) Meeting with Shimei and Mephibosheth, and parting with Barzillai.

(c) The rebellion of Sheba. Jealousy of the ten tribes breaks forth in open rebellion. Death of Sheba in the far north.

7. Closing Years of David's Life

The numbering of Israel may have occurred here, just after Absalom's rebellion, or it may have happened earlier in David's reign. 2 Sam. 24; 1 Chron. 21

(1) He collects vast materials for the building of the Temple. By degrees the feebleness of old age comes on. 1 Chron. 22:2–5; 1 Kings 1:1–4

(2) David organizes the priests and Levites, the singers and the doorkeepers. 1 Chron. 23–26

(3) He directs Solomon to build the Temple. 1 Chron. 22:6–19

(4) Adonijah tries to seize the throne. Solomon is anointed in haste. 1 Kings 1:5–53

(5) He gives to Solomon and the princes of Israel a formal charge, stimulating the princes to generous offerings, and worships God in the presence of the assembly. 1 Chron. 28:1 to 29:22

(6) Solomon is anointed a second time as king, in a more formal and leisurely manner. 1 Chron. 29:22–25

(7) King David dies at the age of seventy. 1 Kings 2:1–12

FIRST AND SECOND KINGS

What we call First and Second Kings was anciently one book, called by the Jews "The Book of the Kings." This is evident from the fact that the division between 1 and 2 Kings occurs in the middle of the short reign of Ahaziah, king of Israel; a severance that no compiler would ever have made, but which first appeared in the LXX and was followed by Jerome in the Vulgate. The Jews did not make the division until controversies with Christians made it necessary for readiness of reference.

These two books are compilations. The editor used source materials that he wove into a continuous narrative. It is certain that he lived after 561 B.C., for he mentions Evil-Merodach, who did not begin to rule until then. He knows nothing of the Return under Cyrus, so we may safely place him between 561 and 539 B.C., in exile in Babylonia. His source materials were (1) the book of the Acts of Solomon, (2) the book of the Chronicles of the Kings of Judah, (3) the book of the Chronicles of the Kings of Israel. These were also compilations from many sources, especially the eyewitness accounts of the prophets like Nathan, Abijah, Iddo, Shemaiah, Jehu, and Isaiah (2 Chron. 9:29; 12:15; 13:22; 20:34; 26:22).

The editor of the books of the Kings has a rigid framework for his accounts. He introduces each king by giving his age, length of reign, mother, etc. Then he gives his own opinion of his reign, after which he discusses the various events. At the close he tells where he gets his source materials, where the king was buried, and who reigned in his stead. The purpose of the compiler was definitely didactic: (1) He judged every king by his conformity or nonconformity to the law of God, especially to the Deuteronomic law of centralized worship. (2) He taught that sin inevitably brings punishment, and faith and righteousness ultimately triumph. (3) He showed an appreciation of the need for social reform, notably in his treatment of Rehoboam and Elijah.

Outline of Book I

1. The Reign of Solomon. 1–11
2. Fortunes of Israel and Judah Down to the Death of Ahab and Jehoshaphat. 12–22

Outline of Book II

1. Fortunes of Israel and Judah Until the Fall of Samaria. 1–17
2. History of Judah Down to the Destruction of Jerusalem. 18–25

FIRST AND SECOND CHRONICLES

In the Hebrew Bible these books are called "the events of days" (daily happenings) and appear at the very end of the third division of the Scriptures. Their position there is due either to the lateness of their composition or to the fact that they were the last books to be admitted to the canon. The LXX gives a better description of the nature of the books— "the things omitted concerning the kings of Judah."

Chronicles was written at a much later date than Kings. The editor refers to a member of the Davidic dynasty of the sixth generation after Zerubbabel (1 Chron. 3:19–24), and uses Persian terms. His style, theology, religious interest, and ethical outlook indicate a date late in the Persian period, probably about 300 B.C. Much time had elapsed since Samuel and Kings had been written. Jewish history needed to be rewritten in light of the conceptions of the editor's day (cf. 2 Sam. 24:1 with 1 Chron. 21:1). Since Northern Israel had long ago disappeared from the scene of history, the editor did not bother to trace its history at all but confined his attention exclusively to the still existent Judah, referring to Israel only as it contacted the Southern Kingdom.

The conceptions of the compiler are even more clearly revealed than those of the editor of Kings, and much more advanced.[1] He stresses monotheism (1 Chron. 29:10–19) and the wrongfulness of idolatry (1 Chron. 14:12; 2 Chron. 14:3), and emphasizes Yahweh's omniscience (2 Chron. 16:9) and omnipotence (1 Chron. 29:10ff.). Worthy of careful attention are

---

[1]Cf. *The Abingdon Bible Commentary* (New York: The Abingdon Press, 1929), p. 440.

his teachings on the conditions which make war justifiable or disastrous (2 Chron. 13:4–20; 14:9–15; 20:1–30), on the fallacy of worldly wisdom (2 Chron. 16:12–14), and the efficacy, duty, and comfort of prayer (1 Chron. 17:16–27; 29:10–19; 2 Chron. 6:1–42; 7:1–3).

OUTLINE OF BOOK I

1. The Genealogies of the Tribes of Israel. 1–9
2. The Reign of David. 10–29

OUTLINE OF BOOK II

1. Reign of Solomon. 1–9
2. History of the Kings of Judah Down to the Destruction of Jerusalem. 10–36

Ezra-Nehemiah

There is little doubt that the books we now know as Ezra and Nehemiah were originally one book, for they actually appear in the LXX as 1 Esdras. Apparently the same author (or authors) is responsible for them and for Chronicles, for the approach and style, as well as the historical perspective, are the same in all these books. The material contained in Ezra-Nehemiah is invaluable, for it furnishes us with the only sacred historical information we possess of the period after the return from Exile. Although the books were completed between 350–300 B.C., they contain authentic materials from the private diaries of both Ezra and Nehemiah, especially from that of Nehemiah.

The book of Ezra begins with the decree of Cyrus for the return of the Jews, then traces the return under Zerubbabel and the first attempt to rebuild the Temple. The subsequent completion of the Temple in 516 is portrayed and is followed by a description of the return of Ezra with a small band of Jews. His attempts at reform apparently end in failure, for when the book of Nehemiah opens, conditions in Judea are indeed hopeless. Nehemiah, the cupbearer of Artaxerxes, is granted permission to leave for Judea to become its governor and to rebuild Jerusalem and its walls. This he accomplishes in spite of serious opposition in an amazingly short period of time. After the walls are completed, Ezra is called in to read the Law to the people and a general reform is brought about. However, when Nehemiah returns to Persia to report his activities, the people fall away. Upon his return to Jerusalem, he is forced to renew his efforts at reform, especially the dissolution of mixed marriages.

Ezra is in general a difficult man to characterize. His is a cold, austere figure, uncompromising in the application of the divine Law. Apparently he was none too popular among the ancient Jews. When Ben Sirach calls the roll of heroes (Ecclesiasticus 49:11–13), he mentions Zerubbabel, Jeshua, and Nehemiah, but not Ezra. In a later book (2 Macc. 1:18–36) Nehemiah is much glorified, but there is no mention of Ezra. A later tradition, however, began to magnify Ezra. He became the founder of the Great Synagogue and the Father of the Scribes. In the apocryphal fourth book of Ezra he is spoken of as the man who restored the Law and rewrote all the sacred works that had been destroyed. To others he was the one who had closed the sacred canon. Concerning all such work of Ezra the Scriptures are completely silent.

Nehemiah was quite human and, with all his faults, possessed much nobility of character. Generous, faithful, with a splendid patriotism, he at once arouses our interest. Nehemiah was a business man with a love for God in his heart. His heart kept him true, and his cleverness kept him successful. His was no mock modesty; he knew his worth and fearlessly made mention of it to God. He concluded his labors with "Remember me, O my God, for good" (Neh. 13:31).

OUTLINE OF EZRA

1. Return of Zerubbabel. The Temple Rebuilt Under Great Difficulties. 1–6
2. Return of Ezra. Effort to Break Up Intermarriage with the Heathen. 7–10

OUTLINE OF NEHEMIAH

1. Nehemiah Returns to Jerusalem, and in the Face of Much Opposition Rebuilds the Walls of the City. 1–6

2. The Great Revival. 7:1 to 13:3
   Law read, Feast of Tabernacles, renewal of covenant, provision for the Levites and for the defense of Jerusalem, dedication of the city wall, separation from the heathen.
3. Reforms Wrought by Nehemiah on His Return from Persia. 13:4–31

ESTHER

The vividness of description and reliability of historical allusions require that the book be placed during the Persian period, not later than 300 B.C. Esther 1:1 shows that the reign of Ahasuerus has long passed away. An explanation concerning him has to be given to the reader of the book. Some claim from 9:20, mistakenly, that Mordecai wrote the book. It must be someone later than he.

Ahasuerus cannot be Artaxerxes, for another Hebrew word is used for him in Ezra 4:7. The Hebrew is *Ashashverosh,* from Persian *Khashayarsha* (mighty eye, or mighty man), whence is derived the Greek *Xerxes*. Several factors make this identification even more certain: (1) Herodotus refers to Xerxes as capricious and sensual as in the book of Esther. (2) The extent of his empire agrees with description given in book of Esther. (3) There are allusions in Herodotus to such a feast as described in Esther just after conquest of Egypt.

The problems of the book are twofold: (1) The fierceness of the Jewish revenge. We have not yet reached the Christian ideal of forgiveness. (2) The divine name wholly absent from book. Elsewhere biblical writers explicitly mention the relationship of God and people. Here the mention of the name of God appears to be censored. Why is it not present? (1) The time of writing is between the prophetic period and enthusiasm of Maccabees when a veil was drawn between the majestic Godhead and mortal man. There was a reluctance to speak of matters beyond man's ken. (2) The writer had in mind the occasion on which the book would be read, a secular celebration, accompanied by excessive conviviality. He did not desire that the holy name of God be taken lightly on such an occasion.

Although the book lacks the divine name as such, it is far from correct to say that it wholly lacks the religious element: (1) God's providential care of his people is plainly taught. (2) Mordecai's warning to Esther reveals an unfailing trust in the overruling hand of God although with a reticence unlike the prophets, who boldly use the name of God. (3) It teaches the law of sin and retribution—Haman was hanged on his own gallows.

In spite of all this, we must admit that the Jewish nation is exalted here at the expense of the exaltation of God. There is no indication of a sense of national sin. When deliverance comes, the people rejoice wildly rather than thanking God. Esther and Mordecai are given the chief credit for the happy end of affairs. All in all, the book reveals the decline in moral insight so characteristic of the late post-Exilic period of Israel's history.

The Jews of the Christian era came to value the book of Esther more and more, and during the Middle Ages it was considered of more importance than the rest of the Writings, the Prophets, and even the Law itself. Its patriotic spirit was responsible, for it strengthened material hopes of the Jews amid persecution. It was called "the Roll." Maimonides, the most eminent Jewish scholar of the Middle Ages, declared that in the days of the Messiah the only Scripture to be left would be the Law and the Roll.

OUTLINE OF THE BOOK

1. How Esther Came to Be the Queen of Persia. 1–2
2. How the Jews Fell Under the Ban of Extermination. 3–5
3. How Danger Was Turned into Deliverance. 6–10

SUMMARY OF ISRAEL'S HISTORY: 931–722 B.C.

When Solomon died about 931 B.C., he left behind many valuable contributions to the history of Israel. (1) The Temple had been established. (2) The transition from an agricultural to a commercial people was hastened. (3) Israel had been placed in the midst of international affairs. (4) The ideal of justice in the courts was exemplified. (5) His proverbs championed common sense in religion.

However, the kingdom easily fell apart when Solomon left the scene. Various elements contributed to this division:

1. An impetuous young man (Rehoboam).
2. A clever labor leader (Jeroboam).
3. Excessive taxation for Solomon's program of building and expansion.
4. Jealousy between the tribes of the North and Judah.
5. Differences in geographical location. Northern Israel was on the great highways to Egypt and Babylonia. Judah was secluded from the rest of the world.
6. The tribes never really united. They came together under Saul and David but only as a loose federation.
7. The fear of dictatorship after the experience with Solomon and the remarks of Rehoboam.
8. The apostasy of Solomon. Sin was having its fruition in disunity.

Upon the death of Solomon, *Rehoboam* (17)[1] became king of Judah, *Jeroboam* (22) king of Israel. Hostilities were continuous between the two. Jeroboam, freshly influenced by the worship of the Egyptians, put golden bulls at Dan and Bethel

[1] Length of reign, usually given in years.

76

to rival worship at Jerusalem. Shishak of Egypt invaded Palestine and plundered the Temple (926). *Abijah* (3), son of Rehoboam, who succeeded him as king, defeated Jeroboam. *Asa* (41), his son, instituted religious reforms in Judah, destroyed idols, deposed his idolatrous mother, put new vessels in the Temple, and defeated Zerah, the Ethiopian, and his mighty host. In second year of Asa, *Nadab* (2), son of Jeroboam, began to rule in Israel and was quickly slain by *Baasha* (24). Baasha prepared to attack Judah, but Asa sent silver and gold from the Temple and palace to Benhadad I of Syria to persuade him to attack Baasha and thus turn him away from Judah. Benhadad obliged, and Baasha abandoned his plan. *Elah* (2), son of Baasha, began to rule in the twenty-sixth year of Asa. He was assassinated by *Zimri* (7 days) who burned the palace down over his own head when besieged by Omri. *Omri* (12) took over Israel and established Samaria as the capital of his kingdom. He made a permanent impression on Assyria, who after his reign always referred to Israel as "the land of Omri." Conscious of international affairs, he married his son Ahab to Jezebel, daughter of the king of Sidon. In the thirty-eighth year of Asa, *Ahab* (22) became king in Samaria. Mesha was king of Moab at this time, the ruler made famous because of his inscription on the Moabite Stone, a record that is of invaluable aid in authenticating biblical accounts, written in a script closely akin to Hebrew.

In his later years Asa was afflicted with gout; but he appealed to physicians instead of to God. *Jehoshaphat* (25), his son, ruled next in Judah, beginning to reign during the fourth year of Ahab. A religious and political reformer, he was a popular king. He had the Law taught throughout Judah. Ahab and Jehoshaphat were always on friendly terms. In fact, Jehoshaphat appears to have been a vassal of Ahab.

When Jezebel came to Samaria, she brought the worship of her god, Baal, along with her, and so Baal worship became the state religion. This resulted in the persecution of the prophets of Yahweh. Elijah appeared before Ahab and the three-year drought followed. Then came the trial of fire at Mount Carmel and the flight of Elijah to Mount Sinai. Later Ahab defeated the Syrians in the *hills* of Samaria and then proved that Yahweh was a God of the *plains*, also, by conquering them at Aphek. Capturing the king, Benhadad, he set him free as protection against Assyria.

The Battle of Karkar (853 B.C.) was the first real contact of Assyria with the Hebrews, with the possible exception of a relation during the reign of Omri. This was a great battle between a coalition of western countries, including Israel and Syria, and Shalmaneser III (859–824), king of Assyria. It probably ended in a draw. This is a pivotal date in Old Testament history.

After the son of Jehoshaphat, Jehoram, married Athaliah, the daughter of Ahab and Jezebel, Jehoshaphat and Ahab allied to go against Ramoth-gilead and Syria. The prophet Micaiah condemned the alliance, and heedless Ahab was killed in battle. From an accidental fall *Ahaziah* (2), Ahab's son, suffered fatal injuries, and his brother *Jehoram* (12) took over Israel. Elisha prophesied during this period. *Jehoram* (8), the son of Jehoshaphat, succeeded his father in the fifth year of Jehoram of Israel. It was just after this time that Benhadad besieged Samaria, and the four lepers discovered his sudden departure in mad flight. Subsequently, Benhadad was slain by Hazael with a wet blanket.

In 845 the Philistines and Arabians defeated Judah and plundered the king's house, taking away his wives and sons. Only his son Ahaziah was left. It is possible that Obadiah prophesied at this time. Later *Ahaziah* (1), son of Jehoram and Athaliah, was slain along with Jehoram of Israel by *Jehu* (28), who destroyed Baal worship and the house of Omri, including Jezebel. In 842 Jehu paid tribute to Shalmaneser III. The Black Obelisk contains this Assyrian record. It refers to Jehu as the "son of Omri."

When Ahaziah was slain, Athaliah, his mother, tried to kill all his sons, but failed to discover the baby Joash. She ruled for six years in Jerusalem, but was slain when Jehoiada, the priest, had the boy *Joash* (40) crowned king. Joash, under the wise guidance of Jehoiada, brought about reforms and repaired the Temple. But when Jehoiada died, Joash lapsed into idolatry, and even killed Zechariah, the priest's son, when he criticized him. The prophet Joel may have prophesied during the early reign of Joash.

The weak king who followed Shalmaneser III on the throne of Assyria could not hinder the oppression of Israel by Syria. Accordingly, *Jehoahaz* (17), son of Jehu, was actually a vassal of Hazael of Syria. Hazael even approached Jerusalem, but Joash bought him off with the palace and Temple treasures. When Adad-nirari III (805–782) became king of Assyria, however, he subjected Damascus and imposed such heavy indemnity on Syria that she bothered Israel no more. In fact, the weakness of Syria enabled *Jehoash* (16), the son of Jehoahaz, to defeat that country in several battles, which resulted in the winning back of previously captured territory.

In the second year of Jehoash of Israel, Joash of Judah was murdered by conspirators. His son *Amaziah* (29) took the throne, and was able to defeat the Edomites. Flushed with victory, he attacked Jehoash and was soundly trounced. The king of Israel plundered Jerusalem and tore down part of the wall. Other weak kings followed Adad-nirari in Assyria. Accordingly, with both Assyria and Syria impotent, Israel and Judah enjoyed prosperity and peace, Israel under *Jeroboam II* (41), the son of Jehoash, and Judah under *Uzziah* (52), the son of Amaziah. Jeroboam restored the former boundaries of Israel from the Dead Sea to Hamath. The prophet Jonah lived during his reign.

Meanwhile Uzziah was reorganizing his government, promoting a department of agriculture, strengthening his fortifications, and conquering the surrounding peoples. During the latter part of the reign of Jeroboam, Amos and Hosea began to prophesy against the corruption resulting from the prosperity of the times. In later life Uzziah committed sacrilege in the Temple and was struck with leprosy. At this time the son of Jeroboam, *Zechariah* (6 months) began to reign. He was soon slain by *Shallum* (1 month), and the period of anarchy began in the Northern Kingdom. It was *Menahem* (10) who killed Shallum.

In 745, Tiglath-pileser IV (Pul, also referred to as Tiglath-pileser III), a usurper, took over the throne of Assyria and ruled until 727. He instituted a new and aggressive policy of organization, unification, and deportation. It was his policy to deport conquered peoples and replace them with captives from some other distant country, thus destroying the spirit of nationalism. In 743–740 he reduced northern Syria and the Phenician coast. In 739 he won over the Hittites, and in 738 received tribute from Menahem of Israel. Soon afterwards the son of Menahem, *Pekahiah* (2), who succeeded him in the Northern Kingdom, was slain by *Pekah* (20). Meanwhile, the son of Uzziah, *Jotham* (16), was followed on the throne of Judah by his son, the idolatrous *Ahaz* (16).

Pekah of Israel and Rezin of Syria combined to invade Judah in 734 and attempted to force her into an alliance with them against threatening Assyria. King Ahaz would not listen to the assurance of the prophet Isaiah, but in fear and trembling appealed to Tiglath-pileser for aid. The king of Assyria welcomed the opportunity and attacked the invaders, carrying away most of the people of the northern and eastern regions of Israel into captivity. It was during this period that Micah probably began to preach. In 732, Damascus fell, and Rezin was slain. *Hoshea* (9), puppet of Tiglath-pileser, killed Pekah. When *Hezekiah* (29) became king of Judah, he conducted important religious reforms. Shalmaneser V (727–722), king of Assyria, besieged Samaria after the rebellion of Hoshea, and after a three-year siege it fell before Sargon II (722–705), in 722. Twenty-seven thousand two hundred and ninety captives were deported and other peoples put in their place. This and the previous deportation of Tiglath-pileser marked the beginning of the Samaritan race, part Jew, part Gentile. The ten "lost tribes" were assimilated among the people with whom they lived by the process of intermarriage. Northern Israel as an entity disappeared forever. Several causes contributed to this collapse of Northern Israel: (1) The division in 931 left Israel too weak to defend herself. (2) Her alliances with other nations dissipated her strength. Her kings were all a bad lot. Not one was approved by the scriptural accounts. (3) The throne was unstable. In a period of about 200 years there were nine dynasties and nineteen kings, ten of whom died violent deaths. (4) Amos and Hosea reveal the shocking immorality of the people and their neglect of God.

Sargon was followed in Assyria by Sennacherib (705–681). When Judah and the other western states rebelled against him, he marched west. Sidon and the cities of the Philistine plain fell quickly before him, and when he came before Lachish in 701, Hezekiah knew that his rebellion had been a great mistake. He sent tribute to Sennacherib, but that did not turn him aside. The taunts of the Assyrian doubting the power of Yahweh caused Isaiah to see that God would never allow Sennacherib to take the city. Just as he prophesied, 185,000 Assyrian soldiers died in one terrible night of plague, and Sennacherib left, never to return. Naturally Sennacherib does not mention this catastrophe. He says only that he shut up Hezekiah like "a bird in a cage," taking away 200,000 captives. However, the fact that he never returned, even though he ruled for twenty more years, and never claimed to have captured Jerusalem is evidence of the fact that some such calamity befell him.

Hezekiah was succeeded by his son *Manasseh* (55), whose reign was characterized by Baalism, gross idolatry, and shedding of innocent blood. In 681, Sennacherib was assassinated and his son Esarhaddon ruled until 669. At that time Assurbanipal (669–626) became king of Assyria. He is famous for his great library with its priceless Assyrian records. Assurbanipal destroyed the Egyptian cities of Memphis and Thebes in 663. In 647 he carried wicked Manasseh to Babylon but later allowed him to return. In 640, the son of Manasseh, *Amon* (2), was slain. *Josiah* (31), his eight-year-old son, was put on the throne. Josiah was a good king and thoroughly reformed his government, wiped out idolatry, and repaired the Temple.

In 626, Cyaxares, king of Media, and Nabopolassar, king of Babylon, allied to make war on Assyria. Assurbanipal had died, and weak kings succeeded him. It was during this year that Jeremiah was called to prophesy. Nahum and Zephaniah also prophesied during this period. In 621 the Law was discovered when the Temple was being repaired by Josiah. This book was probably Deuteronomy. Although the fall of Nineveh occurred in 612 B.C., the Assyrian army was still intact. In 609, Josiah attacked Pharaoh-necho, who was going to fight in behalf of Assyria. Josiah was siding with the new world order, hoping for some share in the spoils. However, the rash king was killed in battle with the Egyptians. The people made his son, *Jehoahaz* (3 months) king, but Necho carried him to Egypt and put *Jehoiakim* (11), his brother, on the throne. Habakkuk prophesied at this time.

The Battle of Carchemish, 605 B.C., marked a great turning point in world history. Egypt and Assyria were defeated, Assyria never to rise again. Nebuchadnezzar (604–561), more correctly designated as Nebuchadrezzar, son of Nabopolassar, became king of Babylon. From the book of Daniel we learn that just after the battle Nebuchadnezzar proceeded against rebellious Jehoiakim and took away a few nobles and treasures. Daniel was among those taken away at this time. A few years later (597), *Jehoiachin* (3 months), son of Jehoiakim, rebelled against Babylonia and was taken captive, along with 10,000 of the blue-bloods of Judah, including Ezekiel. *Zedekiah* (11), brother of Jehoiakim, was made king. When Zedekiah conspired with Egypt against him, Nebuchadnezzar destroyed Jerusalem. The inhabitants were taken captive, including Zedekiah, whose eyes were put out. Gedaliah was made governor of Judah, but was killed by Ishmael. Ishmael was defeated by Johanan, who led most of the remaining Jews into Egypt for refuge.

Evil-Merodach (561–559) succeeded Nebuchadnezzar and treated Jehoiachin with kindness. Then Neriglissar (559–556) became king. He was present at the siege of Jerusalem in 586. (Cf. Jer. 39:3 Nergal-sharezer.) His son, a child, reigned but nine months, and the priestly party put Nabonidus on the throne. He reigned from 555 to 539, a very unpopular king, spending so much time unearthing old relics and rebuilding decaying temples that he neglected the defense of the empire. The government of the city of Babylon was turned over to his son, Belshazzar, the king himself being too preoccupied with religious affairs to take any interest in politics.

Meanwhile trouble was brewing in the east. Cyrus, king of Anshan, was expanding his power in Persia, and in 549 captured Ecbatana, the capital of adjoining Media. Next he turned west against Lydia in Asia Minor, desiring the wealth of its fabulous king, Croesus. Attacking Croesus with camels in his front ranks, he so frightened the famed cavalry of Lydia that he routed the army, seizing the capital, Sardis, in 546. In 539 the gates of Babylon were opened before Gobryas, the general of Cyrus, without a battle. Both Nabonidus and Belshazzar were killed later. In 529 Cyrus was killed in a border skirmish. Invincible in his attacks, brilliant in his tactics, wise in his treatment of conquered peoples, he is rightly called "the Great." Because of his religious toleration, he has been known as "the Baptist of the Old Testament." The return under Zerubbabel (Sheshbazzar) occurred about 537. In the second year of the return (probably 535), the foundation of the Temple was begun but was stopped by opposition of surrounding peoples. In 529 Cambyses, son of Cyrus, became king of Persia. After killing his brother Smerdis, he invaded Egypt, had epilepsy, became insane, and committed suicide. A man who pretended to be the murdered Smerdis (Pseudo-Smerdis) reigned for a few months, but was replaced by Darius the Great (Hystaspis), who ruled from 521 until 485. He was an efficient organizer, and stabilized the hastily won empire of Cyrus, which had begun to fall apart during the reign of Cambyses. How well he did his work is evidenced by the continuance of the kingdom for two centuries more. His deeds are recorded on the Behistun Rock, written in Babylonian cuneiform, Persian, and Elamite. In the second year of his reign (520) the rebuilding of the Temple was resumed under the inspired preaching of Haggai and Zechariah. Four years later the sanctuary was completed.

Darius attacked Greece in 490 B.C., but the outnumbered Greeks defeated him in the Battle of Marathon. He was forced to retreat, but spent his last years preparing to return. He led his son, Xerxes, to promise to continue his efforts. Xerxes (485–465) is mentioned in the Bible as Ahasuerus. In 480, he was engaged in the famous Battle of Thermopylae Pass, where the Spartans made their heroic stand until all were killed. The Persian fleet, outnumbering the Greeks two to one, was wrecked at Salamis. The Persian attempt to control Greece was ended. Artaxerxes Longimanus (465–424) succeeded Xerxes, and completed the conquest of Egypt.

In 458, Ezra led his band of captives back to Judah to teach the Law and encourage the people. He was followed by Nehemiah (c. 444 B.C.). In 433, Nehemiah returned to Persia, and after a year came back to Jerusalem. Malachi may have prophesied at this time.

The kings of Persia who followed Artaxerxes Longimanus were Xerxes II (424), Sogdianus (424–423), Darius II (Nothus, 423–404), Artaxerxes II (Mnemon, 404–358), Artaxerxes III (Ochus, 358–337), Arses (337–335), and Darius III (Codomanus, 335–330). Darius Codomanus was conquered by Alexander the Great, after which the period of Greek dominance began.

PART III

STUDIES IN THE PROPHETS

INTRODUCTION

The roll call of the prophets of Israel includes the most illustrious heroes of her history, from Abraham (Gen. 20:7) to Jesus (Matt. 16:14; 21:11; Luke 4:24; 13:33). Moses, although renowned as lawgiver, was also a prophet (Deut. 18:15; 34:10). Miriam (Ex. 15:20) and Deborah (Judges 4:4) testify that inspiration is not limited by sex. However, the movement that gave rise to the peculiar genius of the canonical prophets seems to have arisen during the days of Samuel, after the dark period described in the book of Judges. Until this time the men of God had been called "seers" (Hebrew, ro'eh) by their contemporaries (1 Sam. 9:9). The term "prophet" (Hebrew, nabhi') came into popular use as a result of the rapid spread of a spontaneous movement that was both religious and political. The Philistine supremacy over Israel resulted in the rise of a loyal group of enthusiasts who believed that if Yahweh were faithfully followed, his people could once again be free. These bands of prophets went from place to place spreading their intense faith in the God of their fathers. The term nabhi' is evidently from a root meaning "to speak"; thus these men were "speakers for God." There is another use of the same root, however, that throws considerable light on this movement. The verb in one of its forms (Hithpa'el) means "to rave" (1 Sam. 18:10). These early prophets were evidently ecstatics, often losing complete consciousness in their frenzy of worship (1 Sam. 19:18–24). Evidently they were not in too good standing in the community, as is often true of such groups today (1 Sam. 10:1–12). The people were surprised that a man of Saul's standing should associate with these underprivileged religious enthusiasts. The names of their fathers were not even known.

Samuel, however, saw that this enthusiasm, once directed into the proper channels, could be of infinite value to Yahweh's purposes. He at once set about this constructive task and soon had gathered a large group about him (1 Sam. 19:20). Elisha many years later took the guidance of these "sons of the prophets" as part of his lifework (2 Kings 4:38–41; 6:1–7).

Many of the early prophets, because of their intense patriotism, became associated with the king's court and were supported by royal funds. This eventually tended to silence any criticism of national policy. Other prophets, born in the same movement, kept their independence and loyalty to the voice of Yahweh (Nathan, Micaiah, Elijah). Although Amos denied that he was one of the professional "sons of the prophets" at Jeroboam's court, his message found its roots in the prophetic enthusiasm of the period of Samuel. Now, however, the dream of Samuel had been realized. Enthusiasm had been channeled into constructive preaching rather than being left to die out in profitless emotionalism.

The canonical prophets were under the influence of the Spirit of God. Their message was from Yahweh. Their mental processes were stimulated and guided by the Spirit, who clothed them with power. Imagination, memory, and reason were no doubt heightened, as well as intuition and spiritual insight. The Spirit of God chose men for his purpose and then turned to account all their powers. The mind of the prophet varied from the extreme of trance and ecstasy all the way to a quiet thoughtfulness over which the Holy Spirit presided.

Contrary to popular belief, the prophets were not primarily predicters of the future. They were "forthtellers" more than foretellers. Prediction was only one aspect of their ministry, and this was seldom in detail. The fundamental principle that undergirded the message of the Old Testament prophets was the necessity of a moral obedience to an ethical God. For them the future was in the hands of God but was in part determined by the free choice of men. Therefore, many details of prophecies are conditional and may never come to pass, although the principles of the utterances will ultimately be realized. Many of the prophecies of the Old Testament are conditional, even where the condition is not stated. (Cf. Jonah 3:4.) Other predictions are couched in poetical language and were never intended to be fulfilled literally. Still others, however, are unconditional and have already come to pass or will take place in the future. These in the main are the great purposes of God for his Messiah and his people that can be delayed by human sin but never defeated.

The Hebrew prophets were not so much concerned with what will happen as with what *must* happen as a result of sin and the nature of God. Prophecies in their noblest sense were contemporary sermons that keep their values for every age because they contain the eternal purposes of God that are ever coming to pass. The prophets were more interested in life than in logic, so their messages often lacked the logical sequence of our modern sermon. Yet they frequently gained thereby in effectiveness.

No true prophet ever spoke by his own authority. They were Yahweh's spokesmen, always preaching by the authority of his Spirit. "Thus saith Yahweh" is their constant refrain. The message that resulted is ageless in its application. God's hand is on the wheel of world history. The individual or nation that opposes his will faces ultimate destruction; those that are faithful will find him true to his every promise.

Each prophet is an individual. As such, his message will bear the stamp of his personality as well as the superscription of the King. To each God revealed that part of his truth most needed by his generation. When the emphases of the various prophetical books are compiled, one is able to grasp more completely the whole picture of God's purpose and plan for the world. Then can be appreciated the divine wisdom in choosing such a method.

OBADIAH

THE BOOK. Obadiah, the shortest book in the Old Testament, has been described as "Obadiah's Indignant Oration" and a "Hymn of Hate." It is not quoted directly anywhere in the New Testament. The occasion of the writing of this bit of prophecy was a calamity that had befallen Jerusalem in which the Edomites had displayed an unbrotherly spirit toward the Jews and had shared in plundering the city, intercepting the fugitives and selling them into slavery. With righteous indignation hot within him, Obadiah predicts retribution on Edom and the eventual exaltation of Yahweh's people.

THE PROPHET. Of the prophet himself nothing is known. His name means "Servant of Yahweh," and he was surely a man of deep convictions, stern, pious, and patriotic, certain that God was in command of the affairs of man. He must not be confused with the Obadiah of Elijah's day (1 Kings 18).

THE DATE. In finding a date for the book, we must first of all find an occasion of a capture and devastation of Jerusalem. There were four such events in Old Testament history. The first is the invasion of Shishak, king of Egypt. This occasion is not likely, for the Edomites remained subject to the Hebrews at this time. Nor is the invasion of Joash of Israel a plausible occasion, since the Israelites would hardly be referred to as strangers (v. 11). The real decision lies between the devastation by the Philistines and Arabians in the reign of Jehoram (c. 845 B.C.) and the destruction of Jerusalem by Nebuchadnezzar in 586 B.C. In favor of the early date is the fact that no reference is made to the destruction of the Temple, the implication that the city may be captured again, the absence of

Aramaic expressions, Jeremiah's quotation of Obadiah 1–6 in chapter 49, and the fact that the prophet is still within the narrow limits of pre-Exilic Palestine. The nations described are not the Exilic neighbors of Israel but the earlier foes. Amos refers to Edom for sins very much like those Obadiah describes (Amos 1:6, 9, 11), although some deny these verses to that prophet. Furthermore, when describing the reoccupation of Palestine, no mention is made of the hill country of Judah, implying that it is already occupied by the Jews, making an Exilic date improbable. In favor of the late date, however, is the fact that the references to a day of distress and calamity naturally apply to the total destruction of Jerusalem in 586. There is additional evidence that the bitter hostility toward the Edomites dates from the Exile, since most of the parallel passages against Edom are found at this date (Lam. 4:21; Ezek. 25:12–14; 35:1–15; Psalm 137:7). Furthermore, the invasion of 845 B.C. is not mentioned in the book of Kings, only in 2 Chronicles 21:16. This would lead one to question the importance of that event. The reference in Chronicles may only be to a border skirmish. No word is said about an invasion of Jerusalem. Finally, both Obadiah and Jeremiah, chapter 49, may be quoting an earlier prophet. Although the evidence is almost evenly balanced, the uncertainty of the historical allusions in Chronicles favors the late date for the book.

THE BACKGROUND. The Edomites were descendants of Esau, and a proud people, living around the mountain fortress of Petra, carved out of solid rock, on a caravan route from the north to the Red Sea, enabling them to be great traders as well as bandits. The city was surrounded by massive cliffs, some as high as 700 feet, and could be approached only by a narrow ravine, terminating in a gorge where two horsemen could scarcely ride abreast. It is natural that the Edomites should feel secure behind such a stronghold. This situation explains the vivid language with which Obadiah opens his prophecies. However, to understand fully his statements, we must also be familiar with the history of these two peoples.

Jacob and Esau were striving against each other from birth. After their death the feud continued unabated. When Moses requested passage through Edomite country, he was refused and had to lead the Israelites around their territory. Saul fought them, and David finally made them a subject people. They continued, however, to rebel under later kings at every opportunity. We do not know exactly the time of the occurrence, but by 312 B.C. the Arabians had driven the Edomites from their stronghold, as prophesied by Obadiah. The descendants of Esau settled in the Negeb, becoming by intermarriage the Idumeans of New Testament times. Herod came from this race, so that in him and Jesus can be seen again the Edomite and the Israelite, and the contrast between the two. In A.D. 70, Titus destroyed the Idumean power completely and the Edomites disappeared from history.

THE TEACHINGS. Obadiah leaves three unforgettable lessons on the reader's mind. His immortal, "Though thou mount on high as the eagle, and though thy nest be set among the stars, I will bring thee down . . ." (v. 4) is a perpetual warning to entrenched evil wherever it may be. The words, "as thou hast done, it shall be done unto thee; thy dealing shall return upon thine own head" (v. 15), are just as surely addressed to the sinners of today as to those in ancient Edom. The cry of hope and faith, "the kingdom shall be Jehovah's" (v. 21), classifies him with the greatest prophetic dreamers of Israel.

OUTLINE OF THE BOOK

1. The Destruction of Edom Inevitable. 1–9, 15b

    (1) Yahweh's ambassador announces punishment for Edom's selfish pride. 1–4
    (2) Edom's allies will be the means of her downfall. 5–7
    (3) Yahweh will continue the slaughter until the destruction is complete. 8–9, 15b

2. The Reasons for the Destruction. 10–14

    (1) Indifference in Jacob's day of trouble. 10–11
    (2) Rejoicing over Judah's calamity. 12

(3) Actively engaging in the pillaging and slave-grabbing. 13–14

3. The Day of Yahweh Near. 15a, 16–21

    (1) The destruction of all God's enemies along with Edom. 15a, 16
    (2) Israel shall possess her old borders and God shall reign supreme in the kingdom. 17–21

JOEL

THE BOOK. The first problem is the time of writing. There are two primary dates suggested, one during the reign of Joash in Judah (c. 837 B.C.) and a late date in post-Exilic times (c. 400 B.C.). The late date is the more natural one in view of the evidence: (1) There is no reference to a king ruling in 1:1, as in other pre-Exilic prophets. (2) There is no mention of the Northern Kingdom; apparently it has long ago disappeared from history. The prophet uses the term Israel for Judah, which no pre-Exilic prophet would do, since the former designation was used for the Northern tribes. (3) Ritual is emphasized more than ethics. (4) The priests are the leaders, as in the post-Exilic society. (5) The reference in 3:6 to the Greeks indicates a time when the Jews were in contact with them. (6) Chapter 3:1, 2, 17 indicate that the Captivity has already taken place.

In favor of the early date, however, it is argued: (1) The prominence of the priests and the absence of the mention of the king are due to the fact that Jehoiada the high priest is really the ruler for the boy Joash. (2) The argument from silence has little weight; the writer is not concerned with what is happening in the Northern Kingdom. The term Israel could certainly be applied to Judah when thought of as the rightful heir to the spiritual blessings of Jacob. (3) "Rend your heart, and not your garments" is surely ethical. (4) It is quite possible that commerce was taking place between Greece and Tyre at this early day. Furthermore, Greece is not spoken of as a nation; but on the contrary the reference is to isolated bands of slave traders, from a distant clime. (5) "Bring back the captivity" simply means, "Restore the fortune" (Job 42:10). There is no description in chapter 3 that will not fit pre-Exilic times. (6) Joel 3:4–6 refers to the same event described in Obadiah. The enemies mentioned are not the Exilic and post-Exilic nations (Assyria, Babylonia, Samaria), but pre-Exilic, Phenicia and Philistia.

The style of Joel is classical, resembling that of Amos and Micah. Either Joel borrowed heavily from earlier prophets, or else he was the well out of which they drew, for the literary affinity is undeniable. Compare Joel 3:18 with Amos 9:13; Joel 1:4 with Amos 4:9; Joel 2:11 with Zephaniah 1:14f.; Joel 2:3 with Ezekiel 36:35 and Isaiah 51:3; Joel 2:11 with Malachi 3:2; Joel 3:10 with Isaiah 2:4.

The occasion of the book of Joel is a devastating locust plague and drought described in chapter 1. Another great problem is presented by chapter 2. Is that locust plague literal or is it apocalyptic, describing an actual invading army in terms of locusts? Does the locust plague in chapter 1 suggest to Joel the invading armies of the Day of the Lord? In favor of the apocalyptic nature is suggested: (1) The description of the locusts far exceeds the bounds of reality. (2) The enemy is referred to as the "northerner," and locusts do not enter Palestine from the north. (3) Chapter 2:17 states that the result of the invasion is that the nations reign over Judah, ruling out the possibility of Joel's speaking of locusts.

In favor of the literal locust invasion is even stronger evidence, however. (1) The description may be somewhat exaggerated, but that is the privilege of graphic poetry. Furthermore, there may be very little exaggeration, for the locusts of the East are sufficiently terrible to defy description. (2) One locust plague has been known to come from the north. Again, the term "northerner" may be idiomatic for "that which is calamitous," since so many invasions came from that direction. (3) Chapter 2:17 should read, "that the nations should not use a by-word against them." (4) In 2:2ff. the locust plague is compared to an army. We could not have here a symbol compared with the reality of which it is intended to be a symbol: a horse would hardly be likened to a horse, but a locust may truly be compared with a horse, for its head resembles that of the horse. (5) When God promises to restore the damage done by the invasion, it is exclusively to the produce of the earth that he refers (2:21ff.).

THE PROPHET. There is no information concerning the prophet except that found in the book itself. His name means, "Yahweh is God." He appears to be a native of Jerusalem. Although he had an intimate knowledge of the service and personnel of the Temple, apparently he was not a priest himself. His close acquaintance with agriculture and intimate contact with the life of the people does not suggest the seclusion of the priesthood. His spiritual discernment was remarkable, for he was always seeing the eternal reflected in the temporal. In the coming of the locust plague he could see the sign of the inevitable Day of Yahweh. The coming of rain upon the parched earth suggested the outpouring of God's Spirit upon man's thirsty soul. The present deliverance from the locusts caused him to see that one day Yahweh would deliver his people from all their enemies. This ability is always the mark of a true prophet of God. To find evidence of God at work in the everyday occurrences of life is the rare gift of one whose eyes have been opened to the spiritual universe.

THE TEACHINGS. Joel has given to the world the invaluable lesson that physical disaster accompanies moral disintegration. How a man lives in relation to his God vitally influences his earthly joys and sorrows. A true repentance ("rend your heart, and not your garments") will not only bring a proper adjustment between man and God but will also improve a man's relation to his environment. The same God who rules our souls rules the world in which we live.

What great comfort to the sinner is the promise, "And I will restore to you the years that the locust hath eaten . . ." (2:25)! For the repentant soul God promises such blessings that the years of heartache will be soon redeemed in the abundance of his favors.

It was Joel to whom was revealed the coming of the Spirit upon all flesh (2:28f.), when all God's people would be prophets and have their eyes opened that they might see the secrets of God. At Pentecost Peter was inspired to say, "This is that which hath been spoken through the prophet Joel" (Acts 2:16).

OUTLINE OF THE BOOK

Superscription 1:1

1. Successive Locust Plagues and Drought. 1:2–20

    (1) The devastation is unparalleled and unprecedented. 1:2–4
    (2) The effect upon various classes is depicted. 1:5–12
    (3) All are called to a "penitential assembly." 1:13–14
    (4) All this is ominous of the Day of the Lord. A prayer for deliverance of all creatures. 1:15–20

2. The Day of the Lord Imminent. Ushered In by a Locust Plague More Terrible Than the Present One. 2:1–11

3. A Call to Repentance. 2:12–17

    (1) It is not too late to avert disaster. Sincere repentance may yet bring blessings. 2:12–14
    (2) The proclamation of a fast urged; the religious leaders to take responsibility. 2:15–17

4. The People Repent, and Yahweh Promises Relief and Restoration. 2:18–3:21

    (1) Material blessings. 2:18–27
    (2) Spiritual blessings. 2:28–3:21
        a. The outpouring of the Spirit of God upon all classes in Israel. 2:28–32
        b. Judgment on all the world. 3:1–21
            (a) The nations destroyed for oppression of Israel. 3:1–16a
            (b) Judah cleansed of her iniquity and blessed forever. 3:16b–21

JONAH

THE PROPHET. The only Old Testament reference that we have to the prophet Jonah is found in 2 Kings 14:25, where it is stated that he was a native of Gath-hepher, a town of lower Galilee, and prophesied concerning the successes of Jeroboam II.

THE BOOK. It is nowhere stated that Jonah himself wrote the book that bears his name. In fact, the evidence is abundant that it was written after his time. The style is marked by Aramaisms. The name of the Assyrian king is not given, as would be done in a contemporary document. It is stated in 3:3 that Nineveh *was* a great city. It appears to be no longer so in the time of the author. In its teaching the book is one of the most advanced in Old Testament history. Jonah is always referred to in the third person. Thus it seems apparent that the author lived later than the days of the events described in the book. The question is, why did he write the book? It is certain that he wrote after 612 B.C., since Nineveh, the capital of Assyria, was not destroyed until then. Missionary ardor among the people had reached a low ebb; they felt no compulsion to bless the world in accordance with their great commission. The conditions just following Nehemiah best suit the facts (c. 400).

The book of Jonah was put in the heart of the writer by God to teach an unforgettable lesson to the people. How was this lesson taught? There are two schools of opinion. One group says we have in the book a literal account of the experiences of Jonah, taken from contemporary records. The story is told in order to impress the people with their missionary obligation to the world. The other group claims that Jonah is an unsurpassed allegory and is no more to be taken as literal history than the parable of the good Samaritan. Jonah stands for Israel. Israel has received a commission to make Yahweh known to the Gentiles. Israel refuses to realize this mission, so she is swallowed up in Exile (of which Jonah and the fish are but figures). As Jonah was delivered from the fish, so Israel has been delivered from Exile. Jonah took his second chance and made the most of it. What will Israel do now that she is delivered?

In favor of the allegorical interpretation is the story of the fish (God *could* have preserved Jonah there, but it certainly is not his usual method of dealing with men), the sudden conversion of all Nineveh upon the preaching of a man who probably spoke in a foreign tongue, and the sudden growth of the vine. It would seem also that such a sudden and complete conversion would leave some permanent effect on Assyria, which it certainly did not. In favor of the literal interpretation, however, are Jesus' references to Jonah's experiences (Matt. 12:38ff.; 16:4; Luke 11:29). The form of the book is a simple historical narrative, not an involved allegory. No other allegory in the Old Testament has as its hero a historical person. If the book is an allegory, it does grave injustice to the real Jonah, who was by every other indication a true prophet of God. Furthermore, if one's God is great enough, the miraculous elements are not disturbing, even to the modern mind.

THE TEACHINGS. It is unfortunate that the remarkable teachings of the book of Jonah have been lost in constant wrangling over the story of the great fish, which is but an event mentioned and soon dismissed. The abiding values of the book are far more important.

Apparently Jonah refused to go to Nineveh for two reasons. The first was his narrow nationalism. He did not want the cruel Assyrians spared when their survival would endanger Israel. Again, he expressed his feelings in 4:2. He did not desire the personal embarrassment of predicting the overthrow of Nineveh and then seeing a gracious God spare it. Both these motives are unworthy of a servant of God. We must seek to view the world from our Lord's position, not from our own selfishly distorted point of view. The accomplishment of the divine purposes is far more important than any personal glory that may come.

The act of Jonah most difficult to understand is his attempt to escape his God by changing his address. Yet much of the restless movement of modern society may be attributed to similar motives. Such attempts will ultimately result in similar experiences. No man can run away from God. He runs only to make the meeting more terrible. One cannot help wondering if Jonah had read Psalm 139:7–12.

The phenomenal results attending Jonah's preaching in Nineveh may be understood in the light of several considerations: (1) Jonah had just known a remarkable experience with God. He was a man come back from the dead. (2) His sermon was terse and to the point. "Yet forty days and Nineveh destroyed!" (3) The revival began among the leaders of the community (3:5–7).

The all-inclusive love of God for his creation is vividly emphasized by his final word to Jonah. And we may note here that God always does have the final word in man's affairs. "And also much cattle" is a cry of pity that makes certain our Lord's unfailing concern for man, made in his own image.

Outline of the Book

1. Jonah's Call and His Fruitless Attempt to Escape from His Duty. Chapter 1

2. A Psalm of Deliverance Followed by Jonah's Being Cast on Dry Land. Chapter 2

3. The Phenomenal Success of the Prophet's Preaching. Chapter 3

4. God's Rebuke of Jonah's Renewed Rebellion. Chapter 4

AMOS

THE PROPHET. The name Amos means "sustained." The prophet lived at Tekoa or in its neighborhood. His occupation was that of herdsman, one who owned or tended sheep. This particular breed of sheep which Amos tended is still known to the Arabs. They are diminutive in size but greatly prized for their wool. His work involved much travel to the markets at Jerusalem and Bethel and considerable moving about in the wilderness of Tekoa, which later was the home of John the Baptist and also the scene of Jesus' temptation. Tekoa was twelve miles south of Jerusalem and 3,800 feet above the Dead Sea. It was shut in on all sides by hills except on the east, where for eighteen miles there was a slope down to the Dead Sea. It is said that Amos was a "pincher of sycomores" (7:14). These trees had a small fig-like fruit, eaten by the poor. The expression "pincher" may mean that he pruned the trees or that he provoked the sluggish lumps of figs to ripen by pinching or bruising them. Some scholars suggest that the fruit was pinched to let out a small insect inside the fruit. Sycomores did not grow at a height greater than 1,000 feet above sea level, so Amos must have had his trees on the eastern slope.

THE CALL OF AMOS. Many times had Amos visited Bethel to sell his wares. There he came face to face with the sins of Northern Israel, especially the worship of the golden calf at Bethel. Finally he could be silent no longer. In the midst of the marketplace he began to prophesy, condemning the sins of Israel, especially those of the leaders, even predicting the death of King Jeroboam II. Amaziah, the priest at Bethel, tried to silence the mountaineer, but he only succeeded in provoking further condemnation. Amos replied that he was not a prophet or the son of a prophet (he was no professional preacher nor the son of one), but he was a man of the soil whom God had called to cry out against entrenched evil. Destruction would surely come on Israel, nor would Amaziah be spared. Because of his attempt to silence the word of Yahweh, his family would be wiped out and he would be taken into captivity.

THE TIME OF THE BOOK. The language of the book is the purest and most classical of the entire Old Testament. It fails to reveal the uncouth shepherd described in some commentaries. There is little difficulty in dating the prophet in Old Testament history. Scholars are almost unanimous in placing him during the middle of the eighth century B.C. The exact limits of his period of ministry are slightly more difficult to define. The title of the book says the prophecies began during the reigns of Uzziah in Judah and Jeroboam in Israel two years before the earthquake. From Amos 6:14 and 2 Kings 14:25 we may conclude that his ministry must have been just after the victories of Jeroboam. This fits well into the picture of prosperity and consequent corruption pictured by Amos. We do not know exactly when the earthquake occurred, but from Zechariah 14:5f., Amos 5:8; 8:9, it appears that a total eclipse of the sun may have accompanied it. Such an eclipse took place June 15, 763 B.C. All this data agrees in placing the beginning of Amos' ministry about 760 B.C. As to the length of time covered by the book, it may be observed that Amos certainly did not prophesy past Jeroboam's death (c. 750), for he is ignorant of the age of anarchy that began at the death of this great monarch.

THE MESSAGE OF AMOS. Jeroboam II was the most successful of all the kings of Northern Israel. Assyria had so weakened Syria that Jeroboam was able to recapture territory that the king of Damascus had taken. A succession of weak kings in Assyria gave him full freedom of movement. Military success was accompanied by great prosperity. The rich grew richer, and the poor, poorer. The courts were corrupt, the prophets asleep. Gross immorality prevailed on every hand. Amos, accustomed to simple life, was disgusted with the pampered lives of the rich nobles and their wives (3:12; 4:1; 6:4). According to Dr. John R. Sampey, Amos "snorted every time he saw a palace." He demanded justice for the poor and oppressed. The theme of the book is found in 5:24: "But let justice roll down as waters, and righteousness as a mighty stream." While Zion was at ease in pleasure, Amos could see the coming of the approaching storm that would destroy Northern Israel—Assyria (6:14).

There has been a considerable amount of discussion in recent years concerning the type of ministry carried on by Amos. Most scholars contend that the book contains only one address of Amos, delivered at Bethel. However, the words of Amaziah to Jeroboam, "Amos hath conspired against thee in the midst of the house of Israel: the land is not able to bear all his words," indicate a larger ministry. Again his words to various groups would have more significance if delivered upon different occasions. Imagine the consternation if the prophet spoke the words found in 4:1–3 to a gathering of the "first ladies" of Samaria, or 8:4–7 actually standing in the marketplace during the "rush hour." If this prophet actually had such a ministry, his various discourses were later written down and compiled into the logical arrangement of the book.

NOTES ON IMPORTANT PASSAGES IN AMOS

1:2 to 2:16. Here is a remarkable passage. The prophet uses the age-old method of taking his hearers by surprise. His crowd gathers as he harangues the surrounding nations for their sins. Loud "amens" come from every corner of the congregation. Then suddenly he reaches his climax and turns upon his hearers, "For three transgressions of *Israel,* yea for four . . ." (2:6).

3:2. Extra privilege demands greater responsibility. Failure requires larger punishment.

3:4–8. Every effect has its cause. Amos prophesies because the Lord is speaking to his heart and he cannot be silent. The testimony of every true preacher of the Word.

4:1. The problem of women and alcohol not a new one.

4:12a. A threat is suggested here but suddenly broken off.

6364

Was Amos interrupted, or were the words too terrible to recall?

4:12b. Prepare to meet thy God in a fight to the finish. Not a call to repentance.

5:21. We could paraphrase, "I hate, I despise your Christmas celebrations, I will take no delight in Sunday services." Ritual without heartfelt religion is mockery before God.

5:25. This much-discussed verse implies a negative answer. The fathers did not do so. They knew, because of their rebellion against God, that mere sacrifice would do no good. At least they were wiser than the people of the day of Amos. They did not waste the animals. This statement does not imply that there was no Levitical legislation in the wilderness, but only states that there was no sacrifice, because of God's rejection of the people, a rejection he was now having to practice again.

7:2, 5. Amos was not a cold, hard-hearted man with no love for Israel. He prayed earnestly for her.

Two Questions Concerning the Teachings of Amos

1. Was Amos a strict monotheist, or did he advocate monolatry, or the worship of one God, while believing in the existence of others? Upon reading chapters 1–2; 5:27; 6:14; 9:1–4, one cannot help concluding that there is no room for a God other than Yahweh in heaven, earth, or Sheol.

2. Did Amos approve calf worship? (See 3:14; 4:4f.; 5:4–6; 5:21–23; 7:9; 8:14–9:1.) Hosea was not the first prophet to oppose the calf worship of Bethel and Dan.

Outline of the Book

Title in 1:1. Text in 1:2—Judgment!

1. A Series of Prophecies Against the Nations, Culminating in the Condemnation of Israel. Chapters 1–2
2. Three Discourses upon Israel's Wickedness, Each Introduced by "Hear this word." Chapters 3–6

3. Five Visions Concerning Israel. 7:1 to 9:10
   (1) Locusts. 7:1–3
   (2) Fire. 7:4–6
   (3) The test of the plumb line. 7:7–9
   (4) Basket of summer fruit. Iniquity ripe for punishment. 8:1–14
   (5) Destruction of Temple and worshipers. 9:1–10
Conclusion—Promise of Restoration. 9:11–15

HOSEA

THE BOOK. Hosea exhibits one of the most confused texts in all the Old Testament. It varies greatly between the LXX and the Hebrew and is almost impossible to outline, being both incoherent and disconnected in many places. This lack of logical arrangement, however, is certainly due to the intense emotion of the prophet. The book has been called "a succession of sobs" (A. B. Davidson), and one does not sob in logical outline. It may be likened to the diary of a soldier at the battlefront, written between shells; or to a ship in a tempest, seeming to be tossing aimlessly, but nevertheless plowing its way toward a determined goal.[1] This book is supremely great; it grows on the reader. It contains some of the noblest passages in the Bible and is frequently quoted in the New Testament. As to the arrangement, we may describe it: (1) the prophet's tragic domestic history and the moral of it (1-3); (2) Hosea's prophetic utterances. All the sins of the people are exposed; he exhorts, using every possible means of persuasion to win them back to God (4-14). Some scholars deny to Hosea the passages of hope and restoration found in the book. It is difficult, however, to comprehend a message of love unless it is accompanied by a word of hope. Such love of God as that described by Hosea cannot fail ultimately in its purpose.

THE PROPHET. Hosea was a northerner, a citizen of Israel. He probably lived in a city (Bethel or Samaria). His name means "salvation" and is equivalent to Joshua and Jesus. The

---

[1]Cf. Rollin H. Walker, *Men Unafraid* (New York: Abingdon-Cokesbury Press, 1923), p. 51.

first prophet of grace, he is also Israel's first evangelist.[2] His prophetic ministry probably extended from c. 750 B.C. to 735 B.C., a little later than Amos, for conditions described in the book agree with the last days of Jeroboam. It cannot be later than 735, for Gilead is still Israelite territory and Assyria her ally. In 732 Assyria took Gilead captive.

Amos and Hosea were very different in their preaching and characteristics. Amos came from Judah to preach in Israel; thus, he was less personal in his preaching. Hosea's heart went out to his own people to whom he was preaching. Amos spoke of justice, to the conscience; Hosea spoke of love, to the heart. This prophet was a poet of the first order, could see things vividly and set what he saw into words of precision and power. In nature he was affectionate, a man of unquenchable love and intense sensitiveness. His was a personality of contrasts. When he thought of God, he was the happiest of men; but when he thought of sinful man, he was the saddest. Thinking of Yahweh, his spirit was gentle as a dove; turning to the ungrateful love of man, he was as fierce as a lion. When he looked at sin, he was a pessimist; when he looked at God, he was a man of faith. Hosea has been called the Jeremiah of Israel and the apostle John of the Old Testament. The keynote of his message was that sin is not so much against the law of God as against his love. So far as we know, Hosea never made a convert. Tradition says he died of heartbreak or martyrdom on the eastern side of the Jordan, on Mount Hosea, where Jews claim his tomb may be seen.

THE BACKGROUND. It was a restless, chaotic age (2 Kings 14:3 to 17:6). The evils which Amos condemned were rapidly growing worse. Pressure from Assyria was increasing. Internally it was a period of anarchy, amid the lying diplomacy of the rulers. However, it was a domestic tragedy that gave Hosea the impetus that made him the great preacher that he was. Just what was the nature of the tragedy? There are several interpretations, all based on the story in chapter 1 and the meaning of "a wife of whoredoms" in verse 2.

1. God commanded the prophet to marry a woman who

[2]Cf. G. A. Smith, *The Book of the Twelve Prophets* (New York: Harper & Bros., 1928), I, 239.

at the time of the wedding was leading an evil life. In opposition to this view is the difficulty of conceiving of God ordering a prophet to marry such a woman. In addition, the Hebrew word describing her would have been singular (whoredom) and not plural.

2. No such marriage took place, but the whole story is an allegory that Hosea used to illustrate the relationship of Israel and Yahweh. However, this does not get rid of the moral difficulty. It is improbable that a man would invent a story that would reflect on his real wife. The theory also implies that Hosea first awakened to the truth that God is love and then wrote the story to illustrate. But verse 2 properly translated should read, "The beginning of that which Yahweh spoke with Hosea. . . ." This implies that the marriage was Yahweh's first word to Hosea. God spoke to him in the object lesson of a broken home. Then he could see how Israel had treated Yahweh in just the same way. Furthermore, the style is that of a narrative and not an allegory. No symbolism can be discovered in the name "Gomer," as would be true if it were allegorical.

3. The woman in chapter 3 is not Gomer. Gomer remained faithful although an idolatress. Hosea brought an evil woman home, separating her from her lovers, to show how God would separate between Israel and her sins. The objection to this theory is found in 3:1. Hosea is commanded to love a sinful woman as Yahweh has loved Israel, although they have turned to other gods. The parallel could only be Gomer, who has left Hosea for other paramours.

4. The marriage really took place, and Gomer was chaste at the time of the marriage. The plural "whoredoms" means that she was an idolatress; she had left God for idols and so was a spiritual adultress. After the marriage her spiritual adultery led to physical sin and she deserted Hosea and her children. This theory recognizes the story as a simple recital of facts, yet avoids the moral difficulty. It gives a reasonable basis for Hosea's love for his wife and better explains the connection between Hosea's experience and his conception of the relationship of Yahweh and Israel. It also is more consistent with the events of chapter 3.

2:15. Achor means troubling. This was the valley where Achan sinned in taking the devoted things from Jericho. This beautiful verse makes the promise that Israel's valley of troubling shall prove to be a door to new experiences of happiness. Such has always been the way of God with man.

4:2. In Hebrew a series of infinitives absolute: "Swearing! Breaking faith! Killing!"

4:6, 9. The people perish because of the failure of their leaders to teach the truth.

4:14. No double standard in morals.

4:16. Lambs do not like too much room. They crave the company of other lambs.

5:13. King Jareb is apparently a nickname. Perhaps "King Pick-a-Quarrel" or "King Fighting-Cock" would be the best rendering. It is evidently applied to Tiglath-pileser.

6:4. A condemnation of seasonal religion that cannot stand the test of time.

6:6. A plea for heartfelt religion that Jesus heartily endorsed (Matt. 9:13; 12:7).

7:8f. Three processes were taking place in Israel that need to be guarded against today: (1) compromise with the world; (2) one-sided development (a pancake not turned); (3) unconscious decay.

9:10b. A law of human nature. Our real interests determine our character.

11:8f. The amazing love of God for sinful man.

12:9. God will reduce Israel to her former nomadic state.

13:14. A decree of destruction effectively reversed by Paul in the New Testament (1 Cor. 15:55). The context demands that verse 14a be read as a question. "Will I ransom them from the power of Sheol? Will I redeem them from death?" The answer is negative, as God calls for the plagues of death and Sheol to punish their sin. Here is an interesting example of eisegesis, whereby a New Testament passage influenced Old Testament translators.

14:5. Dew is the only source of moisture during the dry season in Palestine.

OUTLINE OF THE BOOK

1. Israel's Unfaithfulness Illustrated by the Prophet's Bitter Experience. 1–3

2. Selections from Hosea's Prophecies. 4–14

    (1) The moral decay. 4:1–7:7
    (2) The political decay. 7:8 to 10:15
    (3) The compassion of the Father-God. 11:1–11.
    (4) A final vain appeal to repent. Doom inevitable. 11:12 to 13:16
    (5) The final restoration to follow true repentance. 14

MICAH

THE PROPHET. His name is a rather common one in the Old Testament. It appears in one form or another as the name of more than a dozen persons and has the meaning, "Who is like Yahweh?" His home was in Moresheth, a town near Gath, the site of which is not known with certainty. It was in the Shephelah, close to the gateway to Egypt, where roads converged from all points. Apparently, Micah was a simple countryman, "of the people . . . and for the people." He has been called "Micah the Democrat." A keen observer of nature, he manifested a farmer's instincts for cold facts. Little of the poet was in him; he was usually plain and straightforward. In him, too, was the countryman's dislike of cities. He was quite positive that wickedness and vice concentrated there. A peasant preacher, he felt keenly the wrongs and sufferings inflicted on the common people. A burning passion for justice, right dealing, and holy living possessed him. He believed that all the sins of the people could be traced to one source—the love of money.

Micah was a contemporary of Isaiah, and in these two men we can see considerable differences. Isaiah belonged to the upper classes. He was a native of Jerusalem and in close touch with national and international affairs. The friend and counselor of kings, he took an active part in political movements of his day. His messages were addressed principally to rulers and groups of select disciples. Micah was a quite different kind of preacher. He was a simple farmer, far from the noise and confusion of the city. Whereas Isaiah had received his call amid the pomp of the Temple, Micah heard his in the cry of his oppressed neighbors. He was not a politician like Isaiah. His sermons dealt mainly with social morality and religious duty and not with matters of state and foreign policy. Both prophets paint the picture of the sins of the land, but Micah uses more glaring colors and greater detail. At times Micah exhibits an almost savage vindictiveness, which is absent from the lofty statements of Isaiah.

As different as the men were, they were one in aim and substance of their preaching. They both appealed for justice and morality and preached the inevitable consequences of sin. Strangely enough, neither refers to the other. The only reference to the life and influence of Micah found outside his book is in the book of Jeremiah, chapter 26. Jeremiah was put on trial for his life for predicting the overthrow of Jerusalem. In his defense some of the elders of the city recalled that Micah had predicted an overthrow and was not killed; but rather the people repented of their sins and ruin was averted. As a result Jeremiah also was spared.

No prophet in the Old Testament was able to view the future more clearly than Micah. Among his predictions were the fall of Samaria, fulfilled in 722 B.C.; the destruction of Jerusalem, fulfilled in 586 B.C.; the Babylonian captivity of Judah and the Return (605–537); the birth of the messianic King in Bethlehem.

THE BOOK. There is very little question about the date of chapters 1–3, describing the doom of Samaria and Jerusalem. It is almost universally admitted that Micah wrote these between 724 B.C. and 701 B.C. Many scholars, however, doubt that Micah wrote anything past chapter 3, since they claim that he wrote only words of doom and that the background of chapters 4–7 is not that of the eighth century but of a later era.

A psychological outline of the book, along with numerous other indications, helps defeat the view that Micah wrote only words of doom:

(1) The coming judgment (chapters 1–3). (2) The faithfulness of God. Man may prove false, but God will accomplish his purpose nevertheless. He will save through his Messiah the holy "remnant of Jacob." The "but" in 4:1 clearly sets off the contrast of the two sections (4–5). (3) The final plea. The

preacher of doom says to himself, "Perhaps the wound is not incurable after all. I will make one last appeal" (chapter 6). (4) There is no response from the people, but the prophet dreams that it will not always be so. Better days will come, for Yahweh will be true to his promises to the fathers (chapter 7).

IMPORTANT PASSAGES IN MICAH

1:10–11. In the Hebrew the puns on these names of towns are clearly evident.

2:1. Conditions are so bad that evil men are free to practice their iniquity in open daylight.

2:3. While the wicked of 2:1 are devising evil, Yahweh is busy devising evil against them.

2:10. A call to go into captivity.

3:2f. Micah likens the cruel oppressors of the poor to cannibals.

3:5–7. Prophets whose god is their stomachs, who care more for what goes into their mouths than for what comes out, the quality of whose ministry is determined by the amount of their salary. Their punishment shall be a resultant lack of spiritual insight and a deafness of God to their pleas.

3:8. The contrast with the true prophet who boldly speaks as the Spirit leads.

3:11. The danger of false security.

4:1–4. This prediction of the future is found in almost identical phrasing in Isaiah, chapter 2. The problem of which prophet did the borrowing or whether they both derived it from a third is impossible to solve. Here we find a practical program for world peace.

It is conditioned upon a freedom of worship whereby people voluntarily seek God and urge others to do likewise (2a). This seeking results in their learning the will of God and doing it (2b). As Yahweh's decisions are obeyed, international strife ceases (3a) so that the instruments of war are used for peace. Consequently, this increased production eliminates want. Men no longer live in fear, for everyone has all his heart desires (4).

5:2–5. One of the most remarkable passages in the Old Testament. It was verse 2 that informed the wise men of the place of birth of the child Jesus. Micah indicates in 5:5 that the world peace foreseen in chapter 4 can only be achieved by the Messiah, never by natural development. "And this man shall be our peace."

5:7–8. God's people shall be both a blessing and curse. To those who believe, a blessing; to those who reject, a living condemnation.

6:8. There is not a more magnificent verse in all the Old Testament. In immortal phrasing Micah sums up the message of the other three eighth-century prophets. Amos had emphasized justice; Hosea had preached love; Isaiah urged a humble fellowship with a holy God. (Cf. Deut. 10:12.)

7:1. The prophet longs for just one convert.

7:18–19. The opening phrase is a play on Micah's name. The description of the grace of God is surpassingly beautiful.

ISAIAH

THE MAN. His name means "salvation of Yahweh." Isaiah was born about 760 B.C., about the time that Amos appeared at Bethel. His father was named Amoz (not Amos). When Hosea began to prophesy, Isaiah was a youth. Micah was Isaiah's contemporary. Isaiah was at home among nobility and always a city preacher. By 734 he was married, and his wife was called a prophetess (8:3). His public ministry began "in the year that King Uzziah died" (c. 740), and continued through the reigns of Jotham, Ahaz, and Hezekiah until 698 B.C. In his dealing with political affairs, there were three great crises: (1) In 735 B.C. Rezin, king of Syria, and Pekah, king of Israel, banded together to oppose Tiglath-pileser, king of Assyria. When they tried to persuade Judah to join, she refused. The two kings set out to conquer Judah and to set up a puppet king. Ahaz, frightened, appealed to Assyria for help. Isaiah met him by the waterworks and told him to trust in God and not in Assyria, for the "two tails of smoking firebrands" would soon be destroyed. Ahaz refused to listen but leaned on Assyria. There was little Isaiah could do. Damascus fell, and then in 722 B.C. Israel went to her knees. Ahaz imagined that his foreign policy had accomplished the defeat of his enemies. Even while he was under Assyria he began to make agreements with Egypt against Assyria. Isaiah finally turned him from his folly. He was now in favor. (2) Hezekiah, however, reversed the policy of Ahaz. He joined with Philistia, Edom, Moab, and Egypt in their intrigues against Assyria and barely missed destruction. About the same time he established friendly relationships with the king of Babylon. Isaiah saw in all this a coming doom at the hands of Assyria, and he tried with all his soul to avert it. (3) At the death of Sargon, Judah, along with the other surrounding nations, revolted against Assyria. Isaiah continued to protest. However, when Sennacherib demanded the surrender of the city, challenging Yahweh to prevent it, Isaiah knew the Assyrian would fail. And when he did, once more was the message of the prophet vindicated.

As to Isaiah's character, Valeton[1] describes him: "Never perhaps has there been another prophet like Isaiah, who stood with his head in the clouds and his feet on the solid earth, with his heart in the things of eternity and with mouth and hand in the things of time, with his spirit in the eternal counsel of God and his body in a very definite moment of history."

Isaiah was a member of that select class of men who can dream and not forget the world around them. He could talk of peace and the messianic reign and suddenly burst into a scorching harangue against the wicked immorality and unfaithfulness around him. His was an integrated personality that could brave all the storms of a troublous age and remain unbiased and broad amid the petty provincialism of a narrow nationalistic culture. In spiritual insight he is unsurpassed in all the Old Testament. Though a visionary, he was yet practical. His children's names are object lessons, and his own life was a testimony of what he taught. At one time he wrote a message on a large public board; at another he walked stripped and barefoot through Jerusalem for three years as a living example of what the Assyrians would do to the people they captured. As a reformer he opposed all social injustice.

Perhaps James,[2] in his analysis of the characteristics of Isaiah's style, presents the most significant insight into the prophet's personality when he describes his writings as having majestic impetuosity and piercing beauty of diction, brilliant ever-changing word pictures, trumpet peals of faith, ringing challenges, inexorable demands, white-hot purity, scorn of all base

---

[1]Cited by Geo. L. Robinson, *The Book of Isaiah* (New York: Y.M.C.A. Press, 1910), p. 22.

[2]Fleming James, *Personalities of the Old Testament* (New York: Charles Scribner's Sons, 1939), pp. 268–269.

things, championing of the poor, and tender assurances. In each of the other great prophets some special excellence stands out as his peculiar contribution, but, as Ewald says, in Isaiah "every kind of style and every variation of exposition is at his command to meet the requirements of the subject."[3]

There is no certainty as to the time and manner of his death. Tradition has it that he was sawn asunder during the reign of wicked Manasseh, to which Hebrews 11:37 is probably a reference.

THE BACKGROUND. The economic prosperity that marked the early part of this period was accompanied by every sort of social vice. The chasm between the rich and poor became even wider. Revelling and drunkenness prevailed on every hand. Dishonesty was rampant in public life. At the close of the period the desperate plight of the poor was made even worse by the ravages of war. Hunger stalked the streets of Jerusalem, and little children cried for bits of bread. Dishonesty and immorality showed no tendency to decline. Ungodly men took on the desperate air of those who are doomed to perish for their crimes and yet are ravenously devouring the bitter cup to the last dregs. It was a dark hour, its sole ray of light streaming through the words of a far-seeing prophet who saw his God "high and lifted up." Tugging away at his faithless generation, trying to raise its eyes above, he finally persuaded a desperate king to try the last and only sure alternative, the faithfulness of God.

The religious situation likewise was discouraging. There was a fatal syncretism of Baalism and Yahweh-worship that was nothing more than heathenism. Superstitions and cults from the East were creeping in. In his boldness Ahaz built a heathen altar in place of the altar to the Lord. Worship of Yahweh was a heartless, elaborate ceremonial even during the reign of Hezekiah; else how could the people so quickly follow the sins of Manasseh? The prophets were sottish, speaking with flattery and smooth sayings.

THE BOOK. The book of Isaiah is rightly considered the greatest of the Old Testament prophecies. Here messianic

---

[3]Heinrich Ewald, *Commentary on the Prophets of the Old Testament* (London: Williams and Norgate, 1876), II, 10.

prophecy reaches its peak, causing the book to be the favorite of New Testament writers. The theme of Isaiah is the holiness of God. Yet holiness is not only strict justice and purity but must come down to seek the lost. Thus on one side there is forgiving grace and on the other consuming purity.[4] As for style, the writings give evidence of fine culture, insight, and poetic ability. We may describe the poetry of the book with the words that Isaiah used as he pictured his God—"high and lifted up." Its lofty beauty transcends any passages in the Old Testament.

The majority of scholars today contend, however, that the prophecies found in this book are not all by the same author. Especially questioned are chapters 13–14, 24–27, 36–39, 40–66. By far the most important problem in the analysis of the book is that of the authorship of 40–66. Nowhere is it stated in these chapters that they are written by Isaiah. There is every indication of a difference in authorship. Instead of the stern rebukes of 1–39, here is a sustained body of comfort and assurance. In the earlier chapters the Messiah is pictured always as a king; in chapters 40–66 he is a suffering *Saviour*. The style of Isaiah is direct; here a symphonic literary form prevails.

The destruction of Jerusalem in 586 is not predicted in these chapters. It is presupposed. The Exile is already in progress (64:10; 61:4; 49:19; 52:9; 58:12; 42:22). Zion herself is in exile (49:14–21). The place of the Exile is Babylon (47:1–5; 48:14, 20). The prophet himself is an exile (42:24). The career of Cyrus is not predicted, as it would have been done by Isaiah living 150 years before. He is already on the scene (41:2; 41:25; 44:26; 45:1ff.).

Several references elsewhere in the Old Testament indicate that these prophecies were written by an unknown author during the Exile.

1. References to the decree of Cyrus.[5] In these two identical passages the Chronicler, apparently referring to Isaiah 44:28, says that Cyrus made his decree that the word of Jeremiah might be fulfilled. Duhm takes this to mean that Jeremiah was

---

[4] Cf. A. R. Gordon, *The Prophets of the Old Testament* (New York: Harper & Bros., 1916), pp. 88–91.

[5] 2 Chron. 36:22–23; Ezra 1:1–4.

at that time thought to be the author of Isaiah, chapters 40–66, but there is no hint of this anywhere else. The evident meaning of the passage is that the decree of Cyrus is the fulfilment of the prophecy of Jeremiah that in seventy years the supremacy of Babylon would be ended. Then Cyrus himself cites Isaiah 44:28, a passage with which he was assuredly familiar, as the reason for his action. The absence of Isaiah's name from these references seems to show that neither Cyrus nor the Chronicler thought that Isaiah was the author of the words. Surely, if the Chronicler had known Isaiah had predicted the name of Cyrus and the Return 150 years in advance, he would have used Isaiah's name in preference to that of Jeremiah and his seventy years. It cannot be argued that the Chronicler was not thinking of Isaiah at the time, for he was quoting from his book.

2. The attitude toward Jerusalem and the Temple in Jeremiah's day. When Jeremiah was prophesying, the people in Jerusalem thought their city could never fall, for the Temple of Yahweh was there. In fact, this prophet was arrested for preaching that the Temple would be destroyed. If, less than a hundred years before, Isaiah had written chapters 40–66 with the evident assumption that the Temple would be burned and the people exiled, would not the Hebrew people be living under constant dread of that exile instead of believing Jerusalem could never fall? Could it be that they refused to believe Isaiah? Perhaps, but their attitude can best be explained by the fact that they had gained the idea of the inviolability of Jerusalem from the prophecies of Isaiah against Sennacherib, prophecies which were the last he uttered, leaving the final impression that of the eternity of God's city.

Additional light is cast upon the problem by other passages in Jeremiah. When the prophet was seized for proclaiming the eventual overthrow of Jerusalem, the best defense an elder could make for him was the fact that Micah had prophesied similarly. Why would not the Exilic prophecies of the greater Isaiah be more of a witness—the same Isaiah whom they were undoubtedly quoting for their idea of the inviolability of Jerusalem?

However, objections to this view are very worthy of consideration. Long unbroken tradition assigns 40–66 to Isaiah. The writers of the New Testament attribute these passages to him, although Jesus never does so (Matt. 3:3; 8:17; 12:17; Luke 3:4; 4:17; John 1:23; 12:38; Acts 8:28; Rom. 10:16–20). The section in question has always been associated with Isaiah. We have no record of its ever existing separately. If not by Isaiah, it is strange that its author's identity has been lost when inferior men who wrote at the same time have been remembered.

Most of the scholars who hold the traditional view claim that chapters 40–66 were written from the viewpoint of an exile, but by Isaiah 150 years earlier. A miracle of inspiration transported him through time that he might speak as a contemporary of the Babylonian exiles. Thus the question actually is resolved into theological hairsplitting. Both sides agree that the prophetical voice in chapters 40–66 speaks from the point of view of the Exile. Does this voice proceed from a flesh-and-blood prophet who himself has experienced the misfortune of banishment from the homeland or from the eighth-century Isaiah as a work of imagination? The analogy of other prophecies would indicate that it is an actual prophet speaking to an audience of contemporaries. However, no one can sensibly deny the possibility of God's having inspired a special kind of ministry for Isaiah. Whichever view one takes, he should recognize the fact that the human author of a book is not so important as the God who inspired it.

OUTLINE OF THE BOOK

1. Book of Mingled Rebukes and Promises. Chapters 1–6. (delivered for the most part during the reigns of Jotham and Ahaz)

   (1) "The Great Arraignment." Chapter 1. (The language as to the desolation of the land would suit the time of the invasion of Judah by Pekah and Rezin, or the invasion of Sennacherib.)

   (2) Exaltation of Zion to be attained only through terrific judgments against the proud and sinful. Chapters 2–4

(3) The vineyard and its lessons. Chapter 5
(4) The inaugural vision. Chapter 6
(This vision was given in the year that Uzziah died. We do not know why the account of the prophet's call was not placed at the beginning of his book, as in the writing of Jeremiah and Ezekiel. The book is not arranged solely on the basis of chronological sequence; but it is not without order.)

2. The Book of Immanuel. Chapters 7–12. (delivered during the reigns of Ahaz and Hezekiah)

(1) Important messages in connection with two interviews with Ahaz at the time of the Syrian invasion. Chapter 7. (735 B.C.)
(2) Fresh announcement of desolating judgments, to be followed by great salvation. 8:1 to 9:7. (734 B.C.)
(3) The hand of the lord stretched out for severe judgments upon wicked Samaria. 9:8 to 10:4. (prior to 724 B.C.)
(4) The proud Assyrian shall be brought low, but the people of Yahweh shall be saved. 10:5 to 12:6. (701 B.C.)

3. Book of Foreign Prophecies. Chapters 13–23. (various dates)

(1) Against Babylon. 13:1 to 14:23
(The genuineness of this section has been called into question, inasmuch as it reflects the condition of Babylon long after the time of Isaiah. Unless one believes heartily in supernatural revelation, this conclusion would be unavoidable; and some even of those who believe in the supernatural assign it to the sixth century rather than the eighth. The poetic power and moral energy of the parable or taunt song in 14:3–20 are worthy of the great Isaiah.)
(2) Against Assyria. 14:24–27. Yahweh will surely break the Assyrian in the land of Judah. (date unknown)

(3) Against Philistia. 14:28–32 (727 B.C.). Let not Philistia rejoice over the death of Tiglath-pileser IV; for his successors will smite her even more severely

(4) Burden of Moab. Chapters 15, 16. (From 16:13 we learn that the greater part of this prophecy was delivered sometime prior to the closing prediction. Most likely the whole is from the pen of Isaiah and not merely a long quotation from some earlier prophet.)

(5) Burden of Damascus, with two prophecies concerning Israel and Judah. Chapter 17. (Verses 1–11 were spoken prior to 732 B.C.)

(6) Concerning Ethiopia. Chapter 18. (probably between 705 and 701 B.C.)

(7) The alliance of Judah with Ethiopia to be of no avail. In the coming time Ethiopia will send a present to Yahweh. Cf. 2 Chron. 32:23.

(8) Burden of Egypt. Chapter 19.

(9) Egypt and Ethiopia to be led away captive by the king of Assyria. Chapter 20 (prophecy delivered in 711 B.C. For further earnest warnings against reliance on Egypt, see chapters 30, 31.)

(10) Second prophecy concerning Babylon. 21:1–10. Announcement of its fall in dramatic style; the prophet greatly grieved at the vision. (Was it fulfilled by Sargon or by Cyrus in 539 B.C.?)

(11) Burden of Dumah. 21:11f. No permanent relief for Edom.

(12) Concerning Arabia. 21:13–17. Within a year her caravans shall be scattered by invasion.

(13) The Burden of Jerusalem. 22:1–14 (701 B.C.?)

(14) Shebna (probably a foreigner) to be degraded from his high office. Eliakim to take his place. 22:15–25 (cf. 37:2).

(15) The burden of Tyre. Chapter 23

4. The First Book of General Judgment. Chapters 24–27. (Wide scope reminds us of Joel. Intimate relation to chapters 13–23. Date not known.)

(1) Picture of terrible judgments to come. Chapter 24
(2) Triumph for God's people. Chapter 25
(3) Song of praise to be sung in the land of Judah. Chapter 26
(4) Judgment against the oppressor on behalf of Israel. Chapter 27

5. The Book of Zion (Book of Woes). Chapters 28–33. (delivered during Hezekiah's reign)

(1) The fall of Samaria predicted; also judgments upon sinners in Judah. Chapter 28. (28:1–6 are prior to 722 B.C.; 28:7–29 seem to have been written c. 702.)
(2) Siege and deliverance of Ariel (Jerusalem). Chapter 29. (702 B.C.)
(3) Against the Egyptian alliance. Chapter 30
(4) "The False Help and the True." Chapters 31, 32
(5) Woe to the cruel Assyrian invaders! Chapter 33 (after the return of Hezekiah's ambassadors from Lachish. Cf. 2 Kings 18:13–35; Isa. 33:1, 7–8.)

6. Second Picture of General Judgment. Chapters 34, 35. (date not known)

(1) The judgment. Chapter 34
(2) Glorious counterpart of the judgment on Edom. God shall do wonders for his distressed people, leading them home from exile. Chapter 35

7. The Book of Hezekiah. Historical Interlude. Chapters 36–39

(1) Sennacherib's invasion. Chapters 36, 37. (Cf. 2 Kings 18:13 to 19:37)
(2) Hezekiah's sickness, and the embassy from Babylon. Chapters 38, 39

8. Book of Comfort. Chapters 40–66

(1) Preparation of Almighty God for the deliverance of his people from Babylon. Chapters 40–48. (The doc-

trine of God is unfolded with great fulness and rare charm in the first nine chapters of the Book of Comfort.) Theme of the book, 40:1f.

(2) Salvation comes through the Servant of Yahweh. Chapters 49–55

(3) Promises and warnings. The new heaven and the new earth. Chapters 56–66. (Duhm ascribes these chapters to an author contemporary with Ezra and Malachi, to whom he gives the name Trito-Isaiah. This view has lost in favor in recent years.)

NOTES ON IMPORTANT PASSAGES IN ISAIAH

1:3. Israel unnatural in her affections. Even the dumb ox and ass show more intelligence. One can imagine the effect of these bitter words.

1:6. No place left to chastise.

1:8. A temporary existence.

1:16b–17a. Real reformation twofold.

1:18b. Conditional promise. "They *may be* white as snow . . ." (cf. 1:16, 19). Salvation always conditioned upon man's acceptance of God's way. Or perhaps, "Can they be . . . ?"

1:31. Sin is suicidal. God's moral universe is aflame against all unrighteousness.

4:1. War will destroy most of the men.

5:1. Note the skill of the prophet in securing attention to a love song, and then gliding over into his burning message to a sinful people.

5:7. In Hebrew a play on words, "he looked for *mishpat,* but, behold, *mispach;* for *zedakah,* but, behold, *zeakah.*"

5:8. Isaiah opposed to land monopoly.

5:10. One homer equals ten ephahs. Monopoly leads to eventual desolation.

5:11. Cf. Acts 2:15.

5:18. Harnessed to sin.

5:20. Moral distinctions completely lost.

5:25. His hand stretched out to punish.

6:2. Probably symbolizing reverence, purity, and service.

6:5. It was commonly believed that the sight of God would bring death to sinful man. (Cf. Judg. 13:22; Ex. 22:20.)

6:8. Isaiah a volunteer but not presumptuous.

6:10. Not that the prophet is to do this intentionally. Their hard hearts would result in such a condition upon the reception of his word.

6:11–13. A discouraging ministry for a young man. Yet from the stump the new Israel would sprout.

7:3. There was no natural source of water in Jerusalem, only that which could be stored. Ahaz was inspecting the water supply in preparation for the siege.

7:4. A great amount of smoke but not because of fire. Firebrands smoke the worst when they are going out. "The son of Remaliah" repeated by Isaiah as if to imply, "the son of a nobody."

7:8–9. Governments always depend upon their leaders. No man breathes whom God cannot control.

7:14–16. There are several opinions about the meaning of this difficult passage: (1) Isaiah expects the Messiah to come in connection with the Syrian War. (Cf. 8:8, 10; 7:16.) (2) A child was to be born in the days of Isaiah, who was to be a type of the greater Immanuel. Such a person has not been located. (3) The reference is solely to the birth of Jesus Christ. The two kings were destroyed before he was of age. The length of time between that destruction and his coming is but another indication of the timelessness of God's plan. Of one thing we may be assured: Never was the prophecy *fulfilled* until Jesus had been born of the virgin Mary.

8:16. True religion never popular. The pious kernel. The beginning of the idea of a church within Israel.

8:19–20. No need to consult spiritualists and fortunetellers when God's Word has the answer.

9:6. Omit comma after "Wonderful."

10:5, 7a. God can use men for his purposes who have quite different intentions.

10:19. "so that a child may *count* them."

10:27. The beast of burden becomes so fat that the yoke breaks from being too small.

10:28–32. There is no record of such a campaign. Did the prophecy fail? This may be simply a poetic description never intended to be fulfilled literally, although its essence was accomplished. However, it may have been literally fulfilled during one of the many Assyrian campaigns.

Chapters 13 and 14 strike certain notes often heard in chapters 40–66, particularly the fall of Babylon and consequent return. Hence they are ascribed by many to a prophet in the Exilic period. These chapters show how prophecy often took the form of poetry.

14:12–20. Not a reference to Satan but to the destruction of the king of Babylon. (Cf. 14:16, "Is this the *man* . . . ?")

16:11. No joy in preaching destruction.

18:1. Describes either the numerous flies or sails. Ethiopia was master of Egypt during this period.

19:23–25. A statement of God's relationship to the nations of the world that is remarkable in its scope. This prophet is not bound by Jonah's exclusiveness.

20:2. The prophet removed his outer garments to assume the garb of an exile.

21:3. The fall of Babylon painful to the prophet. Suitable to a Judean prophet in the days of Hezekiah, as Judah and Babylon were in alliance. (Cf. Isaiah 39.)

21:11f. Edom anxiously inquires of the prophetic watchman whether the night is almost past, and receives the comfortless reply that the night is almost over, only to be succeeded shortly by another period of darkness.

22:1–14. Symbolical name for Jerusalem. Vivid picture of the surprise, cowardice, hasty preparation for siege and the revellings of the city.

23:15. The seventy years may be a symbolical number. Tyre was not actually destroyed until the Crusades, when it was demolished by the Saracens. Today it is a small fishing village.

23:16. Referred to as a harlot because she does not care with whom she trades so long as it is profitable.

Chapters 24–27. These passages are distinctly different from anything else in the Roll of Isaiah. They are timeless and universal, impossible to date. Their eschatological character leads some to prefer a post-Exilic background, but this position is impossible to establish with any degree of certainty. Found in this section are many magnificent pictures and glorious promises.

Chapter 24. Man's sin has infected the whole earth, and punishment must include the entire world, with its inhabitants.

25:7–8. A passage of surpassing beauty. There is no promise of a resurrection here, only an assurance of a time when there will be no more death.

26:3. "Thou wilt keep him in perfect peace, whose *imagination* is stayed on thee; because he trusteth in thee." If, when a man relaxes, his imagination instinctively turns to God, he is a blessed believer. During such moments man's true desires come to the surface.

26:9b, 10a. Mankind is much more likely to think of God in adversity than in prosperity.

27:5. The way to make peace with God is not by running away from him, but by laying hold of his omnipotence, as Jacob did at Peniel.

28:1. A reference to Samaria, a city on a hill.

28:4. Too tempting to avoid.

28:9–10. Are we kindergarten children?

28:11–13. The people who cannot understand the prophet will be hearing the Assyrian tongue that will be even more strange to their ears.

28:15–16. The people felt safe behind their covenant with Egypt, but the only real security is found in a faith in God. It has stood the test of endless ages.

28:20. A humorous illustration of the inadequacy of man's best-laid plans.

29:11–13. The lip service of a religion which consists of a human tradition learned by rote always destroys spiritual discernment.

30:15. Isaiah's theme in the Assyrian crisis. Calm neutrality and quiet trust.

30:21. Note that the voice is from behind, not in front. It is based upon experience.

30:33. The image of a funeral pile on which the king of Assyria is consumed. Topheth was a place in the valley of the sons of Hinnom that was desecrated by idolatrous human sacrifices (Jer. 7:31; 2 Kings 23:10). Fulfilled, not by the death of Sennacherib in Judah, but by the destruction of his army there and his own death at home twenty years later.

31:2. You cannot leave God out of history. Politicians do so to their own despair.

31:4. Yahweh a lion and mother-bird, a picture of his power and tenderness.

32:2. Striking figures of speech describing the Messiah as man's refuge.

32:5. Hypocritical flattery shall cease.

32:20. "Blessed are ye that sow *upon* all waters," while the river is still at flood stage, lest there be no harvest—a common practice in the Orient. "Blessed are ye who in times of sorrow prepare for happier days."

33:7f. Sennacherib receives at Lachish the stipulated tribute from Hezekiah but then demands the unconditional surrender of Jerusalem. He captures many cities, breaks up all travel, and sends an army against Jerusalem to enforce his demands (2 Kings 18:13 to 19:37). Hezekiah's ambassadors come home weeping.

33:14. Yahweh is a consuming fire to sinners. No direct reference to hell.

33:17. Just now, all that the people can see as they look over the walls of Jerusalem are the tents of the Assyrians. Hezekiah has put aside his royal robe and donned sackcloth. Soon, however, the scenic view will be unimpeded by alien hosts and the king shall once again be seen in the beauty of his royal robes.

33:20. Isaiah's doctrine of the inviolability of Jerusalem. It appears, however, that he simply intended this truth to apply to Sennacherib's invasion, not for all time. Sennacherib had questioned the integrity of Yahweh with his boastful claim, so could not possibly prevail.

Chapters 34–35. The authenticity of these chapters has been questioned. In chapter 34 the bitterness of the invectives against Edom and its apocalyptic character suggest a late date. Chapter 35 resembles 40–66.

35:7. "And the mirage shall become a pool" means "and what men dream of shall become an actuality."

Chapters 36–39. Probably inserted by a later editor to furnish an historical background. (Cf. 2 Kings 18:13 to 20:21.)

Chapters 40–55. The scene has changed to the Babylonian Exile, c. 545.

40:2b. The kind Father feels the child has suffered twice what she deserved.

40:3–4. The Orient had few good highways. When a great king traveled, the road had to be levelled before him. Here the call goes out to prepare the way across the desert from Babylon to Judea, for Yahweh is coming at the head of his exiles. This prophecy reached its ultimate spiritual fulfilment when John the Baptist prepared the way for Jesus to deliver his people, not from Babylon, but from sin.

40:6–8. All life transient. God alone is permanent. He will keep his promise to his captive people.

40:11. Yahweh's tender care of his returning exiles.

40:22. Did the prophet anticipate modern scientific theories?

40:31. Not an anticlimax; for it is more difficult to keep on with ordinary duties than to soar aloft in seasons of excitement.

41:2. The one from the east is Cyrus, king of Medo-Persia.

41:23. The prophet sarcastically bids the gods of the heathen to do something; whether good or evil, it matters not.

41:25. Cyrus. Media was to the northeast.

42:1–4. The first "servant" poem. There are three others: 49:1–6; 50:4–9; 52:13 to 53:12. The great problem is the identity of this servant. In 41:8 Israel is called Yahweh's servant, thus leading many to refer these passages to God's purpose for Israel. Yet 42:18f. implies the failure of Israel as a true servant. And how could Israel "raise up the tribes of Jacob" (49:6) when she already consists of those tribes? Accordingly, many refer to the servant poems as personifying the pious kernel in Israel, the true Israel. Against this conception is the prophet's inclusion of himself among those benefited by the servant's work (53:5, 8b). Certainly the inspired prophet would be classed among the pious remnant. The passages find their most natural application as applied to the Messiah and his ministry. The thought in 40–55 is that Israel as a nation is to be rejected because of her unfaithfulness. The individual Messiah, who is the true Israel, will accomplish the salvation of both Jew and Gentile.

There is a possibility of a progression in these poems. The nation Israel may be the servant in the first passage, only to retire in the second poem in favor of the individual Messiah who succeeds where she fails. Yet in his success, Israel ultimately achieves God's purposes. Whatever view is correct as to the prophet's identification of the servant, it was surely Jesus who alone fulfilled its intention.

42:22. The fate of the exiles of 586 was much worse than those of earlier captivities.

44:9–20. One of the most caustic condemnations of idols in the Old Testament.

44:28 to 45:6. God's purpose for Cyrus. It is for the sake of his people, who shall rebuild the Temple. This is a marvelous prediction whether by the Isaiah of the eighth century or a contemporary prophet. Cyrus was not a worshiper of Yahweh, but accomplished his will, just as the Assyrians had done.

45:7. Yahweh is not the creator of moral evil. Notice that the "evil" referred to is the opposite of "peace," not of "righteousness." It should be rendered "calamity."

46:1. Bel and Nebo were gods of Babylon. The heathen's religion is a load, not a lift. The picture consists of a frightened people fleeing with their gods.

46:3–4. On the other hand Yahweh carries his people; it is he who rescues them.

46:11. Cyrus again.

47:1–2. The privileged princess becomes a shameless slave.

48:16. Is the "Spirit" the subject or the object of "sent"? If the verse reads "and now the Lord Jehovah and his Spirit hath sent me," we have a hint at the personality of the Holy Spirit in the Old Testament. The Hebrew is ambiguous, so no certain conclusion can be made.

49:1–6. The second servant poem. After this the nation Israel is never referred to as Yahweh's servant. Israel is addressed as wife or son, but never as servant. The followers of the true servant are referred to later in the plural, "servants." This is further indication of the failure of the nation Israel and the recognition of an individual from Israel through whom God's purpose for the world would be accomplished.

49:3. The individual Messiah is the true Israel.

50:4–9. The third servant poem. The servant is faithful but will be rejected.

52:7. The announcement of the Return from Captivity.

52:11. A charge applicable to God's ministers today.

52:13 to 53:12. The fourth and greatest servant poem. Here we have prophesied the rejection and eventual triumph of the Messiah. His vicarious suffering will bring about the salvation of all peoples.

54:2. William Carey's famous missionary text.

Chapter 55. A lovely invitation to partake of the salvation provided by God.

Chapters 56–66. The so-called Trito-Isaiah. Duhm held that these passages were written in the age of Ezra-Nehemiah. At that time, however, the Temple had been rebuilt. Yet 63:18; 64:10–12, indicate that Jerusalem and the Temple are still in ruins. A far better date for the scene of the prophecies, if not by Isaiah, is the Palestine of the period 537–520 B.C., just after the return from Babylon and before the rebuilding of the Temple (520–516). In this view the author of 40–55 returned with the exiles in 537 and wrote 56–66 in Judea.

58:4. Fasting induced an irritable temper, so that the poor servants got many a kick and blow.

59:1–8. A dark picture of human sin. When Paul would draw an indictment against both Jew and Gentile, he quotes Isaiah 59:7f. along with Psalms (Rom. 3:9–18).

60:12. Gentile nations to be servants of the Jews. Not the prophet's final word, for which we are grateful.

61:1–3. Classified by some as a fifth servant poem. Jesus in Luke 4:18ff., at the beginning of his ministry, quotes this passage and announces its fulfilment in him. It is significant that he broke off reading in the middle of 61:2. The quotation in Luke is from the LXX.

62:5. Instead of "thy sons shall marry thee," an incongruous figure, read "thy builder shall marry thee."

62:6–7. As George W. Truett often said, "Plead the promises of God."

63:1–9. Not a picture of Calvary but of the overthrow of Yahweh's enemies. The blood is not that of the Messiah but of the peoples that have been destroyed.

63:10. Another hint at the personality of the Spirit. Only personalities can grieve. Nowhere except here and in Psalm 51:11 is the Spirit of God referred to as "holy" in the Old Testament. The Hebrew idiom is "spirit of holiness."

65:24. Prayer may receive its answer even before it can find expression.

66:3. Sacrifice without the proper spirit is heartless cruelty and brazen blasphemy.

66:13. Here is a rare figure of Yahweh likening himself to a mother.

66:18–21. There is much ambiguity in this passage. However, it presents some of the most advanced Old Testament teachings concerning the place of the Gentiles in God's plan. The thought seems to be that God will save a remnant from the Gentiles who shall bring the scattered Jews to Yahweh as their offering. These Gentile missionaries shall be rewarded for their work by being given equal privileges with the Jews as priests and Levites.

66:22. God keeps his plan for the world ever before him, as an architect surveys his blueprints.

66:24. A hint of eternal hell. This rubbish heap for God's enemies burns but is never consumed. The picture here, however, is an earthly one. The figure is taken from the valley of Hinnom where the dead bodies of the outcasts from Jerusalem were cast to burn and rot.

NAHUM

THE MAN. "Nahum" is a name which occurs nowhere else in the Old Testament. It is based on a root which expresses the idea of consolation. It probably means "the comforter, the consoler, the bringer of consolation." Nahum is called "the Elkoshite." This title suggests that he was a native of Elkosh. Elkosh is not mentioned anywhere in the Bible, so there is considerable difference of opinion as to its location. There are four principal theories: (1) Some have identified it with a modern village, Elkush or Alkosh, a town located about twenty-four miles north of Nineveh. (2) An older tradition locates Elkosh in Galilee, identifying it with modern El Kouze. (Cf. Jerome.) (3) Some have identified Elkosh with Capernaum (Village of Nahum). Those who accept this view believe that the name was changed from Elkosh to Capernaum in honor of the town's first citizen. (4) Most modern scholars hold that Elkosh was in southern Judah, not far from the home of Micah.

The date of Nahum's ministry must be determined on the basis of internal evidence. (Cf. 3:8–10.) It is apparent that Nahum preached after the sack of Thebes (663 B.C.) and prior to the destruction of Nineveh (612 B.C.). Beyond this general statement it is difficult to go. Some scholars maintain that Nahum was active around 630–612 B.C., others that he should be placed about 650. With our present scanty knowledge of both periods, the prophecy of Nahum agrees with either equally well. The earlier date is to be preferred, for it explains the fresh memory of the sack of Thebes revealed in the book.

THE BOOK. Until the latter part of the nineteenth century this prophecy was considered a unity. During recent years it has been the custom among some scholars to claim that prefixed to the genuine prophecies of Nahum (2:3 to 3:19) is an alphabetic psalm of late origin (1:1 to 2:2). Pfeiffer observes: "A redactor living about the year 300 B.C. prefaced Nahum's superb ode . . . with an alphabetic psalm of his own time. Of this psalm he vaguely remembered the first part, substituting for the rest remarks of his own, some of which were Biblical quotations quoted from memory."[1] However, the reconstruction of such a psalm is improbable, and is only a question of academic concern.

Most modern Old Testament scholars assign to Nahum an exalted place among the poet-prophets of Israel. Of all the prophets, Nahum is the one who approaches most nearly to Isaiah in poetic ability. G. A. Smith states: "His language is strong and brilliant; his rhythm rumbles and rolls, leaps and flashes, like the horse and chariots he describes."[2]

THE MESSAGE. The theme of the book is the destruction of Nineveh. Since that city was made the capital of Assyria by Sennacherib, it had been the symbol of treachery and oppression to all the Hebrew people. It was built to endure, located on the eastern bank of the Tigris, fortified with walls and moats. The walls were seven and one half miles in circumference, and they were wide enough for three chariots to drive abreast on their top. Under Assurbanipal the kingdom began to weaken, and upon his death in 626 rapidly disintegrated. Nineveh fell in 612 before an onslaught of Babylonians and Medes. Never was there a more complete destruction. Alexander the Great marched over the ruins without being aware of their presence. Today two great mounds are known to mark its site, but they were not discovered until 1842.

Some writers are very critical of the book of Nahum, even denying its right to be in the canon because of what they consider to be its shallow and narrow vindictiveness. He nowhere accuses his own people of sin as did the other Old Testament prophets. Such a criticism, however, is without imagination or sympathy. Nahum gives expression to more than mere personal

---

[1]R. H. Pfeiffer, *Introduction to the Old Testament* (third edition, New York: Harper and Brothers, 1941), p. 594.

[2]G. A. Smith, *op. cit.*, II, 90.

passion; he bears witness to a great principle. He sees that the universe is so constituted that kingdoms built on force and fraud must eventually collapse, whereas the kingdom of God reared on a foundation of truth and righteousness must ultimately triumph. In the destruction of Nineveh the moral government of the universe was vindicated.

OUTLINE OF THE BOOK

1. The Nature of Israel's God Assures the Destruction of Nineveh. 1:2–15

    (1) Yahweh's personal nature. 2–3a
    (2) His relation to the material world. 3b–6
    (3) His relation to men. 7f.
    (4) Consequent destruction of the Assyrians for the oppression of his people. 9–15

2. Vivid Picture of the Siege and Capture of Nineveh. Chapter 2

3. Cause of Nineveh's Destruction. Chapter 3

    (1) Constant war and violence. 1–7
    (2) She is no better than Thebes, which suffered captivity. In like manner she also shall suffer; for her fortresses are weak, her people like women, and her kings asleep. 8–19

ZEPHANIAH

THE MAN. Zephaniah means "Yahweh hides" or "whom Yahweh has hidden." This name suggests that the prophet was born during the reign of Manasseh when many loyal servants of Yahweh laid down their lives for their faith. Zephaniah's parents may have given him his name with the hope that God would protect and use him. Zephaniah likely had royal blood in his veins. The title verse traces his family back to Hezekiah, king of Judah (727–698 B.C.). If the tradition is trustworthy, Zephaniah was a distant relative of Josiah. He lived in the Southern Kingdom, was probably a citizen of Jerusalem. (Cf. 1:4; 1:10–11.)

Zephaniah prophesied during the reign of Josiah (640–609 B.C.). The question arises, did he preach over this long a time, or was his work confined to a more limited period? It is impossible to answer with absolute certainty. Internal evidence points to the conclusion that most of Zephaniah's preaching was done prior to 621 B.C. (Cf. 1:3–5; 8–9, 12, where the evils described are those preceding the reform of Josiah.) A careful reading of Zephaniah's prophecy brings one to the conviction that the prophecy was delivered in a time of crisis. Some plundering invader was loose, threatening Judah and the surrounding nations. A Scythian invasion of 626 B.C. may have been the historical background of Zephaniah's work. Perhaps as Joel saw in the plague of the locusts a harbinger of the day of Yahweh, Zephaniah saw in the advance of the Scythians a foreshadowing of the great day of divine judgment. If this be true, Zephaniah may have begun his work about the same time as

Jeremiah (626 B.C.). How long he prophesied we do not know.

Zephaniah was not outstanding, but he was earnest, straight-forward, and severe. He has been called the fiercest of the prophets, for he was the herald of universal judgment. Through judgment would come redemption, of his own people first, then of the nations. Zephaniah went beyond Nahum in breadth of view and depth of insight.

THE BOOK. The authenticity of every verse in chapters 2–3 and of several verses in chapter 1 has been questioned by one or more scholars. The passages most generally rejected are 2:1–3; 2:8–11; 3:9–10, 14–20, chiefly upon the ground of Zephaniah's being exclusively a prophet of doom. Regardless of the date of authorship of the passages, we are concerned with the book as we now have it from the Lord. Its present form has the final message intended for God's people. The central emphasis of the book is upon "the day of Yahweh." The ancient hymn, "Dies Irae," was inspired by its atmosphere of fire and brimstone. Its teachings about that day of judgment are significant:

1. The day of Yahweh is imminent. 1:14
2. It will be a day of terror. 1:15
3. It is coming as a judgment for sin. 1:17
4. It will be accompanied by great convulsions in nature. 1:15
5. It will fall upon all creation, man and beast, Hebrew and foreigner. 1:2–3; 2:4–15
6. Only a remnant will survive it. These will enjoy the glories of the messianic age. 2:3; 3:9ff.

NOTES ON IMPORTANT PASSAGES

1:5–6. Three kinds of sinners to be destroyed: (1) those who are divided in their allegiance to Yahweh; (2) those who have once served Yahweh but now do not; (3) those who have never sought the true God.

1:12. Wine, when allowed to remain undisturbed too long, turned to sugar. This was called "settling on the lees." Such wine was useless and distasteful.

2:11. A glorious promise of worldwide worship of the true God.

3:9. Just as the world had been divided by the confusion of tongues at the Tower of Babel, some day its peoples shall again speak the same language and pull together as oxen yoked shoulder to shoulder. The prophet clearly sees that man's differences in language certainly impede his efforts for peace. This unity of language, however, cannot be achieved except as the nations seek to serve the one Lord.

3:12–13. Note the characteristics of those who compose the remnant. They are a thoroughly chastised group, free from insincerity, who put their sole trust in Yahweh.

OUTLINE OF THE BOOK

Title 1:1. Text of the divine message. 1:2–6. The coming day of Yahweh will mean the destruction of all things, especially of idolatry from Judah.

1. Judah Shall Be Punished Severely. 1:7–2:3

   (1) All classes of sinners. 1:7–13
   (2) How terrible the day of Yahweh's wrath! 1:14–18
   (3) Therefore, the meek of the earth must seek the Lord that he may hide them in that day. 2:1–3

2. The Heathen Also Shall Be Punished. 2:4–15

   (1) The Philistines. 4–7
   (2) Moab and Ammon. 8–11
   (3) Ethiopia and Assyria. 12–15

3. Though Richly Deserving Complete Destruction, a Remnant of Judah and of the Heathen Shall Be Saved. 3:1–20

   (1) Picture of Judah's obstinacy in sin and of Yahweh's righteousness. 1–7

(2) Because of Judah's persistency in sin, the heathen are to be cleansed by punishment, and finally converted to Yahweh. 8–10

(3) Zion also shall be sifted and purified, and then honored in all the earth. The people, redeemed, praise Yahweh who abides in the midst of them. 11–20

Habakkuk

THE MAN. The name is derived from a root meaning "to caress, embrace," a designation given either because he was dearly beloved of his parents or because they hoped that he would embrace God and his fellow man in his sympathies. We know nothing of his personal life. The apocryphal work, *Bel and the Dragon* (vv. 33–39), claims he carried pottage to Daniel in the lions' den. According to another such work, *Lives of the Prophets,* he was a man of the tribe of Simeon who fled upon Nebuchadnezzar's advance to take Jerusalem (587) but returned after the fall, dying two years before the return from captivity. Eusebius states in his *Onomasticon* that in his day his tomb was shown both at Gibeah and Keilah!

The time of the prophecy can be determined with considerable exactness. Assyria is off the scene, and Chaldea is coming into power. The time, therefore, must be after 612 B.C. Judah has not yet been invaded, so it must be before the first invasion in 605 B.C. The social and moral evils of the time pictured by the prophet are those of the reign of Jehoiakim. After the death of Josiah the people reverted to the sins they were committing before his reforms.

With Habakkuk a new note appears in prophecy. His utterances are different from those of his predecessors in many respects. The former prophets had addressed Israel on the part of God, but he addresses God on the part of Israel. Their problem was the sin of the people, but his was the inaction of God. In Habakkuk we have the beginning of religious speculation in Israel. His problem is the prosperity of the wicked Chaldeans, while the righteous suffer oppression. The facts of life do not agree with traditional teaching about God, so the prophet begins to ask questions. However, his questions are to God and not against him. As he waits in his watchtower for the answer from God, it comes to him. Evil is by its very nature self-destructive, but the righteous man *lives* in his faithfulness. Though evil seems to prosper for a while, the righteous alone have permanent life.

Notes on Important Passages

1:2–4. Who are these unrighteous mentioned here? Some say Egypt or Assyria. It is most probably the wicked element in Judah. (Cf. "the law is slacked," 1:4, hardly applicable to foreigners.)

2:1. Habakkuk has his reply ready before God answers. He feels his problem is impossible to solve.

2:3. God's reply to man's questions may delay but will surely come.

2:4. The key verse of the book. The wicked is puffed up, unsound, hence transitory, only for a moment. The righteous man has permanence as he abides in his faithfulness to God. The Old Testament has no word for faith; the Hebrews did not think in the abstract ideology of the Greeks. They were a practical people who dealt in concrete terms. Faith to them consisted of a manifestation of righteousness. Yet this manifestation resulted from a trust of God. It remained for Paul to take the concrete Old Testament term, interpret it, enlarge it, and show its fulfilment in the gospel message. In essence, therefore, this immortal statement teaches that the wicked have existence, but the righteous live.[1]

2:14. A majestic assurance of the spread of the Kingdom.

2:20. Perhaps a warning to Habakkuk, also, who in 2:1 was intending to make answer when God replied to him.

Chapter 3. This psalm is denied to Habakkuk, mainly because of the evidence it presents of having been used in Temple worship. (Cf. 3:1a, 19b.) This adaptation could have been made at

[1] Cf. W. J. Farley, *The Progress of Old Testament Prophecy* (New York: Fleming H. Revell Company, 1925), pp. 136–140.

a later date; however, Habakkuk was afraid that retribution upon Chaldea might wait until the latter days. He wanted it immediately—"in the midst of the years."

3:3a. Not a statement of the origin of God but of his coming from Sinai to help his people.

3:16ff. Habakkuk knows now that help will not come immediately but that it will long delay. Until that day, he states in beautiful poetry, *he* will live in *his* faithfulness.

OUTLINE OF THE BOOK

Superscription. 1:1

1. Impending Punishment of Judah. Chapter 1

   (1) The prophet cries to Yahweh for deliverance from violence, iniquity, social disorder.
   The law is slacked and judgment perverted by the wicked. 2–4

   (2) In answer, Yahweh points to the coming scourge of Chaldeans, who are cruel, ambitious, proud, and successful. 5–11

   (3) The prophet's cry to God. How can a holy God use such a cruel instrument as Chaldea? 12–17

2. Impending Punishment of the Chaldeans. Chapter 2

   (1) The prophet takes his stand to see what Yahweh will answer. 1

   (2) Yahweh instructs him to write the vision for clearness and permanence. 2f.

   (3) The oracle of consolation. 4f.
   a. "The just shall live in his faithfulness"
   b. The unjust shall be visited with woes

   (4) Vision of the ultimate destruction of the Chaldeans in five woes. 6–20
   a. Woe because of pride and ambition. 6–8
   b. Woe because of pride and greed. 9–11

    c. Woe because of cruelty. 12–14

    d. Woe because of drunkenness. Yahweh shall now put the cup to their lips. 15–17

    e. Woe because of idolatry. 18–20

3. The Prophet's Prayer (Vision). Chapter 3
   Title 1.

    (1) Prayer to Yahweh: "Revive thy work" 2

    (2) Review of God's work in the past history of Israel, in an exalted strain of poetry. 3–15
        At Sinai (3f.), plagues in the desert (5), terror of the nations at Israel's coming (6f.), crossing the Red Sea and the Jordan (8–10), Joshua at Beth-horon (11), conquest of the land (12–15), all for the salvation of Yahweh's people.

    (3) In view of past wonderful deliverances, the prophet will, in the midst of the most trying circumstances, rejoice in Yahweh his God. 16–19

JEREMIAH

THE MAN. We know more about Jeremiah than any other prophet of the Old Testament. His open soul, and the faithfulness of the scribe Baruch, make the world forever grateful. The name of the prophet means "Yahweh hurls," evidently expressing the hope of his parents that the Lord would use him in helping to alleviate the conditions prevalent during the reign of wicked Manasseh, who was ruling at Jeremiah's birth. From a priestly family, the prophet had the advantage of a cultivated, godly home. Anathoth, but a few miles from Jerusalem, was a quiet, secluded community.

Jeremiah during his youth was a careful student of Hosea, for his earlier prophecies show a direct influence of that prophet. However, he never allowed himself to be the slave of another man's style. Upon all his prophecies is the imprint of his own personality. In later years the influence of Hosea is less noticeable. World conditions were the major factor in the call of Jeremiah. The whole universe seemed to be in a state of flux. In 626 B.C., Assurbanipal died, and Nineveh was under pressure by Babylonia and Media. The Scythians, a savage horde from the northern mountains, were on the loose. Josiah, a young king and ardent worshiper of Yahweh, had succeeded Manasseh and Amon, but the hearts of his people had changed very little.

Later Josiah was to conduct the most complete reform Judah had ever known. In 621, five years after Jeremiah was given his world commission, the book of Deuteronomy, long lost in the desecrated Temple, was discovered by workers repairing the damage done during Manasseh's reign. Most modern scholars hold that the book had been written a few years earlier and was not from the hand of Moses; that it was a "pious fraud," a work composed by the prophetic party and hidden in the Temple so it would be thought to be of ancient authority. The purpose of this attempt was the centralization of worship. They felt that most of the ills of their times were due to the fact that the people were divided in their religious faith. Yahweh was worshiped on every high hill and in many diverse manners. If religion could be centralized at the Jerusalem Temple, it could be made uniform and would help to unite the nation. However, the evidence at hand today seems to indicate that the book of Deuteronomy is older than the reign of Manasseh and was already considered to be of divine authority before discovered in 621 B.C. The scope of this present work, however, does not allow a discussion of this lengthy, involved evidence.

At first Jeremiah seemed to favor the reform, perhaps preaching in its behalf (cf. chapter 11). However, as he began to see that many of the people were trusting in its externals and not the real purpose, he turned upon the worshipers who flocked to divine services (chapter 7, perhaps in Josiah's reign, or the early days of Jehoiakim). Apparently Jeremiah and Josiah were on the best of terms. No one was more grieved than he at the great king's untimely death. However, Jehoiakim was Jeremiah's deadliest enemy. Jeremiah's experiences during the reign of Zedekiah were more disagreeable; however, secretly, Zedekiah respected Jeremiah and sought his advice. Perhaps the most peaceful days of the prophet's life were those in the company of Gedaliah, the son of Ahikam, whose family had always befriended Jeremiah (chapter 26). The prophet died as he had lived, in the heartbreak of preaching to an unresponsive people.

The character of Jeremiah is most complex, for he was a man of conflicting emotions. His experience as a prophet, however, can be best understood as we contrast his call with that of Isaiah. In Isaiah, chapter 6, we see a prophet volunteering for service. In Jeremiah, chapter 1, our prophet shrinks away from the task but lets God have the final word. There is no word of personal consent on the part of Jeremiah. This was a task he had no inclination to perform, but he knew no way of avoiding it. Later he expressed his experience in a heartrending cry of anguish: "O Jehovah, thou hast persuaded me, and I was persuaded; thou art stronger than I, and hast prevailed" (20:7). With such conflicts in his own soul, and a discouraging ministry without, Jeremiah presents a pathetic picture. Yet there was a spark of unquenchable fire within him that challenges the best in every man. He could not play traitor to the God who reigned in his heart. "And if I say, I will not make mention of him [Yahweh], nor speak any more in his name, then there is in my heart as it were a burning fire shut up in my bones, and I am weary with forbearing, and I cannot contain" (20:9).

Many elements contributed to the conflicts within the breast of Jeremiah. Evidently he was a man of considerable culture and nobility. When he was in trouble over his preaching (chapter 26), it was the nobles who saved him. He possessed property and was able to buy land during the siege of Jerusalem. This cultural position produced in him a sensitive nature, further enhanced by a broad education. He was thoroughly familiar with his nation's history and the complicated world situation. Of a shy and gentle nature, therefore, he naturally recoiled against a ministry in which he would be in the limelight and undergo the most harsh treatment and criticism. How he hated to preach the bitter denunciation that his people's sins demanded! How he longed to be able to preach love and peace!

Jeremiah's sensitive nature cried out for companionship and sympathy. Yet he was forbidden to marry and lived in the loneliness that only great men know. Not even faithful Baruch could supply his hunger for friendship and appreciation. Yet all this heartache drove him closer to his God. In him he found companionship and relief. Yahweh's will became the consuming passion of his life and in his doing it, the inner conflict was eventually dissolved.

It is not surprising, as Gordon[1] has so capably demonstrated, that men thought that Jesus was Jeremiah come back from the dead. There are many striking comparisons between the two: (1) The historical situation was curiously alike. Jerusalem was about to be destroyed; religion was buried under the crust of formalism; pressure from without Palestine required a world

---

[1] Cf. T. C. Gordon, *The Rebel Prophet* (London: James Clarke and Company, 1931), pp. 227–256.

message. (2) Both grew up in a Palestinian village, thought in terms of country scenes. (3) Jesus and Jeremiah both came from a distinguished line of ancestors and from godly homes. (4) Each had come to a sense of divine destiny at the time of youth. (5) Neither ever married. (6) The supreme and critical moment of the ministry of each was the condemnation of worshipers in the Temple. (7) They were both opposed by their kinsmen. (8) Neither seems to have written a line. (9) There was a tender, almost effeminate strain in both characters. (10) Loneliness was the lot of each. Both had an intimate and compensating fellowship with God.

Yet there are striking differences between these two. Jesus was loving and sweet to the end. Jeremiah was bitter and revengeful. Jesus never questioned the goodness of God; Jeremiah filled the air with complaints. Jesus was without sin; Jeremiah possessed all the weakness of the human flesh.

THE BOOK. The arrangement of the book is the most confused in the Old Testament. There is a clear grouping of Jeremiah's earlier prophecies (1–25), biographical material (chapters 26–45), oracles against foreign nations (46–51), and an historical appendix (52). Aside from this broad outline it is almost impossible to arrange the material chronologically. Each scholar emerges from the attempt with a different scheme. Yet one would expect, of all the books in the Old Testament, that Jeremiah would be the best arranged, since Baruch so carefully followed his master's every word and act.

It is difficult to discover the reason for this confusion. A clue is found in an examination of the LXX, where the differences between the Hebrew and Greek texts are greater than anywhere else in the Old Testament. In fact, one eighth of the Massoretic text is not in the LXX. Some of these variations may be explained in numerous ways: (1) The LXX makes little attempt at a literal translation of the Hebrew. (2) The manuscripts were often illegible. (3) Many errors were unconscious mistakes of the copyists. (4) Intentional alterations sometimes occurred. When all these matters are considered, many differences are still left unexplained. The foreign prophecies (46–51), for instance, stand in the LXX after verse 13 of chapter 25. Apparently both these texts have been derived from an earlier manuscript, and not the LXX from the Hebrew. Years of copying, therefore, may have resulted in some disarrangement.

During the life of Jeremiah the book went through several editions also. In chapter 36 we learn that Baruch first wrote down his prophecies in 604 B.C. They were burned by Jehoiakim and were dictated again with additions. These prophecies are probably those found in chapters 1–25. In addition, Baruch must have made a further compilation during the closing days of Jeremiah's life. After Jeremiah died, the book went through its final editing as did most of the Old Testament books. Just when this occurred cannot be determined. It could be only through the guidance of our Lord that the books of the Old Testament were preserved as wonderfully as we know them to be over long centuries of editing and copying.

Both prose and poetry are found among the prophecies of Jeremiah, his poetical oracles being his most remarkable. Jeremiah's favorite measure was the *qinah* (dirge) with a 3:2 rhythm. Bernard Duhm has attempted to limit Jeremiah's genuine oracles to those rendered in this measure, but it cannot be denied that he may have used different media for varying situations. A prophet is not always in the mood for poetry.

As a poet Jeremiah does not rank with Nahum or Isaiah. Yet he was a master of metaphor and simile. One can be sure as he reads that each verse is wrung from Jeremiah's own heartagony. The prophet could not have expressed his deepest emotion except through lyric poetry. No other form would do.

LIFE OF JEREMIAH

1. From His Birth Until the Conquest of Palestine by Nebuchadnezzar in 605 B.C. (fourth year of Jehoiakim)

   (1) During Josiah's reign.
       a. Born in a priestly family at Anathoth, about three miles northeast of Jerusalem.
       b. Began to prophesy, while still a young man, in the thirteenth year of Josiah, 626 B.C. Picture his timid-

ity and how God made him strong to speak the truth. Much of the material in Jeremiah 1–6 belongs to this period (Jer. 3:6). Jeremiah's zeal as a prophet seen in 6:10f.

    c. Witnessed the great reformation in the eighteenth year of Josiah. Jeremiah familiar with the Law, especially the book of Deuteronomy.

    d. Was present at the funeral of the good king Josiah, and lamented over his death (2 Chron. 35:25).

(2) During the early years of Jehoiakim's reign.

    a. In danger of losing his life, in the beginning of Jehoiakim's reign, on account of faithful preaching. Read chapter 26 in full. Much of chapters 7–20 belongs to the early part of Jehoiakim's reign. See especially 7:1–20; 9:1f.

    b. Jeremiah's life threatened by men of Anathoth (some place during Josiah's reign, just after 621 B.C.). 11:18–23. His own family also against him. 12:5f. Cursed by all. 15:10

    c. Forbidden to marry. 16:2

    d. Put in the stocks by Pashur. 20:1f. Outburst of the prophet's disappointment and indignation. 20:14–18

2. From the Coming of Nebuchadnezzar in 605 B.C., to the Beginning of the Siege of Jerusalem in 588 B.C.

(1) During the remainder of Jehoiakim's reign.

    a. Great victory of the Babylonians at Carchemish in 605 B.C. See Jer. 46:1–12. Jeremiah preaches submission to Babylon. Chapter 25

    b. Attempt to capture and kill Jeremiah in the fifth year of Jehoiakim (604 B.C.). The roll of his prophecies is burned by Jehoiakim; but Jeremiah is commanded to reproduce it, and many other like words are added. Jer. 36:9–32

(2) Under Zedekiah.

    a. Jeremiah preaches submission to the king of Babylon throughout Zedekiah's reign. He announces to surrounding heathen kings and to Zedekiah that Nebuchadnezzar is to rule over the nations. Chapter 27

    b. Contest with Hananiah. Chapter 28

    c. Contest by letter with false prophets in Babylon. Chapter 29

    d. As the Babylonians draw near to attack Judah, Jeremiah advises Zedekiah to submit to Nebuchadnezzar. Chapter 21

3. Experiences During the Siege of Jerusalem, 588–6 B.C.

    (1) During the first stage of the siege, Jeremiah announces to Zedekiah the certain fall of Jerusalem. 34:1–7

    (2) When the Chaldeans leave the siege of Jerusalem to meet the army of Pharaoh-hophra, Jeremiah predicts their return to capture the city. The prophet is arrested in the gate of the city as he is about to leave for Anathoth, and confined in a dungeon in the house of Jonathan the scribe. 37:3–15

    (3) At his own request, the prophet is transferred by Zedekiah to the court of the guard. 37:16–21. (This court was in the king's house. Jer. 32:2.)

    (4) Shows faith in a return from Exile by purchase of a field at Anathoth. 32:6ff.

    (5) Jeremiah is accused of treason and cast into a pit to die, but is delivered by an Ethiopian and restored to the court of the guard. 38:1–13

    (6) Private interview with Zedekiah in the Temple. 38:14–28

4. Jeremiah's Experiences in the Period After the Capture of Jerusalem

    (1) In chains as far as Ramah. Jer. 40:1 (For brief statement of Nebuchadnezzar's attitude to the prophet, see Jer. 39:11–14.)

(2) Released by Nebuchadnezzar's general, and encouraged to remain in Judah. 40:2–5

(3) Dwells with the new governor, Gedaliah. 40:6

(4) After the assassination of Gedaliah, goes with Johanan to Bethlehem. 41:16–18

(5) Carried into Egypt by force. 42:1 to 43:7

(6) Predicts distress to Jews in Egypt, and the coming of Nebuchadnezzar. 43:8–13

(7) Earnest but futile effort of the aged prophet to wean the Jews from idolatry. Chapter 44

Notes on Important Passages

1:5. Jeremiah a man of destiny. He is to have a worldwide mission.

1:6. A sincere reticence. God does not rebuke Jeremiah as he did Moses. The prophet is not saying "I won't" but "I can't," a deep sense of his unworthiness. The word "child" is best translated "youth," for it is used in the Old Testament of persons varying from infancy to forty-five years of age. Jeremiah was probably about twenty.

1:7–8. Jeremiah told that his success not dependent upon his own strength, but upon the God who would be constantly at his side. God never sends a man unless he goes with him.

1:10. The task of every true prophet of God: to destroy only in order to build a better structure, to uproot only to plant a better seed.

1:11. A play on words in the Hebrew. The almond tree, because of its early awakening in the spring, was called a "wake" tree (Heb. *shaked*). As Jeremiah, wondering when God would intervene in the world, saw the "wake" tree, the word of the Lord came to him, "I, too, am awake (*shoked*), waiting until the proper time."

2:10. Isles of Kittim were the western limits of Jeremiah's world. Kedar, Arabian territory, was the eastern limit. "Go as far west or east as you can . . ."

2:11. The heathen whose gods have no actual existence do

better than Israel. They remain true to these nonentities while Israel forsakes the one living God of the universe.

2:13. The picture is that of a valley at whose head is a wonderfully fresh spring. Yet for their water supply the inhabitants are feverishly digging cisterns that cannot even hold water.

2:23c–25. Translate with *The Abingdon Bible Commentary:* "Thou dromedary in heat, changing its mates. Thou desert wild-ass, snuffing up the wind in its lust, which any male that wants it need not weary itself to discover, since in its season anyone may find it. Do not run your feet sore and your throat dry."

2:36a. An accurate description of modern society also.

3:16. Jeremiah sees the time when the ark of the covenant will no longer be needed. He is the outstanding prophet of spiritual religion which is independent of all externals. As he saw that the Temple must go (chapter 7) and the nation be destroyed, he was driven to the truth that true religion must be independent of all such outward form. The externals of religion are helpful as an aid to expression and a reminder of truth, but they are not the essentials of faith. As externals crumble, a vital religion will create new ones for its expression, and their going, despite the alarmed cries of institutionalism, will never destroy that inner experience that characterizes true faith.

4:5ff. This passage and others in this chapter, continuing through chapter 6, have caused scholars great concern. Jeremiah is speaking of an invasion from the north by some fierce nation. What is this army? There are many suggestions: (1) The Scythians, a primitive, ferocious people from the territory beyond Asia Minor. However, they did not carry on the kind of warfare described in these passages. (2) The Babylonians. However, Babylon was not yet a world threat. (3) First Jeremiah spoke of the Scythians. When they passed by Judah and were bought off by the Egyptians, Jeremiah revised his prophecies to apply to the Babylonians. Such an act, however, would hardly be worthy of the great prophet. (4) Jeremiah did not have any particular nation in mind. He simply knew that one would come from the north. The sins of the people demanded it.

The fourth explanation may be the correct one. However, it is not improbable that by 626 Jeremiah could see that Babylon was on her way to power. Assyria was already crumbling. Indeed, it was Babylon who fulfilled the prophecies.

6:16. Jeremiah urges the people to stop for a moment and examine their way. He urges upon them the old way, not because it is old, but because it has been tested and found good. His hearers, however, prefer novelty to reality.

Chapter 7. Jeremiah's great Temple sermon. Cf. chapter 26.

7:11. Cf. Matt. 21:13. Robbers retire to their den to hide away, just as the Israelites come to the Temple to escape the consequence of their sins, so that they may sin all the more.

7:12. Shiloh, the first permanent sanctuary (1 Sam. chapter 1), was destroyed. Why not this one?

7:21–26. The majority of scholars claim that Jeremiah is denying any Mosaic origin of the sacrificial system. No command was given by God for sacrifice during the Exodus period. The claims of the Pentateuch cannot be taken seriously. More conservative scholars explain the statement in several ways: (1) The prophet spoke relatively, by exaggerated contrast. What he means is that God did not so much command sacrifice as he did obedience. Sacrifice is as nothing in comparison. (2) God urges the people to enjoy the sacrificial feasts themselves, for he did not command Moses *for the sake of sacrifices* (to get to eat them himself) but to assist in obedience. The Hebrew preposition will allow this translation. (3) When God finished bringing the people out of Egypt, he did not first command sacrifice. On the first day he gave the spiritual covenant based on obedience in Exodus, chapter 19; later he gave the sacrificial system. If the people neglect the spiritual basis of the Levitical system, the whole outward procedure is vain.

8:6. God is ready to forgive, but no man will examine his heart for sin.

8:8. Some interpret this as revealing the fact that Jeremiah had discovered that Deuteronomy was a "pious fraud." It has reference, however, to the erroneous scribal interpretations of the Law.

8:22. Medicinal herbs came from the mountains of Gilead, thus also the best physicians (46:11). The medicines and physicians are available, then why not a cure? Simply because the patient will not avail herself of the opportunity. Israel is failing fast because she will not turn to the One who can save her.

9:2. Jeremiah does not desire to get away from people but from responsibility. People who come to the inn will but spend the night and soon be gone, and as soon forgotten. As it is, he must be forever burdened by his hearers' sins. A vain but human desire. Jeremiah stayed with his people.

9:23–24. A true cause for glorying.

10:23–24. Man's inability to direct his own life. Israel's only hope is in the grace of God to forgive and guide.

12:1ff. One of those interesting passages that reveal so much of Jeremiah's inner life and thought. For other insights into his experience, cf. 1:4ff.; 4:10, 19; 6:11; 9:2–3; 11:18–23; 12:1–6; 15:10–21; 16:1–3; 17:9–18; 18:18–23; 20:7–18.

This conflict within the soul of Jeremiah was evidently soon settled, for beyond the reign of Jehoiakim we have no such passages. The solution seems to have been found in Jeremiah's practice of prayer as intimate conversation. He talked with his Lord as he would to a bosom friend, frankly and without reservation. Such sincerity is always rewarded.

12:5. "Take courage, Jeremiah, the worst is yet to come."

12:9. Attacked because she does not resemble the others. Often used to describe the church today.

13:1–7. Did Jeremiah make two trips to the far-off Euphrates just to teach this lesson? Some commentators note that the term "river" is not found here and suspect a textual corruption, since the terrain around the River Euphrates is not rocky. They would suggest an emendation to *Parah,* a near-by town, or to *Ephratah* (Bethlehem).

13:23. The power of habit.

15:10b. A touch of humor. Human nature does not change.

15:15–18. Note one of the causes of Jeremiah's misery. Observe the number of times he uses the first person singular in this passage. He was taking himself too seriously.

17:1. A permanent scar will remain.

17:9–10. The source of the world's ills. Only God can cure the disease. Jeremiah is the prophet of the religion of the heart, using the term more than any other prophet.

Chapter 18. The potter and the clay. Jeremiah's view of predestination. God has a purpose, but it may be resisted by mankind. Such rebellion will result in rejection and destruction. God will form another vessel to meet his demands. He cannot be ultimately defeated.

18:21–23. A terrible indictment. The Old Testament saint had little conception of Christian love. He was unable to hate sin and love the sinner. He hated both with the same fervor.

22:10a. A reference to the untimely death of Josiah.

23:30. Jeremiah opposes those ministers who preach other men's sermons and have no message of their own.

25:12. Not a promise of seventy years of captivity, but a seventy-year world supremacy of Babylon. (Cf. 29:10.)

25:26. Sheshach is Babylon.

28:8–9. Jeremiah, in preaching judgment, is in the prophetic succession. The man who promises peace to a sinful nation is immediately under suspicion. Jeremiah, loving his people, hoped Hananiah was correct (28:6). We note here that Jeremiah was not a bigot; he was willing to revise his theology if necessary, but he must receive orders from above (28:11b). Further word from Yahweh assured him, however, of his previous position.

29:4f. The captives of 597 appear to have had considerable freedom in Babylon.

29:13. Jeremiah anticipates the teaching of Jesus.

30:12, 17. The wound incurable, except by God.

31:20. How great is the love of God for sinful man!

31:26. Jeremiah is permitted in these chapters to preach words of hope and assurance. It was one of the few nights of his life when his sleep was sweet to him.

31:29. Jeremiah's teaching on individual responsibility. As he saw the nation disintegrating, he knew that the individual must be the medium through which God would work in the future, not the nation. This is the first clear formulation of this doctrine in the Old Testament.

31:31–34. The new covenant. It will be an affair of heart, between God and the individual man, based upon the forgiveness of sin. This is certainly in accord with Jeremiah's other teachings, in fact the climax of them.

In instituting the Lord's Supper, Jesus used Jeremiah's term to describe his work. "This cup is the new covenant in my blood. . . ." The early Christians in seeking for terms to distinguish between the older Hebrew Scriptures and the new Christian Writings, used the term "Old Covenant" for the former (describing God's dealing with the nation Israel), and "New Covenant" for the latter (describing the work of Christ in the individual heart). Our English rendering of the Latin as "Old Testament" and "New Testament" has lost this accurate and significant terminology.

32:9–14. This narrative throws valuable light on the business methods of the time: money was weighed; two deeds were made, one of which was closed and sealed, while the other was left open; valuable documents were sometimes preserved in earthen jars. We do not know whether the deed was inscribed on clay tablets in Babylonian fashion or on papyrus after the manner of the Egyptians.

34:17. Ironical play upon the word "liberty."

36:5. Probably means that Jeremiah was able to move about freely, except in the Temple area. (Cf. chapter 26.)

38:2. Jeremiah not a traitor. He had the best interests of his people at heart. A man's patriotism is not determined by his loyalty to the government's policies.

38:10. Why thirty men? Perhaps for protection against interference from Jeremiah's enemies.

39:7. An example of Babylonian cruelty. The last scene that Zedekiah saw before he was blinded was the death of his sons.

40:5. Jeremiah so overcome with grief over the tragedy being enacted in Judah, although the fulfilment of his predictions, that he cannot make a decision. Nebuzaradan in pity sends him to Gedaliah, sensing that it was not out of a love for Babylonia that he had urged his people to capitulate.

42:7. Even Jeremiah must wait patiently for word from God.

45:5a. A warning to every follower of God, as well as to Baruch.

Chapters 46–51. A series of foreign prophecies, most of which are denied to Jeremiah by modern scholars. They are certainly not his best work, and are very dependent upon other prophets. Chapters 50–51 show many elements of Jeremiah's style and may have been written by him after the fall of Jerusalem.

51:30. The army of Cyrus was admitted into Babylon without a battle. Only the citadel within the city resisted.

Outline of the Book

Title 1:1–3
1. Prophecies Belonging for the Most Part to the Reign of Josiah (626–609 B.C.). Chapters 1–6 (As we have them, these chapters may have been reworked during Jehoiakim's reign.)

Introduction.—Call of the prophet, followed by two visions foreshadowing his difficult and thankless task. 1:4–19
   a. Call of Jeremiah. 4–10
   b. Vision of the almond tree. 11f.
   c. Vision of the boiling caldron. 13–16
   d. Jeremiah to arraign princes, priests, and people of Judah. 17–19
(1) Unfaithful Israel rebuked by the faithful Yahweh. 2:1–3:5
(2) Yahweh earnestly urges both Israel and Judah to repent. 3:6–4:4
(3) Repeated and vivid announcement of impending invasion. 4:5–31
   a. Sound an alarm in Judah! A fierce invader is on his way to lay waste the land. 5–9
   b. The prophet complains that the people have been led to expect peace. 10
   c. The invaders, with swift horses and chariots, come from afar to execute Yahweh's judgments against sinful Jerusalem. 11–18
   d. Anguish of the prophet over the terrible destruction about to fall on his foolish people. 19–26
   e. It will be impossible to escape from the cruel spoilers. 27–31

(4) The fruitless search for a righteous man. 5:1 to 6:8

(5) The prophet's unsuccessful efforts to turn his people from their wickedness. 6:9–30

2. Prophecies Probably Belonging to the Reign of Jehoiakim (608–597 B.C.)

(1) Presumptuous Judah, on account of her idolatry and immorality, shall be laid waste. Chapters 7–10 (Chapter 26 gives an account of a dangerous experience through which Jeremiah passed in the beginning of Jehoiakim's reign. Read it, and then turn to 7:1–15 for the message which stirred his enemies to action.)

   a. Warning not to trust in the Temple and its sacrifices to save the land. 7:1 to 8:3

   b. Obstinate and wicked Judah shall be punished by captivity. 8:4 to 9:22. (Some scholars place 8:4 to 9:1 before the reign of Jehoiakim, just before and after the disaster at Megiddo.)

   c. True wisdom of knowing Yahweh contrasted with folly of idolatry. 9:23 to 10:25

(2) Conspiracy of Israel to break the covenant with Yahweh and destroy his prophet. Chapters 11–12

   a. The preaching of the covenant. 11:1–8 (perhaps during the reform of Josiah)

   b. Conspiracy in Anathoth to destroy Jeremiah, even the prophet's own family joining in the plot. 11:9 to 12:6. (Some refer this section to Josiah's reign.)

   c. Judah delivered into the hands of her enemies. In the future the heathen may, by obedience, have part with restored Israel in the blessing of Yahweh. 7–17

(3) Two symbols showing the character and fate of Judah. Chapter 13

   a. The marred girdle, a symbol of the marred pride of Judah. 1–11

   b. The broken bottles, a symbol of the destruction about to overtake Jerusalem. 12–14

   c. Tender appeal of the prophet as the twilight was turning to dense darkness. 15–17

    d. The flock of Yahweh scattered because of habitual unfaithfulness. 18–27

(4) Jeremiah, in opposition to the prophets of peace, announces the impending captivity of Judah. The prophet's trials grow heavier. Chapters 14–17
    a. Concerning the drought. Chapters 14, 15
    b. Jeremiah forbidden to marry, because of impending exile. But there shall be a return. Chapter 16
    c. The sin of Judah has kindled Yahweh's anger. Observance of the sabbath would bring a blessing. Chapter 17

(5) Two symbolical actions pointing to the outpouring of Yahweh's wrath upon Judah, with the prophet's trials in connection with them. Chapters 18–20
    a. The clay in the potter's hand. Chapter 18
    b. The potter's earthen bottle a symbol of Jerusalem, which is soon to be broken. 19:1–13
    c. Jeremiah's trials. 19:14 to 20:18

(6) Other prophecies of the reign of Jehoiakim.
    a. Group dating from the fourth year of Jehoiakim (605 B.C.). Chapters 46; 25; 36:1–8; 45
    b. Fifth year of Jehoiakim. The king burns the roll of Jeremiah's prophecies. 36:9–32
    c. Trials of the Rechabites, and the lesson from their steadfastness. Chapter 35. Cf. 2 Kings 24:2 with Jer. 35:11

3. Prophecies Probably Belonging to the Reign of Jehoiachin (597 B.C.). Against the Kings. 22:1 to 23:8 (of various dates, but in chronological order)

4. Prophecies and Events in the Reign of Zedekiah (597–586 B.C.)

(1) The two baskets of figs. Chapter 24
    a. The vision. 1–3
    b. The captives in Babylonia likened to good figs. 4–7
    c. The people in Jerusalem compared to bad figs. 8–10

EZEKIEL

THE PROPHET. Ezekiel ("God will strengthen") was a priest, son of a certain Buzi (1:3). As such, he belonged to the aristocracy of Jerusalem who, in the year 597 B.C., were deported along with Jehoiachin to Babylon. Here he lived at Tell-abib (3:15) by the Canal Chebar (1:1). Tell-abib ("the mound of corn-ears") is probably from Tel-abubu, "the mound of the flood." The Chebar is probably the modern Shatt-en-Nil, near which were discovered the archives of the banking firm of Murashi and Sons (464–405 B.C.), containing many Jewish names. Ezekiel was the husband of one wife, and, it would appear, childless (24:16–18). His house served as a meeting place among the elders of the exiles; he was, therefore, evidently a person of consideration (8:1; 14:1; 20:1). In the year 592 he was called by an imposing vision to be a prophet (1:2ff.). His prophetic activities fall into two periods, divided by the fall of Jerusalem in 586 B.C. (33:21f.). From 592 to 586 he was exclusively a preacher of repentance and judgment. In discourses and by symbolic action, he foretold the destruction of Jerusalem. In 587 his wife died. From 586 to 570 he was a consoler and a reformer, looking to the coming period of Restoration. The last prophecy was in 570 (29:17).

Ezekiel was a priest and keenly felt the loss of the Temple in which to worship. His initial vision left an indelible imprint upon him. The holiness and glory of God seared the soul of a prophet who had seen but could not describe the glory of what he had seen; he could only try to express his visions. Loving the Word of God (3:3), he fearlessly carried out God's commands, hesitating only once, when asked to eat foul food (4:14).

Ezekiel saw keenly the moral responsibility of each man to God and the terrible duty of God's prophet, for the hand of the Lord was upon him. Known as the Father of Judaism, he helped in the organization of the old laws for the conduct of Temple worship at the Restoration (chapters 40–48). A mystic, his language is often such that the meaning is difficult to grasp. In the interpretation of his visions the finer details must not be taken too literally.

Ezekiel was a new kind of prophet—a prophet of Yahweh in a foreign country. Thrown back on God alone, and able to discern more clearly the coming doom of his country, he could reflect more calmly upon its meaning and purpose; hence, his conviction of the necessity of the Exile is strong. He was always a writer; he had no king's court or chief places of consort and concourse where he could preach as did Isaiah and Jeremiah. Ezekiel was one of the greatest literary artists of the ancient world. (Cf. chapters 16, 17, 27, 28). But he was more than a man of letters; he was pre-eminently a spiritual architect. It was his work to gather and preserve the great prophetic doctrines of his predecessors, to stimulate the hope of the surviving exiles, and to organize new forms of religious life for the future restored community.

Ezekiel is also distinguished from the other Old Testament prophets by the special prominence of the pathological element in his prophecy. Visions, ecstasies, second sight, and striking symbolic actions bulk large in his experience. Some scholars contend that, in addition to certain Babylonian influences (cf. some of his figures in the visions, the banning, etc.), some corporeal ailment is to be brought in by way of explanation; e.g., temporary dumbness with paralytic symptoms, or catalepsy, as Klostermann on the ground of 3:26; 24:27; 29:21; 33:22, has argued. Hermann has contested the literal interpretation of these passages as referring to physical conditions, pointing to 16:63; 29:21, where the "opening of the mouth" is meant symbolically. Ezekiel seems to borrow from Jeremiah. The two prophets are similar in some respects, but in others there is great contrast. Jeremiah is a prophet of tenderest affections; Ezekiel of the most soaring imagination. Jeremiah is a man of feeling and action; Ezekiel, of reason and reflection. We feel we know Jeremiah when we read his book; Ezekiel is little more to us than a name. The prophecies of Jeremiah begin and end with a vision of suffering; Ezekiel's begin and end with a vision of glory.[1] Ezekiel is of the line of Zadok; Jeremiah, that of Abiathar.

THE BOOK. Two difficulties arose among the rabbis as to the presence of Ezekiel in the canon of the Scripture. (1) The one grew out of the dogma generally accepted at the beginning of the Christian era that the Law of Moses was not liable to alteration, and no law was left in heaven to give to man. (Cf. Ezekiel 46:6–7 and Numbers 28:11.) There is no mention of the material in Ezekiel 45:18–20 in the Pentateuch. Some twenty such problems are raised by a comparative study of Ezekiel and the Torah. It was reported that Hananiah ben Hezekiah required 300 jars of oil for his midnight study to arrive at even a temporary conclusion! So serious was the conflict and so many were the problems involved that it was the part of wisdom to waive final decision until Elijah should return and resolve their differences. (2) Speculative difficulties. The strange figures in chapter 1 and the symbolism of later portions of the book easily lent themselves to fanaticism. While pondering these divine mysteries might be invaluable for the initiated and the mature, it might be fatal to the immature. The study of the cherubim, angels, and demons has always, to a certain type of mind, opened the door to fanaticism. Accordingly rabbis prohibited, to those under thirty years of age, the reading of certain parts of Ezekiel: the beginning, the end, and certain other chapters.[2]

Until recently little criticism was made of the book of Ezekiel. Holscher (1924) maintained that Ezekiel, a prophet "standing with both feet on the soil of pre-Exilic religion" had uttered only a few brief *poems*, containing in all 170 verses, the rest of the book being added later until the fifth century B.C. James Smith (1931) claimed Ezekiel prophesied both in Northern Israel and Assyria (722–669 B.C.). A redactor later assembled his utterances. Torrey (1930) claimed no real Ezekiel at

[1]Cf. W. J. Farley, *op. cit.*, pp. 180–181.
[2]Cf. C. C. Torrey, *Pseudo-Ezekiel* (London: Oxford University Press, 1930), pp. 15–18.

all. The book is a work of imagination by a man in Jerusalem about 230 B.C. A later editor introduced Babylonian setting. Herntrick proposed that Ezekiel prophesied in Jerusalem from 593–586 B.C. His prophecies were given a Babylonian setting later by a redactor who added 40–48. Bertholet divides the prophet's activities: (1) Jerusalem before the fall, (2) some city of Judah not far from Jerusalem (12:3ff.), (3) Babylonia. Fisher claimed that Ezekiel prophesied in Babylonia, then returned to Jerusalem until 586, then again went to Babylonia. Later redactors adjusted the text to look as if it all were in the captivity. The problem is that while Ezekiel is represented as being in Babylonia, his eyes (during the first twenty-four chapters) are fixed on Jerusalem. The prophets usually addressed the people before them.

Conservatives take the position that Ezekiel was in the Exile during all his prophetic ministry. He addresses the inhabitants of Jerusalem for the dramatic effect it will have on the exiles before him; i.e., will turn them from their sinful way. There is no hope left for Jerusalem. Ezekiel visits Jerusalem only in spirit after 597, never in the flesh.

Notes on Important Passages

1:1. Much discussion has been made concerning the meaning of "the thirtieth year." This manner of expression usually is applied by prophets to the reign of a king. But verse 2 presents the chronological scheme prevailing throughout the book. Apparently Ezekiel is referring to his own age. Both C. C. Torrey and James Smith use this statement for locating the scene of the prophecies of the book during Manasseh's reign, since he is the only king during this period who ruled as many as thirty years.

1:4ff. This vision is of a chariot borne by four-winged creatures, coming out of the north, the direction from which travelers come when going from Palestine to Babylonia. On this chariot is seated God. The significance is that God, contrary to popular belief, could as certainly be with his people in Babylonia as in Palestine.

1:5. Note the number of times the term "likeness" is used in the chapter. Ezekiel cannot describe what he saw; this is the best description he can make with mortal words. The four creatures symbolize the use God makes of all his creation (eagle, king of birds; ox, king of domestic animals; lion, king of beasts; man, ruler of them all). These creatures at the will of his spirit (verse 12) bear the platform upon which Yahweh sits.

1:16. "Wheel within a wheel." The axes of the wheels were at right angles to one another. Thus the chariot did not need to turn when changing directions but could go immediately. Four of the wheels rolled east or west, the other four north and south. One of these sets of four was within the other set, making four individual wheels.

1:18. Symbolizing the omniscience of God as he watches over the needs of his people.

1:22. "Firmament" should read "platform."

2:1. This verse speaks of both the frailty and dignity of man. The term, "Son of man," which is the favorite title applied to Ezekiel in the book, emphasizes his humanity over against the divine Being. He is commanded to get upon his feet, because God will only speak to his prophet face to face.

3:14-15. Ezekiel is all afire to preach God's judgment until he "sits where the people sit." Then he cannot speak a word. Too often those who condemn people do so from a lack of understanding and sympathy.

3:16. God arouses Ezekiel again with his great responsibility as a prophetic watchman. Although he is overcome with grief at the plight of the exiles, he must nevertheless warn them of their sins lest they perish completely. "But his blood will I require at thy hand" is a terrible indictment that all must heed.

Chapters 4-5. Ezekiel's most effective method of preaching was such object lessons.

6:13. "And *ye* (the exiles) shall know . . . when *their* (inhabitants of Jerusalem) slain men. . . ." Further proof that Ezekiel speaks against Jerusalem for the sake of the exiles.

8:3. Ezekiel in Jerusalem in vision, not in actuality. A vivid description of the experiences of the prophet in a trance or ecstasy.

9:4. The pious were to receive a mark upon their foreheads, that the destroyer might not touch them.

11:13. Did Ezekiel in exile see Pelatiah die in Jerusalem? Perhaps, but it is more likely that Pelatiah died only in the vision, which was prophetic of his actual death in the future.

12:27. It is ever thus. Men always put the day of reckoning into the distant future.

14:14. It is rather singular that Daniel, who was yet a young man, should be named along with the patriarchs Noah and Job. (Cf. Ezek. 28:3.) The recent examination of the Ugaritic records of Palestine has revealed an ancient worthy by the name of Dan'l. This is the spelling in both references in Ezekiel, and not that of the book of Daniel.

Chapter 16. A shocking allegory wherein the prophet describes the sins of Judah as being worse than those of Sodom and Samaria.

16:3. Not a statement of physical descent but of spiritual genealogy. Morally the Israelites are descended from their heathen neighbors, not from Abraham. (Cf. "Ye are of your father the devil." John 8:44.)

Chapter 17. A parable used to condemn Judah's alliance with Egypt. Babylon will destroy Judah as a result.

17:3. Babylon is the great eagle.

17:4. Jehoiachin.

17:5. Zedekiah.

17:7. Egypt.

17:22. The Messiah.

Chapter 18. In chapters 18 and 33 Ezekiel presents in striking fashion his doctrine of individual responsibility. His teaching may be put briefly as follows: (1) No man is necessarily under the dominion of the character and conduct of his ancestors: he can become a wicked man, even though his father was righteous; he may become a righteous man, even though his father was wicked. Yahweh will reward or punish him according to his own deeds and not on account of the conduct of his ancestors. Heredity does not destroy freedom and moral responsibility. (2) No man is necessarily a slave to his own past conduct: he can break away from a righteous life and perish; he can break away from a wicked past and live. Habit is not any more omnipotent than heredity.

18:2. This proverb was invented by the Jews to make it appear that the calamities under which they were suffering were due to the sins of their fathers.

19:4. Jehoahaz.

19:9. Jehoiachin.

20:49. Many students will still agree with Ezekiel's hearers.

22:31. God does not arbitrarily condemn the sinner. His own sins betray him.

24:2. A remarkable knowledge on the part of Ezekiel in exile.

24:15–18. Loyalty to God comes first. Few men, however, could have conducted themselves as did Ezekiel.

Chapter 28. The king of Tyre is not Satan but a poetic description of Tyre's rulers. (Cf. 28:9, "But thou art *man*.")

28:13. Poetic figure for "you had everything heart could desire."

28:15. Tyre's early history was blameless.

33:30ff. Ezekiel was a popular preacher, but it broke his heart because people enjoyed rather than lived in accordance with his sermons.

36:25. Ceremonial cleansing. No reference to New Testament baptism.

Chapter 37. Not a picture of individual resurrection, but of the revival of the nation Israel, seeming hopelessly dead in the Exile. (Cf. 37:11–12.)

Chapters 38–39. Apocalyptic passage teaching the eventual victory of God's people over their enemies, personified as Gog. Any literal identification is difficult and may not be intended.

40:28. There was but one court in Solomon's Temple, but two were included in the Temple built by Zerubbabel. Ezekiel's plan was followed in that respect.

43:8. The old Temple was connected with the palace. The new one would not be so. (Cf. 42:20.) This plan was followed by Zerubbabel.

43:10–11. Ezekiel apparently hoped his plan would be followed literally.

44:9ff. Only the sons of Zadok, of the descendants of Aaron, shall be priests.

Chapter 45. The arrangement of the holy city. In the center is the sanctuary, surrounded by the residence of the priests. To the north the Levites would live, and to the south the ordinary residents of the city. The prince possessed the territory to the east and west of this holy oblation, which was a square 25,000 on each side (holy portion for Temple and priests, 10,000×25,000; Levites, 10,000×25,000; city, 5,000×25,000). Thus the sanctity of the holy place could be observed.

Chapter 47. An inspiring picture of a stream issuing from the new Temple in Jerusalem, flowing toward the Dead Sea, and ever growing deeper. Upon its approach, the Dead Sea and the arid Arabah come to life.

47:11. Ezekiel does not ignore the most minute details. All will not be quickened; some of the marshes of the Dead Sea will be left for salt.

Chapter 48. The whole land of Palestine shall be divided equally among the tribes. These shall be to the north and south of the holy oblation. Judah shall be directly to the north of Jerusalem and Benjamin to the south, since these tribes were the most faithful to Yahweh.

48:35. The name of the holy city shall be changed from Jerusalem to Yahweh-Shammah ("Yahweh is there").

DANIEL

Daniel was of royal or at least noble birth (1:3). He was a fine specimen of physical manhood and had shown marked ability and substantial progress in learning (1:4) when he was carried captive by Nebuchadnezzar in 605 B.C. (1:1f.). He was perhaps twenty years of age and had grown up in the midst of the great religious revival of Josiah's reign. To the influence of this revival he may have owed much of the stability and firmness of his religious character. He was trained in "the learning and tongue of the Chaldeans" for the king's service, and soon established a great reputation for learning and wisdom (1:20f.). So great were his faithfulness, ability, and attainments that Nebuchadnezzar soon "made him to rule over all the province of Babylon and to be chief governor over all the wise men of Babylon" (2:48), and later suffered rebuke at his hands apparently without resentment. During the intervening reigns of Evil-merodach (561–559), Neriglissar (559–556), and Nabonidus (555–539) we hear nothing of him, and he seems to have lost his position and fallen out of public notice. But at the feast of Belshazzar the queen remembers him (5:11f.), and when called, he shows his former fearlessness and wisdom. Darius the Mede recognized his ability and, notwithstanding his great age, made him chief of a board of three presidents, and "thought to set him over the whole realm" (6:2f.). In religion, too, he still manifested the same uncompromising faithfulness, boldly disobeying the king's decree and not even closing his windows to avoid detection. He lived until the third year of Cyrus (10:1; cf. 1:21), being perhaps ninety years of age and still active (6:28).

The date and authorship of the book of Daniel are matters of heated controversy. The majority of modern scholars believe that the book was not written by Daniel, but during the period of the Maccabees (c.167 B.C.). Judah's morale fell low in the second century B.C., when fierce and galling persecutions assailed her under the tyranny of Antiochus Epiphanes. The book of Daniel, it is claimed, was written to warm the blood congealed by the chill night of despondency. Antiochus had sought to introduce among the Jews Greek customs which the high priest Onias III resisted. Onias was deposed in favor of Jason, who desecrated the Temple. In opposition, Mattathias, along with his five sons (the Maccabees), started a rebellion. Finally Judas Maccabeus conquered Jerusalem, and the Temple was purified. It can be understood, therefore, how vast the influence of Daniel's story could be in such a day. That is why a narrative that had been told about the camp fires, or in the gloomy days of exile, would stiffen the powers of resistance and re-energize the nation's will. Although many modern scholars ascribe the book to this period, that does not necessarily deny the historicity of Daniel himself. No one can dispute the fact of the French Revolution. Yet Carlyle's history of it came fifty years later. Even if the book was written long after Daniel lived, Daniel himself is too human, vivid, and convincing to be simply a legendary figure. The scholars who prefer this late date argue:

1. The main interest of chapters 7–12 centers in the times of Antiochus Epiphanes. The analogy of other prophetic writing suggests that it is there one should look for the prophet.

2. In the Hebrew canon, Daniel is not placed among the prophets. It is among the Writings, which, there is reason for thinking, mark the latest stage in the formation of the Old Testament.

3. The series of predictions in chapter 11 are in their minuteness unlike any prophecies in the Old Testament. They read like a literal history of the period.

4. The linguistic phenomena are peculiar. The section 2:4 to 7:28 is in Aramaic; fifteen words from the Persian and at least three from the Greek occur; the Hebrew is late. "The *Persian* words presuppose a period after the Persian empire had been well established; the Greek words *demand*, the Hebrew *sup-*

ports, and the Aramaic *permits,* a date *after the conquest of Palestine by Alexander."*[1]

5. The theology is the most advanced in the Old Testament. There is a hierarchy among the angels; they are even called by name. The doctrine of the resurrection in 12:2 is the clearest in the Old Testament.

6. The book resembles most closely other apocalyptic works of the Maccabean period. This form of literature was natural in a time of persecution; its symbolism and mysticism were created for such dark hours. A similar situation in the first century A.D. called forth the Revelation of John. It was characteristic of apocalyptic writings to treat past history in the form of prophecy, speaking in the name of some ancient worthy. In other words, these writings present a definite type of literature that must be interpreted by its own laws. When the writer of the book spoke in the name of Daniel, he was not regarded as a plagiarist. It was in the spirit of Daniel that he wrote, and his contemporaries were well aware that the work was a recent one. If they respected the literary method enough to canonize the book, one should attempt to view it through their eyes. To them it was the word of God for the hour. We must not impose our modern copyright laws upon a less materialistic age.

Other scholars, however, present persuasive arguments for an Exilic date:

1. The claim of the book that Daniel made the prophecies contained therein must be taken literally. Jesus himself refers to one passage in Daniel (Matt. 24:15). The apocalyptic writers of the Maccabean period followed the method of the earlier book of Daniel, because he spoke of their age.

2. There was time enough for Daniel to acquire a Persian vocabulary of fifteen words. If the book is Maccabean, there should be far more than three Greek words in the book.

3. The theology is late, but not much more advanced than in the books of Zechariah or Job.

4. Chapter 11 is a miracle of inspiration. Antiochus Epiphanes was of such importance in Jewish history as to warrant Daniel's interest.

---

[1] S. R. Driver, *An Introduction to the Literature of the Old Testament* (New York: Charles Scribner's Sons, 1916), p. 508.

5. Daniel is in the Writings because it is wisdom literature or because of the lateness of its acceptance in the canon, due to its Aramaic portion.

Regardless of how one dates the book, its interpretation should be essentially the same. Those who hold the late date usually claim that the kingdoms in chapter 2 and chapter 7 are Babylon, Media, Persia, and Greece. Thus the book of Daniel contains no prophecy except that concerning the later years of Antiochus Epiphanes. The rest of the book is history cast in the form of prophecy as the author writes in the name of Daniel. However, the position of conservative scholars concerning the identification of the kingdoms is true regardless of how one dates the book. The four kingdoms are Babylon, Medo-Persia, Greece, and a fourth kingdom not identified. Persia never succeeded Media as a world empire. The claim that the writer is ignorant of world history cannot stand, for in chapter 8 Medo-Persia is regarded as one kingdom (a ram), with two unequal divisions (two horns). In chapters 2 and 7 the third kingdom (the goat, Greece, chapter 8) is succeeded by a fourth, which is in all probability the power of Rome, on its ascendancy even in the second century B.C.

No matter how the book is dated, therefore, it is a marvelous prediction of the coming of the Messiah and the messianic kingdom and of the eventual triumph of that kingdom (2:44–45; 7:7–28; 9:24–27; 12:1–4). After Antiochus is conquered, the even greater Anti-Messiah shall also meet defeat at the hands of the Messiah. (This king comes from the fourth kingdom, so cannot be Antiochus Epiphanes.)

Outline of the Book

1. History of Daniel. Chapters 1–6

    (1) Daniel's youth and education. Chapter 1
        a. He with others carried captive to Babylon. 1f.
        b. His education and faithfulness. 3–17
        c. His proficiency. 18–21

(2) Nebuchadnezzar's image-dream. Chapter 2

   a. The Chaldeans, failing to tell and interpret the dream, are ordered to be slain. 1–12

   b. Daniel stays the execution, discovers the dream in a vision, and relates and interprets it to Nebuchadnezzar. 13–45

   c. As a consequence, Nebuchadnezzar acknowledges the greatness of the God of the Hebrews, and greatly honors and advances Daniel and his companions. 46–49

(3) The faithfulness of Daniel's companions. Chapter 3

   a. The great image of gold dedicated on the plain of Dura, and all commanded to worship it. 1–7

   b. The three Hebrews refuse to bow down and are cast into the fiery furnace. 8–23

   c. They are miraculously preserved and delivered from the power of the flames. 24–27

   d. As a consequence, Nebuchadnezzar again acknowledges their God, makes a decree to his honor, and again advances these men. 28–30

(4) Nebuchadnezzar's tree-dream related in the form of a decree to all peoples of the earth. Chapter 4

   a. Introduction to the decree; the God of Israel great and powerful. 1–3

   b. How the wise men failed to interpret the dream. 4–7

   c. How the dream was related to Daniel, who interpreted it and exhorted the king to reform. 8–27

   d. The fulfilment, and its effect on Nebuchadnezzar. 28–37

(5) Belshazzar's feast (539 B.C.). Chapter 5

   a. The revelling and sacrilege of the feast. 1–4

   b. The handwriting on the wall, and the failure of the wise men to interpret it. 5–9

   c. Daniel's interpretation and the fulfilment. Belshazzar is slain, and "Darius the Mede" receives the kingdom. 10–31

(6) Daniel in the den of lions. Chapter 6

   a. Daniel again elevated to high political position by Darius the Mede. 1–3

b. Other officers in envy induce Darius to make a decree, and Daniel is caught violating it. 4–11

c. The king reluctantly orders Daniel cast into the lions' den; but he is miraculously delivered, and his enemies are cast into the den. 12–24

d. Darius' decree favoring the God of Daniel. 25–28

2. Visions of Daniel. Chapters 7–12

(1) The vision of the four beasts (first year of Belshazzar). Chapter 7

a. The vision. Four great beasts, differing one from another, come up and out of the sea. Before "one that was ancient of days," seated upon a throne, the books are opened and the beasts are judged, and "one like unto a son of man" comes and receives an universal and everlasting kingdom. 1–14

b. Interpretation of the vision. 15–28

(2) Vision of the ram and the he-goat (at Susa in the third year of Belshazzar). Chapter 8

a. The vision. 1–14

b. Gabriel interprets the vision to Daniel. Antiochus Epiphanes shall be destroyed. 15–27

(3) Daniel's prayer (first year of Darius the Mede, 539 B.C.). Chapter 9

a. Understanding from the prophecy of Jeremiah that the time of the restoration is almost at hand, Daniel confesses the sins of his people and earnestly prays for forgiveness and restoration. 1–19

b. Gabriel reveals to him that his supplication has been heard and the restoration is at hand, and foretells the advent of "an anointed one" and another destruction of Jerusalem. 20–27

(4) Daniel's last vision (by the Tigris in the third year of Cyrus). Chapters 10–12

a. At the conclusion of twenty-one days of fasting, a heavenly messenger appears to Daniel, explains why he had tarried so long, and encourages him. 10:1 to 11:1

b. He foretells the struggles of Persia and Greece. 11:2–4
c. The struggles of the kings of the South (Ptolemies) and the kings of the North (Seleucidae). 11:5–29
d. A king of the North (Antiochus Epiphanes) will oppress the chosen people, exalt himself, and afflict other countries. 11:30–44
e. But he shall come to an end, and the Israelites shall rise again; then the Messianic Age. 11:45 to 12:4
f. The time of the fulfilment is explained to Daniel in enigmatical terms. 12:5–13

HAGGAI

THE BACKGROUND. When the enthusiastic exiles returned in 537 B.C. they found a scanty and dispirited population. The territory of Judah had shrunk—only a small area around Jerusalem, estimated by Kittel to be 20 miles square. On every hand they saw poverty, when they had been accustomed to the prosperity in Babylon. There was no hope of a monarchy. The Temple lay in ruins and the neighboring peoples were hostile. It is no wonder that the rebuilding of the Temple was delayed. The several elements in this delay may be listed:

1. During the stay in Babylon the exiles had learned to do without the Temple.

2. The opposition of the Samaritans and other surrounding tribes would offer a ready excuse to indifferent Jews.

3. The nonfulfilment of the earlier prophecies concerning the glories of the restoration would tend to develop religious indifference and skepticism.

4. Limited resources and poverty resulting from the failure of crops and the devastation wrought by the Persian armies on their way to Egypt were discouraging.

THE MAN. Haggai appears suddenly in 520 B.C. and disappears as suddenly. Nothing is known of his life before or after his preaching. Upon the basis of 2:3, it has been suggested that he was of the small company that had seen the former Temple in its glory; if so, he was an old man when he prophesied. This supposition agrees with the brevity of his public activity. Yahweh had put upon his heart the need for a proper place of worship. When this had been secured his task was done.

The message of Haggai may be summarized:

1. Rebuke of indifference; exhortation to resume building operations (1:1–11).

2. Resumption of building operations (1:12–15).

3. Message of encouragement to the builders (2:1–9).

4. Completion of the Temple a sure guarantee of the return of divine favor (2:10–19).

5. Exaltation of Zerubbabel, the servant of Yahweh (2:20–23).

The ministry of Haggai was quite different from that of earlier prophets. Compared with the glorious messages committed to others, his seems to be a humble one, but no word was ever needed more desperately. Jeremiah had spoken of the time when the Temple would be needed no more, but that day had not yet arrived. The struggling post-Exilic community needed the aid of the Temple influence to unify its people and offset the temptation of heathenism. The Law was needed until the Messiah should usher in the age of the Spirit.

Notes on Important Passages

1:2. Often the cry of God's people today about the need of an adequate church building.

1:4. The people were spending money on their own homes. Why not on God's house?

1:6, 9. When a man neglects his financial responsibility to God, what he keeps for himself never suffices. It was a time of inflation when Haggai began to preach.

1:12b. The reason why the people obeyed Haggai. They were certain he was sent of God.

1:14. Yahweh did not stir up the spirit to build until the preacher had done his part.

2:3, 9. The first crisis in the building operation. The older people were saying that the new Temple did not compare with that of Solomon, and were dampening the enthusiasm of the builders. Haggai assured them that physical appearance is not what is most essential. The days of the greatest glory of that

Temple lay ahead. Of course, this was fulfilled in the ministry of Jesus.

2:19. The second crisis. The prosperity Haggai had promised if they obeyed God had not taken place. They were accusing him of misleading them. He defended himself with a reference to the Law. Uncleanness is more contagious than holiness. It takes a long while after repentance occurs for the results of sin to disappear. Then will come more prosperous days. This truth is constantly applicable. Sin can never be treated lightly. Its consequences continue on earth even after the sinner's reconciliation with God.

2:23. The day of the Lord was always imminent in Old Testament prophecy. The signet was the ring worn to make impression on the wax seals of documents that would guarantee their authenticity. The emblem was different on each ring. The owner never trusted his signet to any but his most intimate associates. The teaching here is that Zerubbabel has Yahweh's guarantee upon his work. There is no indication that Haggai thought Zerubbabel would be the Messiah, as some scholars claim. Yet it is significant that Jesus was a descendant of Zerubbabel.

ZECHARIAH

THE PROPHET. Born in Babylonia, Zechariah saw Jerusalem for the first time when he traveled with the repatriated exiles. He furthered Haggai's advocacy of rebuilding the Temple. Zechariah and Haggai present an interesting contrast. They were as different as could be, with only one thing in common— a passionate enthusiasm for the restoration of the Temple. Haggai was old, conscious that time was speeding by, and that, therefore, he must speak straight and to the point. Zechariah was youthful and a visionary. Haggai was prosaic and practical; Zechariah was idealistic, indulging in colorful word pictures and yet insisting on the necessity of political and religious action. Haggai prophesied from the sixth to the ninth month of 520 B.C.; Zechariah began his work in the eighth month and went on at intervals for several years. The depression alluded to under Haggai was in force. The apathy that resulted was inconceivable to one of Zechariah's temperament. He belonged to the sacred caste of Iddo, a priest, and consecrated his strength to serve the great object that Haggai had so strenuously advocated, throwing himself wholeheartedly into the project. There is a deep-flowing messianic strain underlying his message that gave him confidence that what he urged was in line with God's destiny for the nation. In fact, the fulfilment of those hopes was dependent upon the people's willingness to rebuild the Temple. Zechariah differs from his predecessors in the emphasis which he placed upon visions as a means of divine communication, in apocalyptic symbolism, and in the large place occupied by angelic mediation in his intercourse with God. In his book we see the tendency of later Judaism to emphasize the holiness of Yahweh to such an extent that he no longer comes into direct contact with human beings.

THE BOOK. The criticism of the book began in an attempt to account for the relationship between Matthew 27:9 and Zechariah 11:13. Chapters 1–8 are admittedly Zechariah's. However, in chapters 9–14 there is a problem. One group of scholars claims that these chapters indicate an historical situation within and without Jerusalem different from that which gave rise to the utterances embodied in chapters 1–8. Zechariah 1–8 pictures the whole earth at peace, which was true at least of all Syria; they portend no danger to Jerusalem from the heathen, but describe her peace and fruitful expansion in terms most suitable to the circumstances during the reigns of the earlier Persian kings. This is changed in 9–14. The nations are restless, a siege of Jerusalem is imminent, and her salvation is to be assured only by much war and a terrible shedding of blood. We know exactly how Israel fared in the early part of the Persian period. Her attitude toward the heathen was not that which is reflected in Zechariah 9–14. Some hold that the chapters are pre-Exilic, others that they are post-Exilic at a date not earlier than 350 B.C. However, the best view seems to be that chapters 9–14 have no historical setting but are written by Zechariah in later life as an apocalyptic drama. Cf. Pfeiffer,[1] who, however, does not hold to Zecharian authorship:

(1) A divinely sent invader to devastate Syria, Phenicia, and Philistia, the messianic prince of peace to come (9:1–10).

(2) Restored Judah and Ephraim to defeat the Greeks (9:11 to 10:4).

(3) All Jews will break yoke of oppressors (10:5 to 11:2).

(4) The false shepherds and the true (11:3–17; 13:7–9).

(5) Jerusalem attacked by its enemies but will triumph (12:1 to 13:6).

(6) Sack of Jerusalem and miraculous deliverance of half the people (14).

---

[1] R. H. Pfeiffer, *op. cit.*, pp. 610–612.

1:5. God's Word has stood the test of time. Amos and Hosea have been vindicated.

1:11. No sign of God at work.

1:12b. The glorious promises of the book of Isaiah and the seventy years of Jeremiah do not seem to be ready for fulfilment. Not even the Temple has been rebuilt; Judah's enemies are prevailing still.

2:4. The city is to have no walls (1) because God will protect her, and (2) her rapid growth would find them a hindrance.

2:7. Read, "*To* Zion, escape . . ."

4:6, 10. A comfort to all who are weak and insignificant, as it was to the builders of the Temple.

4:14. Joshua and Zerubbabel.

6:11. Read "crown," not "crowns." The union of the priesthood and kingship in the Messiah. Note that it is Joshua the priest who is crowned, not Zerubbabel who is adorned with priestly robes. The priesthood received a new emphasis after the Exile, and it was believed by many that a priest from the line of Aaron would be the Messiah.

8:4-5. This beautiful scene to replace the deserted condition of the city. In 520, Jerusalem was evidently still unsafe for children or the aged.

9:9. A remarkable prophecy of the Messiah as Prince of peace, literally fulfilled in Jesus.

9:13. Greece was well known in Zechariah's day.

11:12. The price of an injured slave (Ex. 21:32).

11:13. Matthew 27:9 attributes this to Jeremiah, probably a copyist's error in Matthew.

12:11. The mourning for the "pierced One" shall be greater than that for Josiah, one of the saddest moments in Israel's history.

13:2-6. Prophecy had fallen into disrepute because of the prevalence of false prophets. It will be a disgrace to be a prophet, for God will deal directly with his people (13:1).

179

Anyone professing to be a prophet will be recognized at once as being false.

14:7b. A glorious promise.

14:20–21. No more distinction of holy and unclean, but all Israel shall be holy.

OUTLINE OF THE BOOK

Introduction. Return to Yahweh. 1:1–6

1. Messages of Encouragement to the Builders. 1:7 to 8:23

    (1) A series of eight visions, with two messianic prophecies. 1:7 to 6:15

        a. The horseman among the myrtle trees. 1:7–17. Yahweh is preparing to comfort Zion.

        b. The four horns and the four smiths. 1:18–21. Judah's oppressors to be broken.

        c. The measuring line. The nations shall be gathered in. Chapter 2. Jerusalem to be filled with inhabitants; Yahweh Himself its wall.

        d. Satan accusing the high priest. Chapter 3. The priest forgiven, cleansed, and anointed, becomes a sign of the Messiah, Yahweh's servant the Branch.

        e. The golden candlestick. Chapter 4. The royal and priestly lines channels for the Spirit.

        f. The flying roll. 5:1–4. Curse on the thief and the liar.

        g. The woman in the ephah. 5:5–11. Banishment of wickedness.

        h. The four chariots. 6:1–8. Yahweh ready and able to quiet all opposition.

        i. The crowning of the high priest. 6:9–15. Union of the royal and priestly offices of the Messiah.

    (2) About fasting. 7:1 to 8:23

    (Fasting to be converted into feasting. If the restored nation will obey Yahweh and deal justly and truly, the fasts of exilic days will be merged into days of joy and gladness, because back of all is God's love.)

2. The Burden of Hadrach and Other Heathen Cities, Together with Messages of Mingled Promise and Warning for Israel. Chapters 9–11; 13:7–9

    (1) While many heathen cities are to be smitten, Yahweh will protect his land. 9:1–8

    (2) Zion's King enters, bringing peace and universal dominion. Israel to be delivered from captivity and made victorious over all foes. 9:9–17

    (3) In contrast with helpless idols, Yahweh will send rain upon the land, and will deliver, assemble, and lead his chosen people. Chapter 10. Judah and Ephraim now united.

    (4) The good Shepherd and the foolish shepherds. Chapter 11; 13:7–9

3. A Group of Prophecies Concerning Israel. Chapters 12–14. (N.B.—Zechariah uses Israel to designate the people who returned, whether they were of Judah, or of the other tribes.)

    (1) Judah and Jerusalem, by divine aid, will be able to resist all enemies. 12:1–9

    (2) Great mourning in Jerusalem over the "pierced One." 12:10–14

    (3) Jerusalem to be cleansed of idols and false prophets. 13:1–6

    (4) After a terrible chastisement, Jerusalem shall be transformed, and under the protection of Yahweh, shall be the center of worship for the world. Chapter 14

MALACHI

THE PROPHET. By the second century A.D. "Malachi" had come generally to be regarded as a proper noun. But before that date the Hebrew word, which literally means "my messenger" (angel), had been taken by many as a title of the author, whose real name, it was assumed, was not mentioned at all (3:1). For a long time Jewish tradition identified the author of the book with Ezra, while others conjectured that the author was an incarnate angel. Analogy with the other prophetic books would seem to favor the view that the name prefixed to the book is a proper name; on the other hand, the interpretation of the ancients is not without weight.

We know nothing about the author's personal life, except as his writings reveal it. Undismayed by his adversaries, with indomitable bravery, he was ready for what the hour might bring forth. He feared no man because he feared God so much. With rapier thrust he struck home. He faced scorn and antagonism, sure that only through God could the race find serenity and strength. Malachi faced indifference, caused by disappointment and skepticism, that led to a neglect of Temple service. The priests performed their offices perfunctorily, but their hearts were not in their work. Anything was good enough for Yahweh, they thought, and offered the lame and blind on the altar. The people were unwilling to pay their proper religious dues. Mixed marriages and divorces predominated, accompanied by a moral decline. Yet there was a faithful nucleus in the community (3:16).

THE BOOK. There are two principal views of the date: (1) The interval in which Nehemiah had returned to Persia (c.430

B.C.). Malachi denounced the same sins Nehemiah found when he returned. The allusion to the governor in 1:8 points to the presence of a foreign governor rather than to Nehemiah, who refused to avail himself of his official allowances. (2) Preceding Ezra. Malachi does not refer to Ezra's measures against mixed marriage or to the publication of the Law. His language, it is said, is that of Deuteronomy and not of the Priest's Code as would be expected of one following Ezra. To this theory it is objected that the latter argument is from silence and not valid. The teaching of Malachi on marriage and divorce gives more point if he refers them to a covenant made ten years before. The law book of Deuteronomy was very popular after the time of Ezra.

The style of Malachi is didactic, academic, not free as earlier prophets. (1) A charge is made; (2) the people reply; (3) the prophet drives home his truth in true prophetic manner. Prophecy is assuming the temper of teaching, resulting eventually in the scholasticism of the rabbis. In Malachi we have "Prophecy within the Law." He reaffirms truths taught by earlier prophets as to the love and care of God and judgment of the wicked, but on the other hand he places great stress upon the Law as a disciplinary rule of life; its lax performance receives severe condemnation. His final exhortation is, "Remember ye the law of Moses" (4:4).

Notes on Important Passages

1:8. Our offerings to God should be at least as respectable as the taxes we pay.

1:10. Put a lock on the church door! It is better not to have services than to make a mockery of worship.

1:11. There are no verbs in the Hebrew of the verse. This may be a prediction, but usually such a construction demands a verb. If the present time is intended, as the context suggests, the verse means that Gentiles throughout the world (perhaps proselytes) are offering more acceptable worship to the one God than unfaithful Judah.

1:13. Insincere religion is always a burden.

183

2:10. Malachi's conception of the fatherhood of God is applied only to Jews.

2:15. God's purpose in marriage, the rearing of godly children. A broken home destroys this intention of God.

4:2. The most beautiful verse in the book.

OUTLINE OF THE BOOK

Title 1:1.

Introduction.—Yahweh's love for Israel, though called in question, is seen in the history of Israel and Edom. 1:2–5

1. Neglect of Yahweh by Israel, Especially by the Priests. 1:6 to 2:9

   (1) The priests offer worthless and unacceptable sacrifices on the altar of Yahweh. 1:6–9
   (2) Complete rejection by Yahweh of such worthless sacrifices at Jerusalem, with the statement that all over the world more acceptable sacrifices are offered before him. 1:10–14
   (3) Having despised the noble covenant of the priesthood, having perverted justice and led the people astray, the priests themselves are to be rendered contemptible. 2:1–9

2. Taking of Heathen Wives, and Divorcing of Jewish Wives Forbidden. 2:10–16

3. Skepticism Rebuked. 2:17 to 4:3

   (1) The day of the Lord will separate between the righteous and the wicked, and will surely come to priests and laity alike. 2:17 to 3:6
   (2) Bring in the tithes which you are withholding, so that Yahweh may "pour out a blessing" upon the land. 3:7–12

(3) Quit skeptical murmuring; for God will consume the wicked and preserve the righteous. 3:13 to 4:3

Conclusion. Keep the law of Moses, and wait for the forerunner, who will promote love and unity. 4:4–6

PART IV

Studies in the Poetical Books

Hebrew Poetry

The poetry of the Old Testament is the most significant contribution of the Hebrew people to the literature of the world. Like all other people, their earliest literature was poetic. We do not begin to possess in the Old Testament the whole body of poetical writings of the Israelites. Only poems of religious significance were included in the sacred books, and not all of those made their way into the canon. It is said of Solomon that "he spake three thousand proverbs, and his songs were a thousand and five." Biblical writers quote from the collections of poetry known as "The Wars of Yahweh" (Numbers 21:14) and "The Book of Jashar" (Joshua 10:12f.). That lyrical poetry was exceedingly popular in ancient Israel is attested by the number of synonyms in Hebrew for "song," of which there are at least thirteen. Only ideas in common use have many words to express them. The existence in Hebrew, a language by no means rich in synonyms, of thirteen words for "song" indicates a wide cultivation of poetry in early Israel.

Hebrew poetry has two distinguishing characteristics: accentual stress and parallelism. The individual lines are composed in accentual pattern. The usual line has three beats, although often it may be two or four. Unlike the Greek and English poets, the Hebrews considered only the syllables receiving the stress in composing a line, permitting three or even four unaccented syllables to be inserted between the beats. The individual lines are tied together by what is known as parallelism, which is a rhythm of meaning rather than of form. There are three common varieties:

186

1. *Synonymous,* in which a second line simply repeats in slightly altered phraseology the thought of the first line:

"He that sitteth in the heavens will laugh:
The Lord will have them in derision."
—Psalm 2:4.

"My son, hear the instruction of thy father,
And forsake not the law of thy mother."
—Proverbs 1:8.

Job 22:3–11. Most common form in Job.

2. *Antithetic,* in which the second line is in contrast with the first. (See Proverbs 10:1, 5, 7, etc.) Most of the 376 couplets in Proverbs 10:1 to 22:16 are antithetic.

3. *Synthetic* (or progressive), in which the second line supplements the first, both together giving a complete thought. (See Proverbs 1:10; 3:27–30.)

Some other varieties worth naming are:

1. Climactic Parallelism ("ascending rhythm"), in which the second line takes up words from the first and completes them.

"Ascribe unto Jehovah, O ye sons of the mighty,
Ascribe unto Jehovah glory and strength."
—Psalm 29:1

"The rulers ceased in Israel, they ceased,
Until that I Deborah arose,
That I arose a mother in Israel."
—Judges 5:7.

Compare the stair-like poetry in some of the pilgrim psalms (Psalms of Ascents). (See Psalms 121:1–2 [help]; 3–4; 4–5; 7–8; Psalm 122:2–3.)

2. Introverted Parallelism, in which the first line corresponds with the fourth, and the second with the third.

"My son, if thy heart be wise,
My heart will be glad, even mine:
Yea, my heart will rejoice,
When thy lips speak right things."
—Proverbs 23:15f.

3. Emblematic Parallelism, in which the second line brings forward something similar to the first but in a higher realm.

"For lack of wood the fire goeth out;
And where there is no whisperer, contention ceaseth.

As coals are to hot embers, and wood to fire;
So is a contentious man to inflame strife."
—Proverbs 26:20f.
(See also Proverbs 25:4f., 11–14, 19f.)

The lines of Hebrew poetry are variously grouped. In some poems strophes, or stanzas, are easily distinguishable. Occasionally a refrain or chorus comes at the end of each stanza. (See Psalm 107:8, 15, 21, 31.) There are few occurrences of rhyme in Hebrew poetry. In Judges 16:24, we have what has been called "a hymn formed upon a single rhyme." There is a repeated rhyme in the first verse of Psalm 14. The author of Isaiah 40–66 occasionally drops into rhyme for a moment. Otherwise the poetry of Israel lacks this characteristic so essential to our idea of poetry. C. C. Torrey suggests that perhaps the secular Hebrew poetry used more rhyme than the canonical, sacred writers regarding it "as too cheap a device to be employed in serious compositions."[1]

Be that as it may, biblical poetry resembles our free verse more than any other form. Consequently, it suffers very little in translation. However, it often presents a puzzling problem to the translator, as to whether a particular passage is rhythmical prose or prosaic poetry. The Hebrew writers, especially in their more exalted passages, step easily from prose to poetry, their native language being friendly to such transitions. Nevertheless, in such books as Psalms, Song of Songs, and Job, there is no question as to the poetical nature. Scholars have often remarked upon the wide difference between English religious poetry, much of which is considered literary rubbish, and the really great religious poetry of the Bible. There is in these Israelite compositions a force that welds patriotism with moral aspiration, producing a poetry which rings to the height of heaven though cast in the vales of the earth.

The effectiveness of Hebrew poetry is largely due to its freedom from abstractions. It always appeals to the fundamental senses. To express helpless despair, the psalmist names the sensations that characterize it: "my throat is dried"; "mine eyes fail"; "I sink in deep mire, where there is no standing." Terror

---

[1]Quoted in J. A. Penniman, *A Book About the English Bible* (Philadelphia: University of Pennsylvania Press, 1931), p. 95.

in the night is expressed by Eliphaz (Job 4:12–17) as shaking of the bones, hair standing on end, deadly silence, and an object indistinctly discerned. Often, instead of describing the sensation, the poet will simply name the object that invariably produces it. When the author of Psalm 65:9–13 pictures what God is doing in his world, it arouses all the sensations of a warm day in spring.

There is no result so tragic as an interpretation of a poetical passage by a prosaic theologian. Nowhere do the words of Paul, "The letter killeth, but the spirit giveth life" (2 Cor. 3:6) apply better than in a study of biblical poetry. "The poet must be allowed to say things in his own way, and often he deals with feelings and aspirations that 'break through language and escape.' Like Jacob, he wrestles with an angel. He must be read with spiritual sympathy and cooperation. His single words can neither be pressed into etymological niceties nor his separate statements be taken as theological formulae."[2]

It is quite simple to perceive the absurdity of a literal interpretation of poetry. One instinctively knows it should not be so done. When the Song of Deborah says,

> "From heaven fought the stars,
> From their courses they fought
> against Sisera,"

the reader at once realizes that they did not brandish spear and sword and rush into battle. It is poetic imagery that pictures the fact that all God's universe was arrayed against such a man of evil.

Again, when the book of Job refers to the time of creation, "when the morning stars sang together" (Job 38:7), the reader does not summon a vision of the stars assembling to "h'ist a hymn," but realizes that the poet is picturing the joy of God's universe in the language of imagination.

The author of Psalm 114, in describing the Israelite deliverance from Egypt, sings:

> "The sea saw it; and fled;
> The Jordan was driven back.
> The mountains skipped like rams,
> The little hills like lambs."

---

[2]*The Abingdon Bible Commentary* (New York: The Abingdon Press, 1929), p. 23.

Nothing could be more ludicrous than to take the picture literally.

To interpret the poetical passages of the Old Testament in any other way than as the exalted poetry that they are is to ignore the divine method which selects poets above all others to beckon men onward and upward.

KINDS OF HEBREW POETRY

1. *Lyric.* There are many snatches of song in the historical books. Psalms is an imperishable collection of religious lyrics.

2. *Gnomic,* or *Proverbial.* Proverbs, part of Ecclesiastes, and many detached aphorisms in other books of the Old Testament.

3. *Dramatic.* Job, a didactic poem. Canticles, a song of love. Job has been happily called "The Epic of the Inner Life," its chief interest centering in Job's struggle against doubt. Neither Job nor Canticles was ever designed for the stage.

4. *Elegiac.* Lamentations. There are other dirges in the historical books and in the prophets (cf. 2 Sam. 1:19–27; Amos 5:1–3).

The Book of Job

The problem of suffering is the greatest enigma of the human mind. Why is our planet invaded by physical and moral evil? How can an infinite God allow his purposes to be thwarted? Why do the innocent suffer along with the guilty? The traditional Jew had his answer to this enigma. And, like all simple answers to a great problem, it was utterly inadequate for meeting the facts of the case: The righteous always prosper on this earth; the wicked suffer. If a man is suffering, it is an indication that he has sinned. This conclusion was inevitable in light of the traditional idea of immortality found both in the book of Job and throughout the Old Testament. In this view, the afterlife held no attractions for sinner or saint. All were the same in Sheol (grave). It offered only a shadowy existence that could not compare with earthly life, for there was spent an aimless and empty eternity. It was as if a man no longer lived. (Cf. Job 3:17–19; 7:9–10; 10:21–22; 14:7–12; Psalms 39:13; 88:10–12; 115:17; Ecclesiastes 3:19ff.; 9:4ff.)

Since there were no distinctions in Sheol between the reward of the good or the evil man, and since God was righteous, it was necessary for him to reward men in the present world for their deeds. An understanding of this philosophy is essential in interpreting the books of Job and Ecclesiastes. To the author of the book of Job were revealed the errors of this belief and a better solution of the problem. He saw that this view was guilty of two errors. (1) Virtue would be practiced for earthly results. It was this attitude that Satan accused Job of possessing. (2) Religion belonged to the rich, the free, the healthy, the happy, while it had no advantage for the poor, the broken, the defeated, the wretched. When the community flourished, the sufferer was out of place. The leper was shut out from the exercises of religion as well as social life. The mourner was unclean, as was his food (since it was not brought into the house of God). At the very time when religion should be nearest to a man's heart to comfort and sustain, it was denied the ancient Jew. It was to combat their fatal error in the interpretation of suffering that the writer of the book of Job was inspired to compose his great work. Turning from tradition and pious platitudes, he broke through the clouds of doubt into the sunshine of God's purposes for his saints.

The book of Job is the greatest of all dramatic works in the Old Testament. In fact, Carlyle has called it "the world's great book," a description which it richly deserves. At first glance one may conclude that it simply reports events as they happened. However, a closer examination reveals that the writer is using the experiences of Job to impress his readers with the truths God had revealed to him. In other words the Spirit leads him to use the dramatic method to express the revelation. Utterly convincing in this respect is the mechanical arrangement of the speeches into cycles and poetry. No one in the emotional condition attributed to Job would wait politely for each man to speak his piece and then reply to each one in poetical rhythm at the proper moment, repeating this process three times. It is quite apparent, therefore, that the author of the book of Job has investigated the life of the flesh-and-blood Job, and with that raw material has composed his mighty work. He could have simply declared his truth, but by this dramatic arrangement interest is sustained and ideology developed.

Not until this immortal book is recognized as the great dramatic work it is, will it live for the peoples of the world. Not until we see that every line of its splendid poetry is the product of a Spirit-led philosopher who was using every phrase to contribute toward his ultimate goal will we discern the depth of meaning that lies buried in its pages.

When was the book of Job written? There are two main positions:

1. During the reign of Solomon.

This explains its catholic spirit. The three friends were Arabians; perhaps Job was. The setting was in Haran to the northeast of Palestine, near Damascus. There are no references to the Law of Moses or the recorded events of Jewish history. However, this may have been done to allow his break with tradition. Job belongs in thought and form to the wisdom literature that originated with Solomon. It is closer to the book of Proverbs than any other book in the Old Testament (but cf. p. 224).

2. During or after the Exile.

The problem of suffering came to the fore during this period (cf. Jeremiah, Habakkuk). The conception of immortality in the book is a late one. There is considerable Aramaic and some late Hebrew. The picture of Satan is very advanced. This conception is a developing one in the Old Testament. The word "Satan" means adversary. The term occurs only two other times in the Old Testament, both in post-Exilic literature. (Zech. 3:1–2; 1 Chronicles 21:1, the only passage where the article is not used. "Satan" is here a proper name.)

The evidence seems to favor the late date for the book, but is entirely dependent upon arguments from style and theology, which are very precarious.

SUMMARY OF THE BOOK

Prologue.—Story of Satan's effort to make Job curse God (chaps. 1–2). Job's great prosperity and genuine piety (1:1–5). Satan insinuates that Job's piety is inseparable from prosperity and receives permission to test him (6–12). Job's first temptation,—loss of *property and family* (13–22). Second stage in Job's temptation,—loss of *health* (2:1–10). His three friends come to comfort him (11–13). Their words introduce us to the third stage in Job's temptation,—loss of his *good name.*

Job at first is misunderstood, and then openly reproached. The argument continues throughout the poem. There are three cycles of speeches. (Zophar fails to speak on the third round.)

The transition from the prologue to the debate between Job and the three friends is made in chapter 3, *Job's Cry for Death.*

1. Why was I born? 3–10
2. Why did I not die at birth? 11–19
3. Why cannot I die now? 20–26

1. *First Cycle*

The theme is the *nature of God*. Eliphaz emphasizes his holiness and goodness; Bildad, his righteousness; Zophar, his wisdom. Job laments his apparent injustice. He feels that God has deserted him, and has turned to his friends for sympathy; but they see in his suffering an indication of sin and urge him to repent. Job passionately defends his integrity.

First Speech of Eliphaz. Chapters 4–5

No man can be just before God. God is chastening Job in order to correct his sin. If he will admit his guilt, he will prosper again.

Job's Reply to Eliphaz. Chapters 6–7

His friends hurt him rather than help him, with their insinuations. He boldly asks why the mighty God torments a weak man.

Bildad's First Speech. Chapter 8

God is just and discriminating. If he does not heed Job's cry, it is because he has sinned.

Job's Reply to Bildad. Chapters 9–10

A man, though innocent, cannot vindicate himself against the omnipotent God. The sufferer must be misunderstood and counted a wicked man. Job entreats God to let him alone, to give a little comfort before he dies.

First Speech of Zophar. Chapter 11

The boastings of Job amount to nothing in the presence of an omniscient God. If Job will repent and turn to God, he will find prosperity and peace.

Job's Reply to Zophar's First Speech. Chapters 12–14

Job demonstrates that he knows more theology than his friends. He begins to wonder if the traditional idea of immortality is correct. If it is, God is unjust. What if it is wrong? Suppose, if a man died, he continued to live! He could bear his sorrow if that were true. But, no, it cannot be.

2. Second Cycle

The theme is the *Fate of the Wicked Man*. The friends have concluded that Job has added deceit and lying to his other sins. They are more blunt in their accusations. As they begin to lose their tempers, Job becomes calmer, turning more and more to God as his only hope of vindication.

Second Speech of Eliphaz. Chapter 15

Eliphaz asks how Job can claim purity when no man is clean before God. Having tried the love of God in his first speech, this time he preaches wrath upon sinners.

Job's Reply to the Second Speech of Eliphaz. Chapters 16–17

Job does not try to refute Eliphaz. His one hope is in God as the witness of his innocency.

Second Speech of Bildad. Chapter 18

Divine punishment and human execration shall overtake the wicked.

Job's Reply to the Second Speech of Bildad. Chapter 19

After the usual preliminary remonstrances at the reproaches of his friends, Job gives a most touching account of his persecution by God, and the consequent alienation of men, making an earnest plea that his friends have pity upon him. Then comes the mighty climax of the book when Job asserts his faith in his God who will vindicate him even after death. If justice is not done in this world, it will be accomplished beyond the grave.

Second Speech of Zophar. Chapter 20

With passionate haste, Zophar rushes upon Job, and asserts that the triumph of the wicked man is brief; for sin brings its own retribution, and soon God shall bring down the fierceness of his wrath upon his head.

Job's Reply to the Second Speech of Zophar. Chapter 21

After preliminary fencing, Job discusses the difficult theme, *The Prosperity of the Wicked*. God may vindicate beyond the grave, but he certainly is not just in this life.

3. Third Cycle

The theme is the *Sinfulness of Job*. Eliphaz accuses Job of terrible sins. Bildad, able to speak nothing to the point, talks in broad generalities. Zophar will not waste his breath upon such a blasphemer. Note Job's earnest denial of crime at the conclusion of his speech in chapter 31.

Third Speech of Eliphaz. Chapter 22

Since the facts of the case do not agree with the theology of Eliphaz, that worthy tries to change the facts rather than his theology. He accuses Job of sins that he knows he never committed, for they are social sins of which all would have been aware. If, as he believes, only the wicked suffer, Job must have sinned terribly.

Job's Reply to the Third Speech of Eliphaz. Chapters 23–24

Job longs to find God. Although innocent, he cannot do so. Further injustice is shown in the prosperity of the wicked.

Bildad's Third Speech. Chapter 25

God is too great for any mere worm to be just before him.

Job's Reply to Bildad's Third Speech. Chapter 26

I, too, know that God is great. But what light does that throw on my problem?

Job's Concluding Address. Chapters 27–31

(1) Chapters 27 and 28 are difficult to understand, because Job seems to take issue with his own position concerning the fate of the wicked. Possibly he began to see that, in the heat of argument, he had placed too much stress on the prosperity of the wicked. Some commentaries think that imbedded here is a lost speech of Zophar. In chapter 27, Job first protests that he is innocent (1–6), and then pictures the distress and final destruction of the wicked man (7–23). In chapter 28, Job declares that wisdom cannot be found or purchased by man. God alone is in possession of wisdom. To fear him is wisdom. One of the greatest chapters in the book.

(2) Chapters 29–31. Job's review of his case. In chapter 29 is a pathetic picture of his former happiness. In chapter 30 he contrasts his present abject condition. Chapter 31 states a marvelous code of morality that goes beyond anything in the Old Testament. Job proudly challenges God to find sin in him deserving such punishment as he has received.

Speech of Elihu. Chapters 32–37

Elihu, a young interested by-stander, has observed errors in both sides of the argument. Job has already silenced the friends.

Now someone must silence Job. Elihu attacks two arguments of Job that were erroneous: (1) that God is unjust; (2) that God will not speak to him. He shows that God could not run this universe without justice. Chaos would result. God has been speaking to Job all the time by means of his suffering, wishing to teach him every truth. Job has shown a proud spirit, and needs to humble himself. It is significant that Yahweh later condemns the friends but not Elihu. Contrary to the opinion of many scholars, these passages are essential to the argument of the book.

First Address of Yahweh—God's Wonders in Nature. Chapters 38–39

We cannot explain the wonders of God in the inanimate or in the animal world. Job, conscious of his littleness, declines to reply to the Almighty (40:1–5).

Second Address of Yahweh. 40:6 to 41:34

Let Job be careful not to usurp the position of the Almighty, since he cannot overcome or understand even the hippopotamus or the crocodile. Job repents of his rebellious spirit (42:1–6).

Epilogue. Job prays for his three friends, and his former prosperity is doubled (42:7–17). Some scholars claim that this contradicts the rest of the book, teaching that righteousness is always rewarded in this world by prosperity. However, this was done to demonstrate to the friends that Job was correct in his stand. The world knew thereby that there was suffering not due to sin. If Job had died in agony, the friends' position would have been established.

NOTES ON IMPORTANT PASSAGES

1:1. Uz was probably near Damascus. The name Job means "penitent," or "persecuted one"; "a man of sorrows."

1:2. "Seven" and "three" were ideal numbers.

1:3. Job was indeed wealthy. The sheep indicate the size of his pastures. The camels were used for trade; he was a rich merchant. The oxen were beasts of burden and indicate his interest in agriculture. The she-asses were useful because of their milk; Job ran a tremendous dairy.

1:4. The feasts were probably birthday celebrations.

1:5. The Hebrew word for "renounce" is *barak*. It also means "to bless." The play on this word in chapters 1–2 is interesting.

1:6. Satan is among the sons of God. The term "sons of God" is a peculiar Hebrew adjectival construction meaning "divine beings," perhaps angels. Note that it is not said that Satan is one of them, only that he is among them.

1:11. While Job is sacrificing for his sons, lest they renounce God, he himself will soon be put to the same test, little realizing it.

1:16. "Fire of God" is lightning.

1:21. This is only fair. God gave, he can take away as he wills. "Blessed" is the word *barak*, but here Job uses it in the opposite sense from what Satan intended.

1:22. This will not be true later. A hint of what is to come.

2:4. "Skin for skin"—Satan claims that Job is a shrewd bargainer. He will gladly give up all he has as long as he can keep his life. It is still a good bargain.

2:9. It is a matter of interest that Satan did not take away Job's wife. Apparently he felt that she would be his ally. It is natural that she would feel this heartache more intensely than he. The Targum claims that her name was Dinah and gives her a long speech, claiming that it was quite out of propriety that on such an occasion a woman would say so little.

2:13. The sympathy of the friends was deep and sincere.

3:1. Until now Job had kept quiet, but amid the sympathy expressed by his friends, his pent-up grief burst out. He could understand how God could take away what he had given him, but now the situation was different. This suffering of body had no rational explanation, and in addition to all the other sorrow was too much for him to endure. He bared his soul to his sympathizers. When they falsely accused him, he felt that the very citadel of his soul had been betrayed.

4:2a. Would it hurt you too much if I say something?

4:3–5. Why do you not practice what you have preached?

4:17–18. God can see fault even in his angels. How can man be just before him?

6:2–3. My complaints are not out of proportion to my suffering.

6:5–6. Every effect has a cause. My words have a sufficient basis.

6:10. Job exults in pain. The more he suffers, the more he knows he is innocent.

6:21. "Ye see a terror, and are afraid"—If you should agree with me, you are afraid God will strike you, too. Yet you know I am pure.

6:22–23. I haven't asked you for money, so why so harsh with me?

6:26. I know that much of what I say, I do not mean. Please do not hold my wild words against me. Try to understand the reason why I am so upset.

6:27. You would sell my good name to add to your own piety. In condemning me, you feel more holy.

7:11–21. A terrible indictment of God by Job.

7:20. Read, "O thou *spy* of men."

9:20. Job nowhere claims that he is perfect, but only that he has not sinned in *proportion* to his suffering.

9:32–33. Christ has ideally fulfilled this office. The Old Testament saint felt he had no such intercessor.

13:15. A determination, not of trust, but of arguing his case until declared not guilty. Job may die, but he will not deny his own integrity.

13:21–22. Job tells God the only condition upon which he will talk peace with him. He does not exhibit here a proper humility, as Elihu shall mention later.

14:14. Not "shall he live again?" but "will he continue to live?"

14:15b. If there is a reward after death, it would be evidence that You do care.

15:10. We have tradition on our side.

16:4. Criticism is easy when the other fellow is the victim.

16:19. Job is beginning to turn to God again.

18:8–10. Note the number of words used as synonyms for a trap.

18:13. A reference to Job's sickness.

18:15. As had happened to Job's flocks.

18:17. A reference to Job's children.

19:3. "ten times"—a figure of speech, meaning "as much as possible."

19:4. If I have sinned, you have not discovered what it is with all your probing.

19:6. I have not been caught in a net of my own making (cf. 18:8ff.). God has hunted me down without cause.

19:21–22. A touching appeal for sympathy. Finding none, Job makes his immortal declaration of faith in God. Man may desert him, but God never will.

19:23–24. Before, he had not wanted his words remembered (6:26), but what he will say now will be monumental.

19:25. "I know"—Heretofore he had disbelieved or was uncertain, but not so now. "Redeemer"—The Hebrew word *goel* (cf. book of Ruth). The *goel* was a man's closest relative, whose responsibility it was to redeem his property and defend his good name. God will be Job's vindicator, although no man comes to his side. "the earth" (dust)—"my dust," my ashes when I am dead.

19:26. "this"—Job points to his decaying body. "Then without my flesh," when my body has gone back to dust. "Beyond the grave I shall see God."

19:27. Job will not be satisfied with having God vindicate him in this world after he is gone and cannot see it. This verse quite emphatically states that Job shall personally be present. Job is driven to the belief that if God is just, there must be a reward past the grave. What the nature of that reward will be is left for the New Testament to describe. It was enough for Job to know it would come.

A good number of commentators deny that Job asserts a faith in an experience beyond the grave in this passage. The chief argument is that in the chapters that follow he shows no indication of such a faith but continues with his claims of God's injustice. Perhaps this could be better understood by noting that Job is human. Although he now believes in vindication beyond the grave, he still thinks it should also take place in the present world. "Why," he asks, "does God run the *present* world with such injustice?"

21:4. Job calls himself impatient, and the word certainly describes his attitude. The term "patient Job" should more appropriately be "impatient Job." It originated in the expression found in James 5:11. The word there, however, should be translated "endurance," which accurately describes Job. Although impatient, he never quit until he had found God.

21:16. A noble declaration. I had rather have my good conscience than their prosperity.

21:19–21. Recompense is nothing unless the guilty party himself experiences the punishment.

22:2–3. Eliphaz reveals his erroneous basic conception. There can be no such thing as a warm personal relationship between God and man.

26:7. A remarkable statement in light of modern scientific theory.

Chapter 28. Man is able to do wonderful things, but he can never of himself know how to conduct his own life. Only God can give that wisdom.

31:29–30. The attitude Job evidences here toward his enemies surpasses anything in the Old Testament and offers a challenge to the Christian.

31:35. Job personally signs his statement of virtue. He is confident of its correctness.

35:15. A true statement. Job has been wondering why God has not appeared to him. The reason is that Yahweh is merciful. In Job's present spirit of rebellious pride, God could come only in anger. Apparently Job realizes that Elihu is correct, for he does not reply to any statement he makes, even when given opportunity. (Cf. 33:32–33.)

40:8. Job's great sin. He was willing to sacrifice the integrity of God to keep his own.

42:5. Job learns the one lesson he needs, humility. The more intimate the fellowship a man has with God, the more pronounced his sense of unworthiness becomes.

SUGGESTIONS ABOUT THE MEANING OF SUFFERING

1. The Prologue. Satan is allowed to test a goodness that may be only a veneer.

2. The argument of the friends. Suffering is due to past sin. This is often true, but not invariably so.

3. The suggestion of Job. Man suffers because of the indifference of God. This view is shown to be completely erroneous.

4. The Elihu speeches. Suffering is often allowed in order to educate or train, that through it men may learn what otherwise they would not know. Job attained thereby a faith in personal immortality.

5. The Yahweh speeches. Suffering should not produce a spirit of rebellion but an increased faith. Just as man must admit his ignorance of the physical universe, but nevertheless trusts God to manage it, just so he should recognize that God is able to direct his personal life. Whatever happens, we may be sure that God cares for his own.

THE PSALMS

The book of Psalms is the first book of the Hebrew Writings. In the Hebrew it bears the title, "Praises." At one time the psalms may have been considered prayers (Psalm 72:20). The LXX uses the term *"Psalmoi,"* "melodies." In one Codex we have the designation *Psalterion* (whence *Psalter,* songs sung to the accompaniment of stringed instruments). The division of the Psalter is fivefold. Each book closes with a doxology, Psalm 150 being a doxology to the whole Psalter, and Psalm 1 being the introduction. These divisions correspond to the five books of the Law. The designation represents the Psalter as the response of the community to the summons of God in the Law.

First Book (1–41). Consists, with only four exceptions (1, 2, 10, 33), of psalms attributed by their titles to David. This book is distinguished by frequent use of the name Yahweh.

Second Book (42–72). Psalms of "sons of Korah" (42–49), "of David" (51–65, 68–70). This was probably a compilation for tabernacle and Temple services. Here the name Elohim predominates.

Third Book (73–89). "Psalms of Asaph" (73–83) and "sons of Korah" (84–88). Names of deity equally applied. Only one psalm in this book attributed to David (86).

Fourth Book (90–106). The first attributed to Moses, two to David (101, 103). The rest anonymous. Yahweh is the prevailing name.

Fifth Book (107–150). Liturgical, including the Yahweh Hallelujah Psalms. The Psalms of Ascents predominate.

The Titles of the Psalms

1. The Nature of the Titles

(1) Titles descriptive of the character of the poem: (a) *Mizmor* (psalm), a piece of music to be sung with stringed instrument; (b) *Shir*, song of any kind; (c) *Maschil*, a song of special skill (anthem); (d) *Michtam* ("golden, precious"), psalm with idea of atonement, or personal lamentation.

(2) Titles connected with the musical setting or performance: (a) "to the chief musician" (leader of the Temple choir), (b) *selah*, a musical direction, not to be read, either meaning (1) a pause in singing for an instrumental interlude or (2) an elevation (forte); (c) some difficult expressions in the titles probably indicating the tune to which the psalm was to be sung.

(3) Titles referring to liturgical use of psalms to be sung at certain times.

(4) Titles relating to authorship. A Hebrew preposition is used that may mean either "by," "belonging to," or "connected with." One cannot always tell whether it denotes authorship or relationship. "A Psalm to David" may mean "a Psalm by David" or a "Psalm concerning David." However, the regular use of the construction is as a possessive.

(5) Titles describing the occasion of the psalm, practically limited to the psalms that bear the name of David.

2. The Value of the Titles

In the study of the Psalms, much depends upon the opinion of the student as to the general trustworthiness of the superscriptions, or titles. These titles are not part of the inspired text, nor is it probable that they were prefixed by the authors of the various psalms. They are probably the work of ancient editors of collections of psalms. Scholars are quite unscientific in rejecting these superscriptions as wholly worthless; for they represent a very ancient tradition, probably reaching back to the period before the Exile. Davidic titles may have been pre-fixed long before the Exile. The Septuagint translators found the titles in their Hebrew text, and many of the phrases were so ancient and archaic that the translators were wholly at sea as to their meaning. Some of the superscriptions are probably incorrect; but as a rule they are worthy of respectful consideration.

J. W. Thirtle, in *The Titles of the Psalms*, claims that all the musical directions were originally subscriptions, while the notes as to authorship and occasion of composition are true superscriptions. Copyists united the subscription of one psalm with the superscription of the following, without any mark of separation; and later editors placed the two as a long superscription to the second of the two psalms.

3. The Testimony of the Titles as to Psalm Authorship

(1) To David 73 (37 in Book I, 18 in Book II, 1 in Book III, 2 in Book IV, and 15 in Book V).

(2) To Asaph 12 (50, 73–83).

(3) To Sons of Korah 12 (42–49, 84–85, 87–88). Psalm 88 also ascribed to Heman.

(4) To Solomon 2 (72, 127).

(5) To Moses 1 (Psalm 90).

(6) To Ethan 1 (Psalm 89).

4. Classification of Psalms

There are certain natural groups into which the Psalms fall:

(1) Fifteen Psalms of Ascents. 120–134

(2) Seven Alphabetical Psalms: 25, 34, 37, 111, 112, 119, 145. Psalms 9 and 10 give some evidence of conformity to the order of the letters. Psalm 119 is the most complete and elaborate example of an alphabetical poem.

(3) Forty-two Elohistic Psalms. 42–83. All others are Yahwistic, Psalm 84 marking the transition from one class to the other.

(4) Eleven Hallelujah Psalms: 111–113; 115–117; 146–150.

At Passover, in New Testament times, "the Egyptian Hallel," Psalms 113–118, was sung in two parts.

Certain psalms are closely related because of a similarity of subject matter. A study of these groups will enhance the understanding of the teachings of Psalms. This approach has two advantages.

1. The dating of the individual psalms is not imperative. There is such an irreconcilable difference among scholars about these dates that there is a great need for a method that considers what God has to say through all his psalmists to the world today. Regardless of the date of the individual psalms, there is a message of the whole Psalter that mirrors the soul needs of humanity of all ages. It is because of this truth that the book has been so helpful through the ages. Its truth does not belong to time but to eternity.[1]

2. One avoids the repetition in Psalms that gives the impression of sameness to the beginner. In such a study the distinctive teachings of each psalm are noted, and where a whole psalm is distinctive, it can be studied in its entirety. Although all the psalms may be grouped under the following headings, only those that present the more significant ideas will be discussed.

THE NATURE PSALMS

8; 19:1–6; 29; 65:9–13; 104; 147:8–18

To the Hebrew the world was never just so many sticks and stones. Its every wonder testified to the glory of the God who made it.

1. God in the heavens. Psalm 19

The heavens are constantly preaching and teaching (verse 2). Their message is not an audible one (verse 3), yet it has gone through the whole world (verse 4): "If his handiwork is like this, how glorious must be the Artisan" (verse 1).

2. God in the storm. Psalm 29

Modern science has taken the wonder out of the storm. The

---

[1]Cf. A. F. Kirkpatrick, "The Book of Psalms," *Cambridge Bible* (Cambridge University Press, 1910), for an excellent treatment of the dates of the individual Psalms.

thunderbolt is no longer a manifestation of the power of God but simply a rushing of wind into a vacuum created by heat from electric flashes of lightning. But to the ancient Hebrew the storm was an instrument of his God, a reminder of his power. When a storm arose, he thought of God. Note the skill of the poetry of Psalm 29 in swelling to a crescendo as the storm approaches and reaches its climax.

3. God in the earth. Psalm 65:9-13

In the spring a young man's fancy may turn to love, but to the writer of this delightful passage that season turned his thoughts to God, for it was he who prepared the soil through the seasons to ready it for the plowman. The rainfall comes from his river (the clouds), always full of water. By his provision the seed is ready, and at just the right moment showers of blessing fall to soften the crust of the topsoil and allow the tender plants to spring up. At harvest time the psalmist's mind is not upon tearing down barns and building bigger ones, but upon Yahweh, who crowns the year with his goodness. All nature seems to be singing the praise of such a bountiful and gracious God.

4. God in man. Psalm 8

As a psalmist considers the heavens, he is impressed with the smallness of frail man. Then there comes to him the thought that God prefers such insignificant instruments (2). Davids are always slaying their Goliaths. In fact, God has made man the crown of his creation, only slightly below himself (verse 5, Hebrew, *Elohim*; the LXX translated "angels," but this is the usual word for God in the Old Testament). As he thinks of such grace shown to man, he shouts a grand doxology. When the psalmist considers man, he is constantly reminded of his gracious God.

THE CHARACTER PSALMS

1, 15, 24, 50, 75, 82, 101, 112, 127, 128, 131, 133

These are the psalms that state the characteristics of the man who pleases God. Note these significant traits:

1. Sincerity, purity of motive. This is one of the highest

ideals among the Hebrews. It is the opposite of deceit and hypocrisy. If the stream is to be pure, the source must be pure. The ideal man is pure of heart (24:4a) and speaks truth in his heart (15:2b). He does not set his affections on vanity or false-hood (24:4b).

2. Purity of motive is not enough. Right actions must result. The man approved of God walks uprightly and works right-eousness (15:2). This upright and righteous life is character-ized by several traits:

(1) He is careful of his companions (Psalm 1:1)—observe the types of men he avoids. He does not listen to the advice of the ungodly (Hebrew, "off-center folk," abnormals, whose view of life is distorted), nor does he follow the life of the sinner (Hebrew, "those who miss the mark" or fail in God's intention for their lives). The scoffer, who sits on the sideline of life and mocks those who play the game, finds him indiffer-ent to his complaints. On the other hand, God-fearing men are those whose friendship he desires (15:4b). To them he is a loyal friend. Psalm 133 extols the value of brotherly unity. It will bless the whole community, like the anointing oil of Aaron, the dew of Hermon. Naturally the good man is not a gossip. He does not travel on his tongue (15:3). Stories injurious to his neighbor's reputation stop with him. Psalm 120 is a caustic con-demnation of a deceitful tongue.

(2) He is a man of principles. His word can be relied upon (15:4); nor can he be bribed (15:5). He does not take unfair advantage of the misfortune of others by charging interest. In Israel no one borrowed money unless he was in desperate cir-cumstances. The word for "interest" means "something bitten off."

(3) He finds his chief delight in meditating upon the Word of God (1:2).

Psalm 1 states that the results attendant upon the God-approved life are worth every effort expended:

1. Stability. The ideal man is like a tree firmly planted (1:3). He shall never be moved (15:5). The Hebrew word "never" comes from a root meaning "to conceal," and means "that which is concealed either in the past or future." The expres-sion means, therefore, "The one doing these things will not be

moved, even beyond the dim unknown." The world may reel or rock, but this man will not be shaken.

2. Exhaustless supply of strength. He is like a tree planted between streams of water, with abundant nourishment on every side.

3. Fruitfulness. Since he is planted firmly and bountifully supplied, good fruit is inevitable.

4. Perpetual beauty and attractiveness. He is like an evergreen, whose leaf never withers. Men will marvel at his source of strength.

5. The power to see it through. Read, "Whatever he begins, he will bring to a successful conclusion" (1:3). This is accomplished by the direct aid of God, but also by the assistance of the numerous children with which Yahweh blesses him (Psalm 127). It is vain to build without God, but with him on your side. peace of mind and abundance of children result.

THE PENITENTIAL PSALMS

6, 25, 32, 38, 39, 40, 51, 102, 130

Underlying the psalms is a deep sense of human sin. "For in thy sight no man living is righteous" (143:2). "If thou, Jehovah, shouldest mark iniquities, O Lord, who can stand?" (130:3). "There is none that doeth good, no, not one" (53:3).

In Psalm 51 we find sin graphically characterized as:

1. Rebellion against the will of God (verse 1, ASV, "transgression").

2. Missing the mark set for life (verse 2, ASV, "sin").

3. The perversion of the image of God (verse 2, ASV, "iniquity").

4. Pollution (2, 7).

5. A haunting spectre (3b).

6. Primarily an affront to God (4).

7. Transmitted by the race (5).

8. Breaking fellowship between God and man (11a).

9. Destroying the joy of living (12).

10. Sealing the lips of testimony (14–15).

11. Hurting our fellow man (14).

Since sin is such a terrible master, there is only one hope for its victim—the grace of God. The favor of God can never be won by good works alone (16–17). The sinner's only hope is to come to God with a humble and contrite spirit, begging for mercy. Even then he will never master temptation until a new creation is achieved (51:10). In this process there are four steps:

1. A broken spirit (17a), when the sinner admits his sin and begs for mercy.

2. A willing spirit (12b). Whatever cure is suggested will be followed.

3. "Spirit of thy holiness" (verse 11, ASV, "thy holy Spirit"), whereby man is separated from the world and dedicated to God.

4. Steadfast spirit (10). Now that he has become separate, the power is given to endure.

In Psalm 32 we have the joy of the soul forgiven of sin. It is the companion of Psalm 51.

1. The joy of the forgiven soul (32:1–2). His rebellion has been removed, his missing the mark blotted out, his moral perversion forgotten. He has hidden nothing from God but has confessed all (2b).

2. The contrast of the state of sin with that of forgiveness. Before the sinner acknowledged his guilt, he was in absolute misery. God's hand was heavy upon him. Life held no joy; both soul and body were shrivelling (32:3–4). Immediately upon the confession of sin, the weight was gone, and he knew the joy of forgiveness. He that had been hiding from God now hides in him (32:5, 7). The pardoned sinner leads others to repent (51:13) and calls upon the righteous to take new courage (32:6). God further instructs him to be stubborn no longer but freely to follow his leading. Responsibility to God does not cease with the sinner's pardon for sin.

PSALMS CONCERNING THE WORD OF GOD

119; 19:7–4

The psalmist's love for God's Word (his revealed truth) was as intense as the modern love for comics. Psalm 119, each section of which begins with the successive letters of the Hebrew alphabet and which is the longest psalm in the Psalter, has this affection as its entire theme. The teachings of God are the constant thoughts of the psalmist (119:97). He rejoices over each new-found truth as one who has found great spoil (119: 162). Sweeter to his taste than honey is the thought of God's Word (119:103). He cannot wait until night, when he can be alone to meditate (119:148). It is to the Scriptures that he goes when he needs advice (119:24). Wherever he goes, he speaks of his affection, even before kings (119:46). When he sees others disregarding Yahweh's commands, he weeps with sorrow at their neglect (119:136).

The characteristics of the Word are vividly portrayed in these psalms. (1) It is faithful. When once it is decreed in heaven, it will be carried out, for all things are servants of God (119:89ff.). (2) It is unlimited in its application. All other things have a limit, but the Word of God is an ideal that has never been attained (119:96). (3) All of truth is found therein (119:160), for the ordinances of the Lord conform to an absolute standard (19:9). (4) The law of God has been tested and proved by the ages (119:140). (5) It is sure, not relative or variable; therefore, it makes wise the man who lacks convictions (ASV, "simple"), assuring him of the existence of fixed principles (19:7). (6) The law of the Lord is perfect; that is, it always accomplishes its purpose of restoring the soul (19:7). When the soul is lost from God, it shows the way back; when it is discouraged, refreshment is brought. (7) In contrast to the immorality of the heathen, the fear of the Lord taught by his Word is clean. It demands the highest of moral standards (19:9), assuring its application to every people and age as it challenges the best in man (19:8b).

The work of the Word of God is invaluable. (1) It guides a man through the problems of life. The young man needs its voice of experience (119:9). To the mature it is the light that shines through the darkness to show the way (119:105). (2) Its comfort in the time of trouble is immeasurable (119:50). Without its assurance, hope would be lost (119:92). As it tells of God's help to the saints of old, new courage comes in the present (119:132). In fact, it often takes sorrow to cause a man to discover the comforts found in the Word (119:67, 71). (3) True wisdom is bestowed by the truths of God more than by all man's learning (119:98-99, 104).

The Scriptures can never be understood by human wisdom alone; God must open eyes that see but do not understand (119:18). Not until the heart is enlarged by Yahweh does man find room for his commandments (119:32). When understanding is bestowed upon man, then for the first time he will know how to live (119:144).

The psalmist's method of study is worth noting. Reading the Word is not mentioned a single time. He is so familiar with the Law that he knows it by heart and constantly repeats it to himself (119:97; 1:2). It is hidden in his heart (119:11). He does not forget what it says (119:16). A mere reading of Scripture is useless unless its truth is appropriated and carried over into life. When one studies so diligently that the Word of God is actually a part of himself, then its true value can be realized.

However, something more is needed than just a knowledge of Scripture. There must be the power to follow the truth one knows. The author of Psalm 119, with all his knowledge and affection for the Law of God, concludes his magnificent eulogy with a surprising confession. He forgets not the commandments of God; yet he has gone astray in the weakness of his flesh. God must seek him or he is lost (119:176). In Psalm 19, after describing the glories of the Word and taking warning from its teachings (19:11), the psalmist still cannot see all his errors. Only wisdom from above can enlighten him. Else hidden faults will grow into wilful sins, which will eventually result in open rebellion against God. How important it is to stamp out sin in its beginnings! Only a closer walk with God will make the recognition of its presence possible.

Psalms Concerning Worship

26, 73, 84, 100, 116, 122

The book of Psalms is rich in its teachings about the reasons why a man should attend worship services. The modern might not appreciate the slaughterhouse atmosphere of the Jewish Temple, but to the devout Hebrew it was the most precious spot upon God's earth. Surely those of us who follow Christ should love his church as devotedly.

1. The psalmist loved to go to the Temple for the sense of fellowship with God. His one desire was to be able to spend his whole life there (27:4). One cannot help thinking of those people who claim to love God but cannot bear the thought of being present at church for one hour a week. It is true that God is everywhere, but man needs a special place and time to worship, lest he forget to think of God at all. In Psalm 84 the psalmist is pining away for lack of that spiritual strength bestowed upon him when he worships God in his house. As the sparrow and the swallow find no rest until their nest is made, so his soul knows no quiet except the peace found in worship in the Temple (84:3). One day spent there is worth ten thousand elsewhere. Its most meager positions surpass all the glory man can offer (84:10). The presence of the Temple gives Jerusalem its place of honor. For its sake prayer should be lifted up for the peace of the city. The existence of the state is justified by the presence of the church within its boundaries and under its protection (Psalm 122:1–9).

2. Not only does the godly man go to worship services because it is there that he feels closest to God, but also because of the opportunity of communing with fellow worshipers. There is a virtue in communal worship that private devotion can never know. In sharing the experience, each worshiper is the more enriched. On the one hand the psalmist despised the assemblies of the wicked (26:5). On the other he found special

delight in the congregations of the Lord (26:12). Those who love the Lord will seek the companionship of his friends.

3. It is at divine services that life's greatest problems are often solved. Psalm 73 has this great truth as its theme. As the psalm begins, the author is praising the goodness of God to the pure of heart. However, he was not always of this conviction. He had almost slipped into the abyss of a lost faith in God. The source of his doubt was the problem of the book of Job, the prosperity of the wicked (73:3). Evil men seem to live charmed lives (5). When they die, it is without pain (4). They are so well fed that their eyes bulge out (7). Insolent (8–9) and skeptical (11) they challenge God himself to punish them, yet remain secure (12).

The righteous psalmist on the other hand had been plagued and chastened (14) and was seriously questioning the wisdom of trying to live a clean life (13). Yet he kept his doubts to himself lest he destroy someone else's faith (15). Try as he did, he could find no solution to this problem until he went into the sanctuary of God (16–17). Then the whole matter was solved in the atmosphere of worship. Some problems intellect can never solve, but a close walk with God can. Life has to be viewed in its ultimate as well as its present aspect. The wicked have no real permanence (18–20). God, however, stays by the side of his suffering servants and will eventually reward them (23–26). As a result of this vision in the Temple, the psalmist sees that he has been a *"dummox"* (verse 22 Hebrew, "hippopotamus," hence "dumb ox"), and his conscience condemns him for his lack of faith. As a result of this attendance upon a worship service, he knows that his feet cannot slip, for he is held by God's hand (23). He is filled with a desire for fellowship with God that will brook no rivalry (25).

4. The worshiper also finds refreshment and strengthening not known by others. The man in whose heart are the highways to Zion (the one who constantly thinks of the path that leads to the Temple that he may follow it) may pass through the valley of weeping (misfortune, sorrow), but it will become a place of springs (nourishment, source of strength) (Psalm 84:5–6). He it is who has found the secret of serenity. Those who worship before God in Zion also have the secret of eternal

youth (84:7). As the outward man decays, the inner man is constantly renewed.

5. One of the chief aims of worship is to praise God. Psalm 100 calls all the people of the earth to come together to praise God as the true God, Creator of mankind and Provider of all good things.

6. Another reason why the psalmist goes to worship at the Temple is to testify to others concerning the peace of God bestowed upon him. The author of Psalm 116 has just experienced such an act of grace. He had been depressed, and God restored him (116:6). Losing his faith in God (116:8), he had also lost his faith in man (116:11). Now that he has been delivered, he wishes to express his gratitude (12). He will proclaim (ASV, "call upon") the glory of God by paying his vows in the presence of the congregation (13–14). To him, presenting his offering is an opportunity of praise, his testimony to others of appreciation for God's bounty. Those who do not desire that others know what they are offering to God have little in common with this psalmist. Perhaps the size of their gifts could not possibly be considered as indicative of a spirit of gratitude. The verbs in verses 13–17 are interesting, "I will take, I will proclaim, I will pay, I will offer."

THE PSALMS OF SUFFERING

37, 42–43, 49, 77, 90, 109, 137

The list could be extended far more.[2] Most of the Psalter reveals the saint as enduring suffering of some kind. Throughout these psalms runs a sense of the transitoriness and pathos of life, best expressed in Psalm 90. With tears set to verse, the psalmist "preaches man's mortality in immortal words" (Maclaren), contrasting the eternity of God with the brevity of man (90:1–6, 10). The same refrain is repeated in Psalms 39, 49.

In these psalms suffering is portrayed with every imaginable

---

[2]Cf. Psalms 5, 7, 10, 12, 13, 14, 17, 28, 35, 41, 44, 53, 54, 55, 56, 58, 59, 60, 64, 69, 70, 71, 74, 79, 80, 83, 86, 88, 89, 94, 120, 123, 129, 132, 140, 141, 142, 143, 144.

figure of speech. The sufferer makes his bed swim with the water of his tears (6:6). He feels like a worm (22:6) and can count all his bones (22:17). Great floods have engulfed him (42:7); the tempest roars (55:8). God holds back his eyelids to prevent his sleep (77:4); his bones burn like a firebrand (102:3). He is like a sparrow alone upon a housetop (102:7), in such agony that he forgets to eat (102:4). Upon his back plowers have plowed, making long furrows (129:3).

The causes of suffering are four:

1. Mental anguish. The psalmist is disturbed because of God's inaction. One problem was the prosperity of the wicked and the suffering of the righteous. We have already seen this in Psalm 73. Psalm 37 and Psalm 49 present a similar situation. Here, however, the psalmist is not a doubter himself but is giving advice to those who are. "Fret not thyself" (Hebrew, "Do not get hot"), Psalm 37 suggests. Another disturbing element was the matter of unfulfilled promises. The author of Psalm 89:19-51 wonders why God has not kept his promise to David to bless his seed (cf. 33–38).

2. Physical disease (41:8; 77:10). This is not as frequently mentioned as the other causes.

3. Sin. Psalm 90:7ff. attributes the brevity of life to God's wrath upon sin. The sufferer in Psalm 102 is under the wrath of God (10), as is the author of Psalm 39 (8–11). In Psalm 32 the psalmist is in anguish because of unconfessed sin.

4. Persecution. By far the greatest number of these psalms present the psalmists as being under persecution by evil men (Psalms 5:8; 42:9; 43:1–2; 55:3; 140:1). Psalm 137 describes the sad condition of the exiles in Babylonia.

Conspicuous by their absence in the Psalter are complaints because of the death of loved ones. The psalmists did not express selfish problems. Death was to be expected. However, when the innocent suffered, or the sinner repented, the reputation of God was at stake.

It is helpful to note the attitudes toward suffering revealed in Psalms. Psalm 37 suggests two procedures in problems of mental anguish: (1) Trust: "Roll thy way upon the Lord" (5a); "silence your complaints and wait patiently" (7a). (2) Keep busy (37:3).

In the matter of disease, the psalmist bears it with stoic endurance (77:10, read, "and I said, This is my infirmity, the change of the right hand of the Most High"). God had blessed, and now he was permitting suffering. It was the lot of the sufferer to endure. His remembrance of past blessings lightens his dark hours (77:6), and he has faith that just as God has delivered in the past, he will do so again (77:11–12).

The psalmist has learned the lesson of sin: His only hope is in the grace of God (90:15; 102:13). The brevity of life should teach man to live well his few days (90:12). His only opportunity of permanence is found in the work he may do. He will soon depart, but the psalmist prays that his work may endure (90:17).

Under persecution the attitude of the psalmist was twofold. He first voiced imprecations against his enemies. The Imprecatory Psalms present one of the greatest problems of the Old Testament. How could even an Old Testament saint speak of his enemies in such terms as those found in Psalms 55:15; 137:9; 139:22; 69; 109? Several considerations aid in understanding the attitude in these psalms:

1. These men would not have treated their enemies in such a manner if they had fallen into their hands. Both Psalm 69 and Psalm 109 are attributed to David, yet one is well aware of his treatment of Saul (cf. 7:4). Jeremiah, who voices similar imprecations in his book, would certainly not have been guilty of such a sin.

2. The Hebrews did not deal in abstractions. They hated the sinner as much as his sin. If he were an enemy of a saint, he was God's enemy and should be hated as such.

3. Although in some ways these men were far advanced in their concepts, they did not possess the Christian concept of love that is available only through Christ.

4. The traditional idea of immortality had a great deal to do with the matter. If a man were to be punished, it must be in the present world. (Cf. 30:9; 39:13; 88:9ff. 115:17ff. and the introduction to the book of Job in this volume.) Some of the psalms seem to indicate a belief in a future life (16:10; 49:15; 73:24). These are few and questionable. Psalm 49:15 is the most probable indication of a faith in an afterlife, in light of

its context. In verses 13 and 14 the psalmist mentions the fate of the sinner in Sheol. In verse 15 it is stated that God will redeem his servant's soul from the power of Sheol and will receive him. Then verse 20 states that the man who understands not perishes like a beast. It is implied, therefore, that the righteous man lives on.

The second reaction of the psalmist to persecution is a confident faith in deliverance. The psalmist sleeps soundly, not afraid even of ten thousand enemies (3:5–6). Though mother and father forsake him, God will take him up (27:10). He casts his burden upon his Lord, who will not suffer him to be moved (55:22). Having put his trust in God, what can flesh do unto him (56:4)? His heart is fixed, set like concrete, trusting in God's deliverance (57:7).

The Psalms of Assurance

3, 4, 11, 16, 20, 23, 27, 31, 36, 46, 52, 57, 61, 62, 63, 85, 91, 108, 121, 125, 126

There is a close relationship between this group and the Psalms of Suffering, for these are not the utterances of inexperienced optimism but the result of passing through the vale of heartaches and sorrow. They are like the rainbow after the storm. Through experience with God in every trial of life the psalmists describe Yahweh's dealing with them.

1. God is Protector of his own. He makes peace (46:9ff.). He is a tender shepherd (23:1) and a gracious host (23:5). Like an eagle's protecting wings, God hides those who trust in him (91:4). He is their shield against pestilence and destruction (91:4ff.), and their fortress when refuge is sought (91:2). As a keeper he never sleeps but constantly watches over his ward (121:4–5, 7–8). Yahweh is the shade that protects his own, both from the sun by day (sunstroke) and the moon by night (insanity) (121:5–6).

2. God is Provider. He gives length and joy of life (91:16; 34:12). Like a life-giving river, he sustains the besieged city (Psalm 46). In fact, he is the giver of all good gifts (Psalm 34:8–10). Psalm 23 mentions the various provisions God makes

for the needs of his people. The Lord is shepherd, his sheep will lack none of these: (1) Nourishment ("He maketh me to lie down in green pastures"). God richly provides, for it is tender young grass. He satisfies, for the sheep lie down only when they have enough to eat. (2) Rest ("waters of quiet places"). (3) Restoration, refreshment ("He restoreth my soul"). (4) Guidance (23:3). God is always ahead, not behind. The course is never uncharted. His paths are straight, always lead to the intended destination. He does this because of what he is. Being God, he can do nothing else. (5) Security. In the gloomiest gorge his sheep are adequately protected. As a gracious host he favors and protects his guest even while enemies look on. The psalmist shall never be evicted from *his* house.

PSALMS OF PRAISE

87, 103, 107, 114, 139, 150

The psalmists compensated for their complaints with their praise.[3] Never did a people love their God so much. His character defied description. Nevertheless his various attributes could be gratefully acknowledged.

1. Yahweh is praised for his grace. "His anger is but for a moment; his favor is for a lifetime; weeping may tarry for the night, but joy cometh in the morning" (30:5). He hears the prayers of men and is merciful (65:2–3). Even Gentiles shall be considered as native citizens of Zion (Psalm 87). The beauty of Psalm 103:7–18 is well known to all.

2. His possessions are unlimited. The earth is the Lord's and all that dwell therein (24:1). The bullocks of the sacrifices already belong to him (50:7–15).

3. He heals diseases and provides for every need (Psalm 103:3–5).

4. He is the deliverer from every distress. Psalm 107 calls upon those redeemed by God to declare it (107:2). These are the lonely and despairing (4–9), those bound by sin (10–16),

---

[3]Cf. Psalms 9, 18, 30, 33, 34, 47, 48, 65, 66, 67, 68, 76, 78, 81, 92, 93, 95, 96, 97, 98, 99, 105, 106, 111, 113, 115, 117, 118, 124, 134, 135, 136, 138, 145, 146, 147, 148, 149, 150.

the afflicted (17–22), the storm-tossed (23–32). Note the recurring refrain in each stanza that makes this psalm one of the most artistically constructed and hauntingly beautiful in the Psalter.

5. His omniscience is beyond man's ken (139:1–6).

6. His presence is everywhere. There is no escape from him. This is either the most terrifying or most comforting thought men may have (139:7–12).

7. His omnipotence is demonstrated in the wonders of the formation of a human being (139:13–18). Delightful Psalm 114 describes his mastery of nature in beautiful poetry. Psalm 115 declares his supremacy over other gods.

8. His holiness manifests itself in the destruction of the wicked (Psalm 139:19–24).

The Psalms suggest various ways in which such a God should be praised. (1) Psalm 65:1 may be read, "Silence is praise before thee." There are times when man can best praise his God by being quiet. (2) Psalm 150 calls upon the various orchestral instruments to join in praising God. (3) Psalm 107 urges that men praise God with their lips (107:2). (4) Psalm 100 calls upon the people of the earth to join in praise by singing. (5) The attitude one has while serving God may praise or belittle him. To praise him properly, one should "serve Jehovah with gladness." (6) The psalmist in 103:1 praises God with his whole personality: "all that is within me."

THE MESSIANIC PSALMS

These psalms are very difficult to interpret, yet their importance in the plan of God cannot be overestimated. Three designations of the Messiah occur.

1. The Messiah as King (Psalms 2; 20; 21; 45; 72; 110). Psalms 20, 21, 45 seem to have as their immediate object a contemporary king, although the true significance of the passages was fulfilled in Christ. Psalms 2, 72, 110, however, go beyond the possibility of an ordinary earthly king. Psalm 2 is divided into four equal stanzas. In the first (1–3) we see the great tumult of nations preparing for war. They are in insurrection

against God and his anointed (Messiah), seeking to free themselves from their service. The bonds and cords are not those of slavery but those used in yoking oxen. The nations are refusing to serve God in his purposes for the world. The next stanza pulls back the curtain on a scene in heaven. There all is unperturbed. As the nations throng, God is sitting securely enthroned. In a bold figure the psalmist pictures him in laughter at the foolishness of attempts below. Then suddenly Yahweh will act in his wrath, establishing his King upon the holy hill of Zion (4–6). Now the Messiah speaks (7–9). He has been acknowledged as Yahweh's Son and will attain universal dominion. The last strophe draws the practical application from these events (10–12). Let the leaders of the nations take warning and pay obeisance to the Son. Those who trust in him will find refuge.

Psalm 72 describes a king that no earthly person ever approximated until the advent of Jesus. "They shall fear thee while the sun endureth, and so long as the moon, throughout all generations" (72:5). "He shall have dominion also from sea to sea, and from the river unto the ends of the earth" (72:8). "His name shall endure forever . . . and men shall be blessed in him" (72:17; cf. Gen. 12:3).

Psalm 110 is most certainly messianic in its primary reference. Verses 1–2 picture the Messiah's dominion and dignity. Verse 3 describes those who constitute his all-conquering army. They are volunteers, and a holy, priestly people, with the vigorous, life-giving qualities of youth. The psalm concludes with a further description of the ultimate victory of the Messiah (5–7).

2. Psalm 110 also pictures the Messiah as priest. He is to have an eternal priesthood like that of Melchizedek. The writer of Hebrews demonstrates how Jesus fulfilled this prophecy (chapters 5–7).

3. The Messiah as sufferer (Psalms 22; 31:5; 69:7–9, 21). All these passages have reference to the experiences of Jesus upon the cross, allusions too detailed (especially Psalm 22) to be coincidental. The problem that arises is that apparently the psalmists are not consciously predicting events at Calvary but are speaking of their own experiences. If the cross had not

occurred in human history, no one would ever have considered these psalms as messianic. The only logical explanation is that God in his wisdom was guiding the psalmists in writing down their own experiences for a purpose they did not realize themselves. When one day the Messiah suffered and died, the world would know that it was in the eternal plan of God. Because he had been faithful to God, the Old Testament saint aroused the opposition of all those who were enemies of Yahweh. More than any other, Jesus, by his perfection, made evil men conscious of their sin. Accordingly, his experience was both similar and more terrible.

THE PROVERBS

The Hebrew term *"mashal,"* which is translated by the English word "proverb," comes from a root meaning "to be like," and therefore has primarily the meaning of comparison, similitude, and is applied to many discourses, sentences, and expressions which we should not class under the head of proverbs as we commonly use the term ("a pithy saying"). Balaam's prophecy (Num. 23:7) is so called; likewise Job's didactic poem; also the parables in Ezekiel 17:2 and 20:49. There are in the book of Proverbs many passages which are proverbs in the strictest sense (cf. 13:12; 14:10; 14:12; 16:2; 16:3; 17:22; 22:1). However, there are many others that are not of such a nature. Even if, as the Hebrew meaning implied, the "proverbs" were at first restricted to sayings containing a simile, they soon moved out of the bounds of such limitation. A Hebrew proverb is simply a *wise saying* of any form. Proverbs may be divided into five classes: (1) *Historical proverbs*, wherein an event of the past has passed into a popular saying. (Cf. "Is Saul also among the prophets?") However, there seems to be no instance of this type in the book of Proverbs. (2) *Metaphorical proverbs*. These are what we should most appropriately call proverbs. (3) *Enigmas*. These are either riddles or obscure questions (chapter 30). (4) *Parabolic proverbs*. Herein are presented truths in allegorical form. The best example of this class is the treatment of Wisdom. (5) *Didactical proverbs*, which give precise information and instruction on points of behavior (especially chapters 1–9).

The book assumes that there is but one God. There are no

allusions to the Temple, priests, angels, or idolatry. The Messiah is not mentioned, nor is Moses, the Captivity, or any events in Israel's history. The book concerns itself with wisdom, of which there are two different meanings in its passages: (1) practical religion, intelligent uprightness, a human quality (10–31); (2) wisdom personified as the sovereign over life, the helper of Yahweh in his creation, director of the affairs of men (1–9). The picture of wisdom in chapter 8 is similar to the concept of the *Logos* in John 1:1ff. This conception is certainly the embryo out of which the later doctrine developed. It is a groping after a great idea that only centuries of revelation would finally clarify.

Tradition has ascribed the whole book to one author, Solomon, the king of Israel. It is true that three sections of the book are prefaced with his name, but two sections are attributed, one to Agur, and the other to Lemuel. Thus, the book itself claims three different authors by name and includes two sections containing the "words of the wise." Even though some try to explain the preceding by saying that Agur and Lemuel are other names for Solomon, they have no basis for their explanation, whereas there is a mass of evidence for the opinion of divided authorship for the book. Just as in Psalms, however, and even more so, the interpretation and value of the Proverbs do not depend upon their date of writing. What we are concerned about is the truth contained in these inspired passages.

SUMMARY OF THE BOOK

1. Praise of Wisdom

    The style is flowing and poetical. Longer passages prevail. 1–9

2. Collection of Short Proverbs Attributed to Solomon

    Contrasting couplets predominate. 10:1 to 22:16

3. Two Groups of Sayings of the Wise

More a body of maxims than strict proverbs. Longer proverbs prevail. 22:17 to 24:34

4. Several Collections of Proverbs Attributed to Solomon

Comparative couplets predominate. There is more grouping by subject than elsewhere. 25–29

Discourses. Of Agur (30), mother of Lemuel (31:1–9), and an acrostic poem on the ideal housewife (31:10–31)

CLASSIFICATION OF PROVERBS

It is profitable to group the passages of the book according to their teachings concerning moral conduct.

1. On Laziness: 6:6–10; 10:4–5; 10:26; 15:19; 18:9; 19:24; 22:13
2. The Tongue: 6:12–19; 14:29; 15:1; 16:32; 18:8; 18:13; 18:21; 26:2; 26:20; 29:20
3. Contrast of the Fool and Wise Man: 9:8; 11:14; 12:15; 13:20; 14:7–8; 14:15; 15:20; 17:10; 20:3; 26:1; 26:3; 29:9.
4. Drunkenness: 20:1; 23:29–35
5. The Righteous Life and Treatment of Enemies: 1:10–19; 3:1–12; 4:18–19, 23; 11:17; 11:30; 12:10; 13:15; 14:34; 15:16; 23:17; 24:12; 24:29; 25:21, 22; 28:13; 29:1
6. Treatment of Friends and Neighbors: 3:27–29; 10:12; 17:9; 17:17; 18:19; 18:24; 21:14; 25:17; 25:19; 25:20; 26:18; 27:5; 27:6; 27:14; 29:5
7. On Pride and Boasting: 16:18; 25:14; 26:12; 27:1; 27:2
8. Parent-Child Relationship: 1:8; 4:2–4; 10:1; 13:24; 20:11; 22:6; 22:15; 30:17
9. Success in Business: industry (20:4; 24:30–34); honesty (11:1; 15:27; 20:10, 14); truthfulness (12:19, 22); caution in speech (12:16; 13:3; 16:24; 19:11); avoidance of security debts (6:1–5; 11:15; 22:26f.); a wise beneficence (11:24–26; 13:7; 14:31; 19:17); good companionship (15:22; 27:9–10); trust in God (3:5–6; 16:3)

10. Women: the strange woman (5:6–7; 9:13–18); contentious woman (15:17; 17:1; 21:9, 19; 25:24; 27:5, 15–16); indiscreet and foolish woman (11:22; 12:4; 14:1); the worthy woman (18:22; 31:10–31), who is industrious (31:13–16, 19, 24, 27), a good housekeeper (verses 21–22, 25), wise and kind (26), charitable (20), religious (30), rewarded in success of husband and children (23, 28–31)

THE BOOK OF ECCLESIASTES

The book is called in the Hebrew, *"Koheleth,"* a title taken from its opening sentence, "Words of Koheleth, the son of David, king in Jerusalem." In the Latin and Greek versions, however, it is called "Ecclesiastes." Jerome tries to explain this by saying that in Greek a person is so called who gathers the congregation, or *ecclesia.* Symmachus gives it a title which is probably best translated, "Proverb-monger." Martin Luther plainly gives the name, "The Preacher, Solomon." The modern versions entitle it "Ecclesiastes," or "The Preacher."

Koheleth comes from a Hebrew root which means "to call," or "to assemble." We would do well to compare the Latin *calo* and the Greek *kaleo,* which mean to call or to assemble, especially for religious purposes. *Koheleth* is a feminine participle. However, the feminine gender of the word does not necessarily mean that the writer was a woman. Words in Hebrew writings which are used to describe attributes are often in the feminine. An example of this may be found in the book of Isaiah (40:9), "O evangelist (feminine) of Zion." Various meanings have been advanced for *Koheleth.* Some declare its meaning to be "one who assembles an audience," thus lecturer; i.e., preacher. Others say he is a debater or discusser. Some give it the force of a uniter or reconciler (God's people with God). Also, the idea of a collector or gatherer of truths has been advanced as the real meaning.

Few biblical scholars have been able to discern that Ecclesiastes is a matchless essay, an informal essay on the highest good. This quality may account in part for Renan's estimate of it as "the only charming book a Hebrew ever wrote." The characteristics found in this Hebrew work are those already familiar to us in essays of Montaigne, Lamb, or Stevenson. To those men the essay was an informal revelation of the processes of the writer's mind as he reflected upon some subject that interested him. The very term, *essai*, that Montaigne chose, means trial, attempt. The informal essayist might treat of serious subjects as well as lighter ones.

If scholars had perceived the true nature of the book of Ecclesiastes, a great deal of trouble could have been avoided. Most of them have insisted on demanding that it originally was a logical treatise that for some reason is now hopelessly disarranged, and have attributed its apparently contradictory statements to scribal insertions or multiple authorship. Dr. Lyman Abbott is much more accurate in his analysis:

> Thus the Book of Ecclesiastes is a dramatic monologue portraying the complicated experiences of life; these voices are conflicting, but they portray the conflict of a single soul at war with itself. In this monologue the man is represented as arguing with himself; weighing the contrasted experiences of life over against one another. . . . Thus the Book of Ecclesiastes is deliberately and of intention confused because it is the portrayal of the confused experiences of a soul divided against itself.[1]

Much of the difficulty in interpreting the book is due to the inability of many to recognize the literary device that opens the masterful essay. The statement, "I Koheleth was king over Israel in Jerusalem" (1:12) has led many to claim that Solomon is the author. To this view, however, there are grave objections. There never was a time when Solomon could say, "I *was* king over Israel," for he remained king until his death. Would Solomon (the wise man) boast unrestrainedly of his intellectual acquirements (1:16) and his possessions and greatness (2:7–9)? Is he satirizing himself when he denounces the royal spendthrift and glutton and describes the misery which he brings on the land (10:16–19)? These, and other considerations, have led even the conservative Delitzsch to say, "If the Book of

---

[1]Lyman Abbott, *Life and Literature of the Ancient Hebrews* (New York: Houghton Mifflin and Company, 1901), pp. 292–293.

Koheleth were of old Solomonic origin, then there is no history of the Hebrew language."[2]

Every school pupil knows that the speaker in a literary work is not necessarily the author of it. The author of Ecclesiastes has sought "to evoke Solomon from his tomb and make him tell what has been the experience and the outcome of his intellectual, practical, and emotional life."[3] If the richest and wisest man in Jewish history found his attainments vain and unsatisfying, then the partial accomplishments of others certainly could impart no permanent values. In its grasp of life's fundamentals, Ecclesiastes ranks with the world's greatest philosophical works.

The purpose of Koheleth is to discover what is the highest good in life. He tries pleasure, wisdom, and wealth, but finds them vain. Is there anything that is worth-while in the world? Some scholars claim that the answer is negative. (Cf. 1:2–3.) Yet there is a positive note recurring throughout the book. Koheleth constantly advises moderation in the enjoyment of God's gifts as the *summum bonum* of life. Since all worldly pursuits are vain, let man enjoy what comes his way in his labors from day to day, since that is God's blessing. If one plans for the future, or worries about philosophical problems, it is in vain. The past is gone, the future uncertain. The present is the time for enjoyment. (Cf. 3:13; 3:22; 5:18; 8:15; 9:7; 11:7.) Yet man must live so that he will be able to enjoy his labors. If he is too righteous (perhaps self-righteous), his neighbors will be antagonized and make his life miserable. If he is too wicked, God will strike him down. The best thing to do is to follow a happy mean between the two extremes (7:16–17). The only way a man can have the power to enjoy life from day to day is to receive it from God (2:24). Therefore, the *summum bonum* can be achieved only as one fears God and keeps his commandments (12:13). This fear, however, does not require perfection (7:18).

What keeps Koheleth from reaching the Christian standard

[2]Franz Delitzsch, *Commentary on Song of Songs and Ecclesiastes* (Edinburgh: T. and T. Clark, 1877, p. 90.

[3]D. B. MacDonald, *The Hebrew Literary Genius* (Princeton: Princeton University Press, 1933), p. 197.

of morality is his traditional conception of immortality (3:18–21; 9:1–6). The expression in 12:2 simply states that man's spirit came from God and to him returns. (One cannot say that it does not refer to an afterlife, nor can he prove that it does.) Since there are no rewards after death, his happy mean is a sensible procedure, for in this world the most wicked and the best men are the most sorely beset. However, the Christian's hope of life after death as well as the peace assured him in this life can leave no room for this popular doctrine of common sense.

The permanent values of the book of Ecclesiastes explain why God inspired its writing. There are two valuable lessons taught that were needed in the history of revelation. First, Koheleth ably demonstrated the fallacies of the traditional idea of immortality. If there is no afterlife, then the present life is in the main a drab, colorless, aimless existence. As one reads the book, he is made eternally grateful for the assurance of immortality provided by Jesus Christ. The book of Job presents the positive arguments for a doctrine of immortality; Ecclesiastes demonstrates the need for such a doctrine. The second value of the book is found in its argument that in this life it pays to serve God. God's rewards come in the present as well as the future. To the one who serves him, he gives an added capacity to live life to its fullest.

OUTLINE OF THE BOOK

Prologue. Chapter 1

1. The Pursuit of Pleasure (2:1–11)

2. The Pursuit of Wisdom (2:12–17)

3. The Pursuit of Wealth (most of 2:18 to 6:12)

   This is the most devastating argument in the Scriptures against the accumulation of worldly goods. Koheleth gives at length his objections to seeking wealth (cf. *The Abingdon Bible Commentary*):

(1) After a man labors his whole life, he must leave his goods to one who has never worked for them and who may use them foolishly (2:18–21).

(2) There is a time for everything, but that is known only to God. Man is always choosing the wrong moment and losing all he possesses (3:1–11).

(3) The unjust courts take away hard-earned possessions after they have been acquired (3:16).

(4) The government seizes what is left with oppressive taxation (4:1).

(5) Success causes jealousy and the loss of friends (4:4).

(6) After a man gains wealth, it will not satisfy his soul (4:7–8; 6:1–12).

(7) The more a man gains, the more ways there are to spend it (5:11).

(8) Wealth for which a whole life has been spent can be lost in a moment (5:13–17).

4. Sundry Practical Observations from the Experience of Koheleth (7:1 to 11:8)

5. Advice to the Young Man (11:8 to 12:12)

(1) A life of pleasure will bring retribution. Youth is nothing in itself (11:9–10). (11:9 is ironical.)

(2) Remember God in youth before it is too late to find joy in living (12:1–8). In this passage is a remarkable allegory describing the complete disintegration of the body that accompanies old age. Some of the identifications are difficult, others are very clear.

(3) True wisdom cannot be found in books (12:11–12).

Conclusion. Fear God and keep his commandments, for judgment is inevitable (12:13–14).

THE SONG OF SONGS

The book is traditionally ascribed to Solomon. A few critics assign it to an author living in Northern Palestine shortly after the death of Solomon, while others place it much later. Although parts of the book refer to Solomon (1:5; 3:7–11), it is written about Solomon rather than by him.

Controversy has raged around this book for many centuries. Three viewpoints concerning its nature are to be found. The allegorical view is the most ancient one. The rabbis as early as A.D. 90 were interpreting the poems as describing in figurative language the relationship between Yahweh and Israel. The Church Fathers continued this method and taught that the Song is descriptive of the love between Christ and his church. This view has been modified in recent times into the typical viewpoint, which holds that the poem is descriptive of human love, but was written in order to provide a prototype for the future relationship of Christ and his church. Scholars in general today take the literal view that the poems simply describe human love.

Setting out with the theme of fidelity in love between man and woman, the author, by means of dialogue, dramatically prepares the reader for the final climactic declaration:

"Set me as a seal upon thine heart,
As a seal upon thine arm:
For love is strong as death . . ."

Although it is difficult to find in the Song of Songs a dramatic structure continuous and complete, one can readily see that the purpose of the writer is, by means of repetitious dialogue, to illustrate the strength and fidelity of woman's love.

When once this is realized, then all the fanciful allegorical interpretations of the book disappear. Why should a book exalting fidelity in love not be in the canon? And if human love is as strong as death, surely we are led to conclude that divine love is even stronger.

The language of the poem is considered eminently chaste among Orientals. What a pity that such a gem should sometimes be perverted!

THE BOOK OF LAMENTATIONS

In the Hebrew Bible this book appears among the Writings, but in the LXX, the Syriac, and the Vulgate it appears with the book of Jeremiah. The tradition is ancient that connects these words with that prophet, the LXX making the statement that he wrote Lamentations. At the present time scholarship is reluctant to attribute the work to Jeremiah, mainly because of the artificial structure of the poetry. The poetry of Jeremiah was spontaneous; this is studied. There are five poems in the book, corresponding to the five chapters. The first four are alphabetical poems, chapter 3 being a triple acrostic.

Each of the five elegies treats of the sorrows of captive Zion. There is considerable variety in the monotony of the grief, the short lines of the fifth chapter standing in marked contrast to the longer lines in the second and fourth. Captive Zion, though claiming that her sorrow is without parallel (1:12), yet recognizes the perfect justice of Yahweh in her fate (1:18). While the poet sometimes sinks into despair (5:22), he also comforts himself with thoughts of Yahweh's goodness and faithfulness (3:21-39).

Suggested Reading List for
Introductory Old Testament Study

1. GENERAL READING

Adams, J. McKee, *Biblical Backgrounds*. Second edition; Nashville: Broadman Press, 1938

Davidson, A. B., *The Theology of the Old Testament*. Edinburgh: T. and T. Clark, 1904

Dodd, C. H., *The Authority of the Bible*. New York: Harper and Brothers, 1929

Hebert, A. G., *The Authority of the Old Testament*. London: Faber and Faber, 1947

Knudson, A. C., *The Religious Teaching of the Old Testament*. New York: The Abingdon Press, 1918

Robinson, H. Wheeler, *Inspiration and Revelation in the Old Testament*. Oxford: Clarendon Press, 1946

Rowley, H. H., *The Re-Discovery of the Old Testament*. Philadelphia: The Westminster Press, 1946

Snaith, H. H., *The Distinctive Ideas of the Old Testament*. Philadelphia: The Westminster Press, 1946

Tasker, R. V. G., *The Old Testament in the New Testament*. Philadelphia: The Westminster Press, 1946

2. INTRODUCTIONS

Cartledge, Samuel A., *A Conservative Introduction to the Old Testament*. Athens: University of Georgia Press, 1944. A valuable presentation of the progressive outlook of the Old Testament

Pfeiffer, Robert H., *Introduction to the Old Testament*. Third edition; New York: Harper and Brothers, 1941. A liberal treatment of the Old Testament

Watts, J. Wash, *A Survey of the Old Testament Teaching.* Nashville: Broadman Press, 1947. Two volumes. A conservative survey of the teachings of the Old Testament. Designed primarily for classroom use

3. BIBLE DICTIONARIES

Hastings, James, *A Dictionary of the Bible.* New York: Charles Scribner's Sons. Five-volume edition, 1904; one-volume edition, 1909. Deals with the language, literature, and contents of the Scriptures

The International Standard Bible Encyclopaedia. Revised edition; Grand Rapids, Mich.: William B. Eerdmans Publishing Company, 1939. Five volumes. A conservative presentation of the material of the Old Testament with maps, illustrations, etc.

4. COMMENTARIES

One-volume Commentaries

The Abingdon Bible Commentary. Cincinnati: The Abingdon Press, 1929. Edited by Eiselen, Lewis, and Downey. A progressive view of the Bible. A *must* on every student's desk

Old Testament Commentary. Philadelphia: The Muhlenberg Press, 1948. Edited by Alleman and Flack. A progressive general introduction to the Old Testament

Complete Sets

It is seldom advisable to buy a complete set of commentaries, since individual volumes in each set surpass others. If this is contemplated, however, the best general commentaries are listed below according to importance:

The Cambridge Bible for Schools and Colleges. Cambridge: University Press, 1886–   . This is the best commentary for general use

The Westminster Commentaries. London: Methuen and Company, 1914–

The Expositor's Bible. New York: Funk and Wagnalls Company. Twenty-five volume edition 1900; six-volume edition 1940. This set of books is more of an exposition than a commentary.

The American Commentary on the Old Testament and New Testament. Philadelphia: American Publishing Society, 1881–   . Seven volumes in New Testament; ten volumes in the Old Testament

The International Critical Commentary. New York: Charles Scribner's Sons, 1903. Forty-four volumes. An invaluable set to advanced students, but too technical for the average reader

5. BOOKS ON OLD TESTAMENT HISTORY

Breasted, James H., *A History of Egypt from the Earliest Times to the Persian Conquest.* Second edition; New York: Charles Scribner's Sons, 1909

Oesterley, W. O. E., and Robinson, T. H., *A History of Israel.* Oxford: Clarendon Press, 1932. Two volumes. A liberal view of Old Testament history

Olmstead, Albert T. E., *A History of Assyria.* New York: Charles Scribner's Sons, 1923

Olmstead, Albert T. E., *History of Palestine and Syria to the Macedonian Conquest.* New York: Charles Scribner's Sons, 1931

Price, Ira M., *The Dramatic Story of Old Testament History.* Second edition; New York: Fleming H. Revell Company, 1935

Rogers, R. W., *Cuneiform Parallels to the Old Testament.* Cincinnati: Jennings and Graham, 1912

Rogers, R. W., *A History of Ancient Persia, from Its Earliest Beginnings to the Death of Alexander the Great.* New York: Charles Scribner's Sons, 1929

Rogers, R. W., *A History of Babylonia and Assyria.* Sixth edition in two volumes; New York: The Abingdon Press, 1915

Robinson, David M., *A Short History of Greece.* New York: Huxley House, 1936

6. BOOKS ON PENTATEUCHAL CRITICISM

Allis, Oswald T., *The Five Books of Moses.* Philadelphia: The Presbyterian and Reformed Publishing Company, 1943. An able defense of the conservative position

Driver, S. R., *Introduction to the Literature of the Old Testament.* Revised edition; New York: Charles Scribner's Sons, 1906. The standard critical introduction

Eiselen, F. C., *The Books of the Pentateuch.* Cincinnati: The Methodist Book Concern, 1916. An invaluable presentation by a renowned progressive scholar

Orr, James, *The Problem of the Old Testament.* New York: Charles Scribner's Sons, 1905. A valuable conservative treatment for the student with patience

Pfeiffer, Robert H., *Introduction to the Old Testament*. New York: Harper and Brothers, 1941

7. COMMENTARIES AND STUDIES IN THE PROPHETS

(1) General Works

Briggs, A. C., *Messianic Prophecy*. New York: Charles Scribner's Sons, 1886

Eiselen, F. C., *The Christian View of the Old Testament*. Cincinnati: Jennings and Graham, 1912

Eiselen, F. C., *The Prophetic Books of the Old Testament*. New York: The Methodist Book Concern, 1923. Two volumes

Hyatt, J. Philip, *Prophetic Religion*. New York: Abingdon-Cokesbury Press, 1947

Kirkpatrick, A. F., *The Doctrine of the Prophets*. Third edition; London: The Macmillan Company, 1901

Scott, R. B. Y., *The Relevance of the Prophets*. New York: The Macmillan Company, 1944

Yates, Kyle M., *Preaching from the Prophets*. New York: Harper and Brothers, 1942

(2) Isaiah

Delitzsch, Franz A., *A Biblical Commentary on the Prophecies of Isaiah*. Fourth edition; Edinburgh: T. and T. Clark, 1927. Two volumes

Driver, S. R., *Isaiah, His Life and the Times and the Writings which Bear his Name*. New York: Fleming H. Revell Company

Jefferson, Charles E., *Cardinal Ideas of Isaiah*. New York: The Macmillan Company, 1925

Scherer, Paul, *Event in Eternity*. New York: Harper and Brothers, 1945

Skinner, John, "The Book of the Prophet Isaiah," *The Cambridge Bible for Schools and Colleges*. Revised edition; Cambridge: The University Press, 1930

Smith, George A., *The Book of Isaiah*. Revised edition; New York: Harper and Brothers, 1927. Two volumes

Wade, G. W., "The Book of the Prophet Isaiah," *Westminster Commentaries*. London: Methuen and Company, 1911

(3) Jeremiah

Binns, L. Elliott, "The Book of the Prophet Jeremiah," *Westminster Commentaries*. London: Methuen and Company, 1919

Calkins, Raymond, *Jeremiah the Prophet*. New York: The Macmillan Company, 1930

Gordon, T. C., *The Rebel Prophet*. London: James Clarke and Company, 1931

Jefferson, Charles E., *Cardinal Ideas of Jeremiah*. New York: The Macmillan Company, 1928

Meyer, F. B., *Jeremiah: Priest and Prophet*. New York: Fleming H. Revell Company, 1894

Morgan, G. Campbell, *Studies in the Prophecy of Jeremiah*. Chicago: Fleming H. Revell Company, 1931

Peake, A. S., "Jeremiah," *The New Century Bible*. New York: Henry Frowde (no date). Two volumes

Robinson, H. Wheeler, *The Cross of Jeremiah*. London: Student Christian Movement, 1925

Skinner, John, *Prophecy and Religion*. Cambridge: The University Press, 1922

Smith, George A., *Jeremiah*. Revised edition; New York: Harper and Brothers, 1929

(4) Ezekiel

Davidson, A. B., and Streane, A. W., "Ezekiel," *The Cambridge Bible for Schools and Colleges*. Revised edition; Cambridge: The University Press, 1916

Lofthouse, W. F., *The Prophet of Reconstruction*. London: James Clarke and Company, 1920

Matthews, I. G., "Ezekiel," *An American Commentary on the Old Testament*. Chicago: American Baptist Publication Society, 1939

(5) Daniel

Boutflower, Charles, *In and Around the Book of Daniel*. London: Society for Promoting Christian Knowledge, 1923

Charles, R. H., *A Critical and Exegetical Commentary on the Book of Daniel*. Oxford: Clarendon Press, 1929

Wilson, R. Dick, *Studies in the Book of Daniel*. Second edition; New York: Fleming H. Revell Company, 1938

Young, Edward J., *The Prophecy of Daniel*, Grand Rapids: Wm. B. Eerdmans, 1949

(6) Minor Prophets

Calkins, Raymond, *The Modern Message of the Minor Prophets*. New York: Harper and Brothers, 1947

Davidson, A. B., "Nahum, Habakkuk, and Zephaniah," *The Cam-*

bridge *Bible for Schools and Colleges*. Revised edition; Cambridge: The University Press, 1920

Driver, S. R., "Joel and Amos," *The Cambridge Bible for Schools and Colleges*. Revised edition; Cambridge: The University Press, 1915

Eiselen, F. C., *The Minor Prophets*. Cincinnati: Jennings and Graham, 1907. This is the best one-volume study on the Minor Prophets; however, it is out of print.

McFadyen, J. E., *A Cry for Justice, a Study in Amos*. New York: Charles Scribner's Sons, 1912

Merrill, W. P., *Prophets of the Dawn*. Chicago: Fleming H. Revell Company, 1927

Morgan, G. Campbell, *Hosea, the Heart and Holiness of God*. New York: Fleming H. Revell Company, 1934

Robinson, George L., *The Twelve Minor Prophets*. New York: George H. Doran Company, 1926

Smith, George A., *The Book of the Twelve Prophets*. Revised edition; New York: Harper and Brothers, 1928

Storer, J. W., *The Major Messages of the Minor Prophets*. Nashville: Broadman Press, 1940

8. COMMENTARIES AND STUDIES IN THE POETICAL BOOKS

(1) Job

Davidson, A. B., "Job," *The Cambridge Bible for Schools and Colleges*. Cambridge: The University Press, 1886

Morgan, G. Campbell, *The Book of Job*. New York: Fleming H. Revell Company, 1909

Reichert, V. E., *Job*. Hindhead, Surrey: The Soncino Press, 1946 (a Jewish publication)

(2) Psalms

Eiselen, F. C., *The Psalms and Other Sacred Writings*. Cincinnati: The Methodist Book Concern, 1918

Kirkpatrick, A. F., "The Book of Psalms," *The Cambridge Bible for Schools and Colleges*. Cambridge: The University Press, 1910

Maclaren, Alexander, "The Psalms," *The Expositor's Bible*. New York: Funk and Wagnalls Company, 1900. Two volumes

Oesterley, W. O. E., *The Psalms*. London: Society for Promoting Christian Knowledge, 1939

Walker, Rollin H., *The Modern Message of the Psalms*. Cincinnati: The Abingdon Press, 1938

Yates, Kyle M., *Preaching from the Psalms*. New York: Harper and Brothers, 1948

(3) Proverbs

Horton, R. F., "Proverbs," *The Expositor's Bible*. New York: Funk and Wagnalls Company, 1900

Perowne, T. T., "Proverbs," *The Cambridge Bible for Schools and Colleges*. Cambridge: The University Press, 1916

Toy, Crawford H., "A Critical and Exegetical Commentary on the Book of Proverbs," *The International Critical Commentary*. New York: Charles Scribner's Sons, 1910

(4) Ecclesiastes

Cox, Samuel, "Ecclesiastes," *The Expositor's Bible*. New York: Funk and Wagnalls Company, 1900

Gordis, Robert, *The Wisdom of Ecclesiastes*. New York: Behrman House, 1945

(5) Song of Solomon

Eiselen, F. C., *The Psalms and other Sacred Writings*. Cincinnati: The Methodist Book Concern, 1918

Waterman, L., *The Song of Songs*. Ann Arbor: University of Michigan Press, 1948

9. OLD TESTAMENT ARCHAEOLOGY

Adams, J. McKee, *Ancient Records and the Bible*. Nashville: Broadman Press, 1946

Albright, W. F., *The Archaeology of Palestine and the Bible*. New York: Fleming H. Revell Company, 1932

Albright, W. F., *Archaeology and the Religion of Israel*. Baltimore: The Johns Hopkins Press, 1942

Albright, W. F., *From the Stone Age to Christianity*. Baltimore: The Johns Hopkins Press, 1940

Barton, G. A., *Archaeology and the Bible*. Seventh edition; Philadelphia: American Sunday School Union, 1937

Burrows, Millar, *What Mean These Stones?* New Haven, Conn.: The American Schools of Oriental Research, 1941

Finegan, Jack, *Light from the Ancient Past; The Archaeological Background of the Hebrew-Christian Religion*. Princeton: Princeton University Press, 1946

Frankfort, H. and H. A., Wilson, J. A., Jacobsen, T., and Irwin, W. A., *The Intellectual Adventure of Ancient Man*. Chicago: The University of Chicago Press, 1946

Glueck, Nelson, *The Other Side of the Jordan*. New Haven, Conn.: American Schools of Oriental Research, 1940

Glueck, Nelson, *The River Jordan*. Philadelphia: The Westminster Press, 1946

Heidel, A., *The Gilgamesh Epic and Old Testament Parallels*. Chicago: The University of Chicago Press, 1946

McCown, C. C., *The Ladder of Progress in Palestine*. New York: Harper and Brothers, 1943

Wright, G. E. and Filson, F. V., *The Westminster Historical Atlas to the Bible*. Philadelphia: The Westminster Press, 1946

CHRONOLOGICAL CHART OF
THE KINGDOM OF ISRAEL

DATE	EVENTS AMONG THE ISRAELITES
B.C. c.1020	Saul anointed at Mizpah.
1000 970 935	David king of all Israel. Accession of Solomon. . . . .

FROM THE DIVISION OF THE KINGDOM

DATE	JUDAH	PROPHETS IN JUDAH
B.C.	I. From the Death of Solomon to the Accession	
931	1. *Rehoboam* [17]. Mistake at Shechem (1)	Shemaiah forbids war with the Ten Tribes (2).
	Fortifies many cities (8). After three years of obedience and prosperity, Judah lapses into idolatry (9).	
926	Invasion of Shishak. Jerusalem plundered (11).	Shemaiah predicts the victory of Shishak (10).

(1) 1 K. 12:1–19; 2 C. 10:1–19.   (9) 1 K. 14:21–24; 2 C. 11:17;
(2) 1 K. 12:21–24; 2 C. 11:1–4.   12:1.
(8) 2 C. 11:5–12.   (10) 2 C. 12: 5–8.
                                    (11) 1 K. 14:25–31; 2 C. 12:2–9.

CONTEMPORARY EVENTS

> Twenty-first (Tanite) Dynasty in Egypt. Assyria
> weak.
> Abibaal (Hiram I) king of Tyre.
> Assyria slowly revives. Hiram II of Tyre.
> . . . . Tanite Dynasty expelled by Sheshonk (Shishak), the
> founder of the Twenty-second Dynasty.

TO THE FALL OF SAMARIA. 931–722 B.C.

PROPHETS IN ISRAEL	ISRAEL (TEN TRIBES)	CONTEMPORARY EVENTS
of Jehu, Athaliah and Hazael. 931–842 B.C.		
Man of God from Judah rebukes Jeroboam and curses his altar (6).	1. *Jeroboam* [22]. Builds Shechem and Penuel (3). Sets up golden calves at Bethel and Dan (4). Changes time of feast (5). Appointment of new priesthood and consequent exodus of the Levites into Judah (7).	Shishak of Egypt. Rezon of Syria.
Ahijah predicts the death of Jeroboam's son and destruction of his house (12).		

(3) I K. 12:25.
(4) I K. 12:26–31.
(5) I K. 12:32–33.
(6) I K. 13:1–32.

(7) I K. 13:33–34;
   2 C. 11:13–17.
(12) I K. 14:1–18.

DATE	JUDAH	PROPHETS IN JUDAH
914	2. *Abijam* [3]. Defeats Jeroboam at Zemaraim (1).	. . . .
911	3. *Asa* [41]. Great religious reforms (2). Fortifies cities and organizes a great army (3). Ten years of peace in Judah (5).	. . . . Iddo writes the lives of Rehoboam and Abijah (4).
910	2d year.	. . . .
909	3d year.	
c.900	(a) Asa defeats Zerah's army of a million (8).	(b) Azariah encourages Asa, and stirs up a revival (9).
	(b) Asa bribes Ben-hadad to attack the dominions of Baasha (11).	. . . .
	(c) Destroys Ramah and with the material builds Geba and Mizpah (12).	(d) Hanani rebukes Asa (13).
886	26th year.	. . . .
885	27th year.	. . . .
885	. . . .	. . . .

(1) 2 C. 13.
(2) 1 K. 15:9–15; 2 C. 14:1–5.
(3) 2 C. 14:6–8.
(4) 2 C. 12:15; 13:22.
(5) 2 C. 14:1.

(8) 2 C. 14:9–15.
(9) 2 C. 15.
(11) 1 K. 15:18–21; 2 C. 16:1–5.
(12) 1 K. 15:22; 2 C. 16:6.
(13) 2 C. 16: 7–10.

Prophets in Israel	Israel (Ten Tribes)	Contemporary Events
. . . .	18th year.	
. . . .	20th year.	
. . . .	2. *Nadab* [2]. Son of Jeroboam 1. Nadab slain at siege of Gibbethon by (6)	
. . . .	3. *Baasha* [24]. He destroys the house of Jeroboam (7).	
. . . .	. . . .	Zerah the Ethiopian.
. . . .	(a) Baasha builds Ramah to stop the exodus into Judah (10).	Ben-hadad I of Syria.
Jehu's prophecy against house of Baasha (14).		
. . . .	4. *Elah* [2]. Slain in Tirzah by Zimri (15).	
. . . .	5. *Zimri* [7 days]. Besieged by Omri, he burns palace over his head (16).	Ashurnatsirpal II (884–860) first Assyrian to sweep to Mediterranean Sea.
. . . .	6. *Omri* [12]. Civil War with Tibni for four years (17).	

(6) 1 K. 15:25–28.   (15) 1 K. 16:9–13.
(7) 1 K. 15:29–30.   (16) 1 K. 16:15–19.
(10) 1 K. 15:17.   (17) 1 K. 16:21–22.
(14) 1 K. 16:1–4, 7.

DATE	JUDAH	PROPHETS OF JUDAH
881	....	....
874	38th year....................	....
	In his 39th year Asa diseased, but not relying on Jehovah (4).	
	Buried in Jerusalem with great honors (5).	
871	4. *Jehoshaphat* [25]. Religious reforms (6).	....
	Fortresses and army greatly strengthened (7).	
869	The law of God taught in his 3rd year (9).	
	Tribute from Philistines and Arabians (10).	
853	....	....
852	17th year. (a) Alliance with Ahab (15)......................	(d) Jehu rebukes Jehoshaphat (18).
	Jehoram regent (2 K. 1:17; 3:1).	

(4) 1 K. 15:23; 2 C. 16:12. (9) 2 C. 17:7-9.
(5) 2 C. 16:13-14. (10) 2 C. 17:10-11.
(6) 2 C. 17:3-6. (15) 1 K. 22:44; 2 C. 18.
(7) 2 C. 17:2, 12-19. (18) 2 C. 19:1-3.

PROPHETS IN ISRAEL	ISRAEL (TEN TRIBES)	CONTEMPORARY EVENTS
. . . .	Omri builds Samaria and transfers his capital thither (1). Makes Moab tributary.	
. . . . . . , ...	7. *Ahab* [22]. Marries Jezebel of Zidon (2).	Mesha of Moab.
	Rapid introduction of Baal worship into Israel (3).	
. . . .	4th year.	
	Elijah's appearance and the drought of three and one-half years (8).	
Elijah	Destruction of the 450 prophets of Baal at Mt. Carmel (11).	
	Flight of Elijah to Horeb (12).	
	War with Syria. Ahab victorious at Samaria and at Aphek. Makes treaty with Ben-hadad (13).	Ben-hadad II of Syria. Shalmaneser III (859–824).
. . . .	Naboth's vineyard (14).	Battle of Karkar.
(b) Micaiah versus 400 false prophets (16).	(c) Ahab slain in battle at Ramoth-gilead (17).	

(1) 1 K. 16:24.	(12) 1 K. 19.
(2) 1 K. 16:31.	(13) 1 K. 20.
(3) 1 K. 16:31–33.	(14) 1 K. 21.
(8) 1 K. 17.	(16) 1 K. 22:5–28; 2 C. 18:4–27.
(11) 1 K. 18.	(17) 1 K. 22:1–40.

Date	Judah	Prophets of Judah
852	Jehoshaphat improves the administration of justice (1). (a) Great invasion of Moabites, Ammonites, and Edomites (3). (c) Navy broken up (7)	. . . . (b) Jahaziel encourages the people (4). (d) Eliezer predicts the destruction of the navy (6).
851	18th year.	. . . .
849	5. *Jehoram* [8]. Daughter of Ahab for wife (11). Slays his brethren (12). Revolt of Edom and of Libnah (13). Letter from Elijah (14). Death of Jehoshaphat. Invasion of Arabians and Philistines, who plunder and kill (15). Loathsome disease for two years (16).	. . . . Obadiah (?).

(1) 2 C. 19:4–11.	(12) 2 C. 21:1–4.
(3) 2 C. 20:1–30.	(13) 2 K. 8:20–22; 2 C. 21:8–10.
(4) 2 C. 20:14–17.	(14) 2 C. 21:12–15.
(6) 2 C. 20:37.	(15) 2 C. 21:16–17.
(7) 1 K. 22:48–49.	(16) 2 C. 21:18–20.
(11) 2 C. 21:6.	

PROPHETS IN ISRAEL	ISRAEL (TEN TRIBES)	CONTEMPORARY EVENTS
. . . .	8. *Ahaziah* [2]. Revolt of Moab (2).	
. . . .	(e) Unites with Jehoshaphat in building merchant vessels at Eziongeber (5). Jehoram regent with Ahaziah. Inquires of Baal-zebub. Attempts to arrest Elijah (8).	
. . . . Elisha	9. *Jehoram* [12]. Combines with Jehoshaphat to recover Moab (9). 55th year.	Mesha, king of Moab, attacked by kings of Israel, Judah, and Edom (10).
	Terrible siege of Samaria by Benhadad. Remarkable flight of Syrians (17).	

(2) 2 K. 1:1.
(5) 2 C. 20:35–36.
(8) 2 K. 1:2–17.

(9) 2 K. 3:4–8.
(10) 2 K. 3:9–27.
(17) 2 K. 6:8–7:20.

Date	Judah	Prophets of Judah
842	6. *Ahaziah* [1]. Affinity with house of Ahab (1).	....
842	Slain by Jehu (5)	....

II. From the Accession of Jehu to the

Date	Judah	Prophets of Judah
842	(0) Athaliah [6] usurps the throne. Destroys seed royal except Joash (6).	....
836	Athaliah slain (8).	
	7. *Joash* [40]. Baal worship uprooted (9). Under the tuition of Jehoiada, Joash is faithful to Yahweh (10).	....
		Joel (?).
814	23rd year. The Temple repaired (12)	....
	Death of Jehoiada, quickly followed by lapse into idolatry (13).	Zechariah, son of Jehoiada, rebukes Joash, and is murdered (14).
	Hazael threatens Jerusalem, but is bought off by large presents (17).	....
800	37th year................	....

(1) 2 C. 22:2–4.
(5) 2 C. 22:5–9.
(6) 2 K. 11:1–3; 2 C. 22:10–12.
(8) 2 K. 11:4–20; 2 C. 23.
(9) 2 K. 11:17–20.
(10) 2 K. 12:1–3; 2 C. 24:1–3.

(12) 2 K. 12:4–16; 2 C. 24:4–14.
(13) 2 C. 24:15–19.
(14) 2 C. 24:20–22.
(17) 2 K. 12:17–18;
     2 C. 24:23–24.

PROPHETS IN ISRAEL	ISRAEL (TEN TRIBES)	CONTEMPORARY EVENTS
. . . .	12th year. Wounded in battle with the Syrians (2).	Murder of Ben-hadad II (Hada-dezer) by Hazael (3).
. . . .	Slain by Jehu at Jezreel (4).	

Fall of Samaria. 842–722 B.C.

PROPHETS IN ISRAEL	ISRAEL (TEN TRIBES)	CONTEMPORARY EVENTS
. . . .	10. *Jehu* [28]. Exterminates house of Ahab and uproots Baal worship, but retains calf worship (7). Pays tribute to Shalmaneser III of Assyria.	Shalmaneser III attacks Hazael.
. . . .	7th year.	
	Hazael's inroads. Takes possession of country east of Jordan (11).	Shamsi-adad (824–805).
. . . .	11. *Jehoahaz* [17].	
	Hazael keeps Israel in subjection (15).	Adad-nirari III (805–782).
. . . .	. . . .	Hazael captures Gath, and threatens Jerusalem (16).
. . . .	12. *Jehoash* [16]. Associated two years with his father.	(Maria of Syria, 803).

(2) 2 K. 8: 28–29.	(11) 2 K. 10:32,33.
(3) 2 K. 8:7–15.	(15) 2 K. 13:1–7.
(4) 2 K. 9.	(16) 2 K. 12:17–18.
(7) 2 K. 10:1–29.	

Date	Judah	Prophets of Judah
799	Amaziah regent with Joash. Conspiracy against Joash. Slain in Millo (1).	
797	8. *Amaziah* [29]. Slays his father's murderers (2).	....
	(a) Hires large army of mercenaries from Israel to fight against Edom (5).	(b) Man of God forbids the league with Israel (6).
	(c) Defeats Edom, but worships the idols of the conquered nation (7).	(d) Prophet rebukes Amaziah (8).
790		
785	Challenges Israel, but is captured at Bethshermesh, and Jerusalem is plundered (9).	....
785	15th year..................	....
	Decline of Amaziah. Uzziah regent. Amaziah slain by servants in Lachish (11).	
c.770	9. *Uzziah*, or Azariah [52]. Conquers the Philistines and Arabians. Builds Elath. Receives tribute from the Ammonites. Fortifies Jerusalem and Judah. Fond of husbandry. Organizes and equips a great army (14).	Zechariah instructs Uzziah (13).
750	38th year..................	....
	Uzziah's sacrilege and leprosy.	

(1) 2 K. 12:20–21; 2 C. 24:25–26.

(2) 2 K. 14:5–6.

(5) 2 C. 25:5–6.

(6) 2 C. 25:7–10.

(7) 2 K. 14:7; 2 C. 25:11–14.

(8) 2 C. 25:15–16.

(9) 2 K 14:8–16; 2 C. 25:17–24.

(11) 2 K. 14:19–20.

(13) 2 C. 26:5.

(14) 2 C. 26:1–15.

PROPHETS IN ISRAEL	ISRAEL (TEN TRIBES)	CONTEMPORARY EVENTS
. . . .	2nd year. Visits Elisha (3). Three victories over the Syrians (4)	Ben-hadad III of Syria.
. . . .	Jeroboam regent with Jehoash. 15th year. Defeats Judah and breaks down part of the wall of Jerusalem (10).	
. . . . Jonah.	13. *Jeroboam II* [41]. Great warrior. The boundaries of Israel greatly enlarged (12).	
. . . .	27th year (?)	
Amos. Hosea.		
. . . .	14. *Zechariah* [6 mos.] Slain by (15)	

(3) 2 K. 13:14–19.   (12) 2 K. 14:25–28.
(4) 2 K. 13:22–25.   (15) 2 K. 15:8–12.
(10) 2 K. 14:8–16;
     2 C. 25:17–24.

DATE	JUDAH	PROPHETS OF JUDAH
	Regency of Jotham (1).	
748	39th year..........	
738	50th year..........	
736	52nd year	
		Isaiah.
735	10. *Jotham* [16]	
	Fortifies Judah and Jerusalem (5).	Micah.
	Keeps the Ammonites in subjection (6).	
734	11. (*Jeho*) *Ahaz* [16]	
	Given up to idolatry (8)......	
	Defeated by Syria and Israel (9).	
	(a) Captives taken to Samaria (10)........................	
	Edomites and Philistines capture many towns (12).	
734	Ahaz calls upon Pul to assist him (13).	
732	Ahaz at Damascus (16).......	
	Introduces Syrian idolatry (17).	

(1) 2 K. 15:5.
(5) 2 C. 27:3f.
(6) 2 C. 27:5.
(8) 2 K. 16:1–4; 2 C. 28:1–4.
(9) 2 K. 16:5f; 2 C. 28:5–7.

(10) 2 C. 28:8.
(12) 2 C. 28:16–19.
(13) 2 K. 16:7–9; 2 C. 28:20f.
(16) 2 K. 16:10.
(17) 2 K. 16:11–18; 2 C. 28:22–25.

PROPHETS IN ISRAEL	ISRAEL (TEN TRIBES)	CONTEMPORARY EVENTS
. . . .	15. *Shallum* [1 mo.]. Slain by (2)	
. . . .	16. *Menahem* [10]. Tributary to Pul of Assyria (3).	Tiglath - pileser IV (Pul) of As-
. . . .	17. *Pekahiah* [2]. Slain by (4)	syria (745–727).
. . . .	18. *Pekah* [20]. Long reign in Gilead, perhaps 15 years.	
. . . .	2nd year.	
	Pekah and Rezin enter into an alliance against Judah (7).	Rezin of Syria.
. . . .	17th year.	
(b) Oded encourages the men of Israel to send back the cap- tives (11).		
. . . .	Northern and eastern districts of Israel carried captive by Pul (14).	
. . . .	. . . .	Damascus cap- tured and Rezin slain (15).

(2) 2 K. 15:13–15.	(7) Is. 7:1–9.
(3) 2 K. 15:17–22.	(11) 2 C. 28:9–15.
(4) 2 K. 15:23–26.	(14) 2 K. 15:29.
	(15) 2 K. 16:9.

Date	Judah	Prophets of Judah
731 730	12th year............................	....
727	12. *Hezekiah* [29]................ Great reforms (3). Remarkable observance of the Passover (4). Idols destroyed (5). Restores Temple service (6).	....
	....	....
724	....	....
722	6th year....................	....

FROM THE FALL OF SAMARIA TO THE FIRST CAPTURE

Date	Judah	Prophets
720	....	....
717 713	.... Hezekiah's sickness (11). Psalm of Thanksgiving (13).	.... Isaiah predicts recovery of Hezekiah (12).

(3) 2 K. 18:3–6; 2 C. 29:2–36.   (11) 2 K. 20:1–11; 2 C. 32:24–26;
(4) 2 C. 30.   Is. 38:1–8.
(5) 2 C. 31:1.   (12) 2 K. 20:4–6; Is. 38:1–6.
(6) 2 C. 31:2–21.   (13) Is. 38:9–20.

Prophets in Israel	Israel (Ten Tribes)	Contemporary Events
. . . .	Hoshea slays Pekah (1). 19. *Hoshea* [9]. Confirmed in his kingdom by Assyria.	So, (Sibe) of Egypt.
. . . .	3rd year. Alliance with So (Sibe) of Egypt (2).	Shalmaneser V of Assyria (727–722).
. . . .	Hoshea imprisoned (7).	
. . . .	7th year. Shalmaneser besieges Samaria (8).	
. . . .	Fall of Samaria (9). Inhabitants carried away by Sargon to the far East (10).	Sargon II of Assyria (722–705).

OF JERUSALEM BY NEBUCHADNEZZAR. 722–605 B.C.

Assyria and Babylon	Other Nations
Sargon captures Karkar. . . . . Sargon destroys Carchemish.	Egyptians defeated at Raphia by Sargon.

(1) 2 K. 15:30.   (8) 2 K. 17:5.
(2) 2 K. 17:4.   (9) 2 K. 17:6.
(7) 2 K. 17:4.   (10) 2 K. 17:6.

DATE	JUDAH	PROPHETS
712	Merodach-baladan sends an embassy to Jerusalem (1).	Isaiah predicts a Babylonian captivity (2).
711	. . . .	. . . .
710	. . . .	. . . .
705	. . . .	. . . .
701	(a) Sennacherib invades Philistia and Judah (4). (b) Hezekiah prepares Jerusalem for a siege (5). (c) Hezekiah submits, and pays tribute (6). (d) He twice refuses to surrender his capital (7). (g) Great disaster to the Assyrian army (9).	(e) Isaiah announces the safety of Jerusalem (8).
698	13. *Manasseh* [55]. Plunges into gross idolatry, superstition and cruelty (10).	
681	. . . .	. . . .
681	Manasseh tributary to Esarhaddon	. . . .
670	. . . .	. . . .
669	. . . .	. . . .
668	Manasseh tributary to Assurbanipal	. . . .
663	. . . .	. . . .

(1) Is. 39:1–2; 2 K. 20:12–15; 2 C. 32:31.

(2) Is. 39:3–8; 2 K. 20:16–19.

(4) 2 K. 18:13; 2 C. 32:1; Is. 36:1.

(5) 2 C. 32:2–8.

(6) 2 K. 18:14–16.

(7) 2 K. 18:17–19:19; 2 C. 32: 9–20; Is. 36:2–37:20.

(8) 2 K. 19:20–34; Is. 37:21–35.

(9) 2 K. 19:35–36; 2 C. 32:21; Is. 37:36–37.

(10) 2 K. 21:1–16; 2 C. 33:1–10.

ASSYRIA AND BABYLON	OTHER NATIONS
Sargon's general captures Ashdod (3). Sargon overthrows Merodach-baladan. Death of Sargon. Sennacherib reigns.	
	(f) Battle with Tirhakah at Eltekeh. Sennacherib claims the victory.
Sennacherib slain by his sons (11). Esarhaddon of Assyria (681–669).	
Esarhaddon conquers Egypt.	Tirhakah flees into Ethiopia.
Assurbanipal of Assyria (669–626).	Tirhakah regains Egypt. Egypt snatched from Tirhakah.
Assyrians invade Egypt.	Sack of Thebes (No-Amon).

(3) Is. 20:1.
(11) 2 K. 19:36–37; 2 C. 32:21; Is. 37:37–38.

DATE	JUDAH	PROPHETS
c.647	Manasseh carried in chains to Babylon (1). Restored to his throne, he reforms (2). Heathen gods removed, and Jerusalem fortified (3).	
642	14. *Amon* [2]. Wicked like his father (4). Slain in a conspiracy (5).	
640	15. *Josiah* [31]. Seeks after Yahweh at the age of fifteen (6).	
629	Destroys idols in Judah (7).	Nahum (?).
626	. . . .	Jeremiah commences his ministry (8). Zephaniah.
621	(a) Repairs the Temple (9). (b) Book of the Law found (10). (d) Renews covenant with Yahweh (12). (e) Thorough reformation extending even to Bethel and Samaria (13). (f) Great Passover (14).	(c) Prophecy of Huldah (11).
609	Josiah slain by the Egyptians at Megiddo (16)	. . . .
608	16. *Jehoahaz* [3 mos.]. Deposed by Necho on his return from the Euphrates, and carried to Egypt (17).	

(1) 2 C. 33:11.
(2) 2 C. 33:12–13.
(3) 2 C. 33:14–16.
(4) 2 K. 21:19–22; 2 C. 33:21–23.
(5) 2 K. 21:23–24; 2 C. 33:24–25.
(6) 2 C. 34:1–3.
(7) 2 C. 34:3–7.
(8) Jer. 1:1–2.
(9) 2 K. 22:3–7; 2 C. 34:8–13.

(10) 2 K. 22:8–11; 2 C. 34:14–19.
(11) 2 K. 22:12–20; 2 C. 34:20–28.
(12) 2 K. 23:1–3; 2 C. 34:29–33.
(13) 2 K. 23:4–20; 2 C. 34:33.
(14) 2 K. 23:21–23; 2 C. 35:1–19.
(16) 2 K. 23:29–30; 2 C. 35:20–25.
(17) 2 K. 23:31–33; 2 C. 36:1–3.

Assyria and Babylon	Other Nations
	Cyaxares founds the Median Empire (633).
	Scythian invasion?
Nabo-polassar (625–605) king of Babylon.	Nineveh destroyed (612 B.C.)
	Necho of Egypt (609–594).
. . . .	Pharaoh-necho marches through Palestine to the Euphrates (15).

(15) 2 K. 23:29.

DATE	JUDAH	PROPHETS
608	17. *Jehoiakim* [11]. Enthroned by Necho (1).	Habakkuk.

THE EXILE

DATE	JUDAH	PROPHETS
605	Nebuchadnezzar captures Jerusalem (3). Carries some of the sacred vessels to Babylon (5).	Daniel carried to Babylon (4).
604	. . . .	. . . .
602	Jehoiakim rebels against Babylon (6).	
597	18. *Jehoiachin* [3 mos.]. Carried captive by Nebuchadnezzar (7).	Ezekiel carried captive to Babylon (8).
597	19. *Zedekiah* [11]. Placed on the throne by Nebuchadnezzar (9).	
593	Zedekiah visits Babylon (10).	
592	. . . .	Ezekiel begins to prophesy (11).
588	Zedekiah, along with other petty kings, rebels against Babylon (13). Nebuchadnezzar invades Jerusalem (14).	Jeremiah sorely persecuted (16). . . . .

(1) 2 K. 23:34–35; 2 C. 36:4. (9) 2 K. 24:17; 2 C. 36:10.
(3) 2 K. 24:1; 2 C. 36:6. (10) Jer. 51:59.
(4) Dan. 1:3–6. (11) Ezek. 1:2.
(5) 2 C. 36:7. (13) Jer. 27:1–3; 2 K. 24:20; 2 C.
(6) 2 K. 24:1. 36:13.
(7) 2 K. 24:10–16; 2 C. 36:10. (14) 2 K. 25:1–2.
(8) Ezek. 1:2. (16) Jer. 37:11–38:28.

ASSYRIA AND BABYLON	OTHER NATIONS

605–537 B.C.

BABYLON AND PERSIA	OTHER NATIONS
Nabo-polassar dies..............	Pharaoh-necho defeated by Nebuchadnezzar at Carchemish (2).
Nebuchadnezzar (604–561).	
	Pharaoh - hophra (Apries) of Egypt (589–564).
....	Encourages Judah to rebel against Babylon (12). Tries to raise the siege of Jerusalem (15).

(2) Jer. 46.
(12) Jer. 37:5–10.
(15) Jer. 34:8–22; 37:5, 11.

Date	Judah	Prophets
586	Jerusalem captured and destroyed (1). Gedaliah appointed governor of Judah (2). Slain by Ishmael (3). Johanan defeats Ishmael (4).	Jeremiah carried by force into Egypt (5).
581	Nebuzaradan carries away a band of Jews (6).	
561	. . . .	. . . .
559	. . . .	. . . .
555	. . . .	. . . .
549	. . . .	. . . .
546	. . . .	. . . .
539	. . . .	. . . .
537	Jews allowed to return to Judah.	. . . .

(1) 2 K. 25:3–21; 2 C. 36:14–21; (4) Jer. 41:4–18.
     Jer. 39:1–8.   (5) Jer. 43:1–7.
(2) Jer. 40:5–12; 2 K. 25:22.   (6) Jer. 52:30.
(3) 2 K. 25:23–25; Jer. 40:13–
     41:3.

BABYLON AND PERSIA	OTHER NATIONS
Death of Nebuchadnezzar. Succeeded by Evil-merodach (561–559). Jehoiachin released from confinement, and treated with honor (7). Neriglissar (559–556). Nabonidus (555–539). Belshazzar prince regent (8). . . . . Cyrus captures Babylon. Darius made ruler for two years. Daniel promoted by Darius (9). Cyrus sole ruler in Babylon (537–529). Edict for the benefit of the Jews (10).	 Cyrus unites Persia and Media. Cyrus conquers Croesus of Lydia.

(7) 2 K. 25:27–30.   (9) Dan. 6:1–3.
(8) Dan. 5:1, 16.   (10) Ezra 1:1–4.

Date	Judah	Prophets
537	The Jews under Zerubbabel return home (First Return) (1). They attempt to rebuild the Temple, but are discouraged by opposition (2).	
529	....	....
525	....	....
522	....	....
521	....	....
520	The prophets urge the people to rebuild the Temple (3). Building resumed (4). Darius protects and aids the builders (5).	Haggai and Zechariah.
516	Temple dedicated (6). Passover observed with joy (7).	
490	....	....
485	....	....
480	....	....
465	....	....
458	Ezra leads a caravan of Jews to Jerusalem (Second Return) (9). Shortly after his arrival induces the people to give up their heathen wives (10).	

(1) Ezra 2:1, 64–67.
(2) Ezra 2:68–4:6.
(3) Ezra 5:1.
(4) Ezra 5:2.
(5) Ezra 5:3–6:14.

(6) Ezra 6:15–18.
(7) Ezra 6:19–22.
(9) Ezra 7–8.
(10) Ezra 9–10.

PERSIA	OTHER NATIONS
Accession of Cambyses (529–522).	Cambyses, defeated in Ethiopia, devastates Egypt.
Pseudo-Smerdis (8 mos.). Accession of Darius Hystaspis (521–485), after the overthrow of Pseudo-Smerdis.	
Accession of Xerxes (485–465). Accession of Artaxerxes Longimanus (465–424).	Battle of Marathon. Battle of Salamis.

DATE	JUDAH	PROPHETS
445	Nehemiah, after earnest prayer, secures appointment as governor of the Jews in Palestine (1). Begins to rebuild the walls of Jerusalem, in the face of serious opposition (2). Relieves the poor from oppressive interest (3). Though harassed by foes, Nehemiah completes the wall after 52 days (4). Reading of the Law and observance of the Feast of Tabernacles (5). Social and religious reforms inaugurated (6). Dedication of the city wall (7).	
433	Nehemiah returns for a season to the court of Persia (8).	Malachi (?).
432	Returns to Jerusalem. Certain evils corrected (9).	

(1) Neh. 1:1–2:10.	(6) Neh. 9, 10.
(2) Neh. 2:11–4:23.	(7) Neh. 12:27–43.
(3) Neh. 5.	(8) Neh. 13:6.
(4) Neh. 6.	(9) Neh. 13:31.
(5) Neh. 8.	

PERSIA	OTHER NATIONS
	Herodotus (444 B.C.).
	Pericles in Athens.

The author is especially indebted to Ira M. Price, *The Dramatic Story of Old Testament History* (New York: Fleming H. Revell Company, 1935) and Wright and Filson, *The Westminster Historical Atlas to the Bible* (Philadelphia: The Westminster Press, 1946) in the preparation of this chart.